Between Men

GENDER AND CULTURE

Carolyn G. Heilbrun and Nancy K. Miller,
editors

GENDER AND CULTURE
A SERIES OF COLUMBIA UNIVERSITY PRESS
Edited by
Carolyn G. Heilbrun
and
Nancy K. Miller

BETWEEN MEN

English Literature and Male Homosocial Desire

With a new preface by the author
EVE KOSOFSKY SEDGWICK

COLUMBIA UNIVERSITY PRESS
New York

To
Hal Sedgwick

The Andrew W. Mellon Foundation, through a special grant,
has assisted the Press in publishing this volume.

Library of Congress Cataloging-in-Publication Data

Sedgwick, Eve Kosofsky.
Between men.

(Gender and culture)
Bibliography: p. 229
Includes index.
1. English literature—History and criticism.
2. Men in literature.   3. Sex in literature.
4. Sex role in literature.   5. Masculinity (Psychology)
in literature.   6. Feminism and literature.   I. Title.
II. Series.
PR409.M38S4 1985   820'.9'353   84-17583
ISBN 0-231-05860-8
ISBN 0-231-08273-8 (pbk.)

Casebound editions of Columbia University Press books are
printed on permanent and durable acid free paper.

Columbia University Press
New York   Chichester, West Sussex

p 10 9 8
c 10 9 8 7 6 5 4 3

CONTENTS

PREFACE

I WONDER if it's obvious, reading *Between Men* now, what reckless pleasure went into its writing: The Osborne computer ("portable" at thirty-five pounds), whose tiny screen evoked the undefrostable windshield of a Volkswagen Beetle; the waxy takeout cartons of double-cooked pork that, far into the night, nourished me in my lit-up cell in the humming beehive of the Bunting Institute. My mantra was "I could be bagging groceries"—inexplicably cheering at a time when jobs were scarce, feminist criticism the most embattled of enterprises, and tenure nowhere on the horizon. I felt confident of nothing, nothing at all, but there was not a day when it didn't seem an adventure and privilege to be writing this particular book.

Between Men intended two main interventions. The most immediate audience I had in mind was other feminist scholars. I started work on the book at a moment when feminist scholarship seemed like a single project: little enough of it was being done then that it seemed possible, as well as urgent, to undertake feminist restructuring of a whole range of disciplines according to a relatively small number of powerful axioms. As a deconstructive and very writerly close reader, I was surprised, exultant, grateful to be lifted into the whirlwind of that moment of activist grand theory. I was, as well, acutely responsive to the empowering utopian intimations and the sustaining day-to-day excitements of working with communities of women thinkers. At the same time, like many other feminists, I also wanted—needed—feminist scholarship to be different. In particular, I found oppressive the hygienic way in which a variety of different institutional, conceptual, political, ethical, and emotional contingencies promised (threatened?) to line up together so neatly in the development of a feminocentric field of women's studies in which the subjects, paradigms, and political thrust of research, as well as the researchers themselves, might all be indentified with the female. Participating in each of these contingencies, I still needed to keep faith, as best I could, with an obstinate intuition that the loose ends and crossed ends of identity are more fecund than the places where identity, desire, analysis, and need can all be aligned and centered.

I intended *Between Men* very pointedly as a complicating, antiseparatist, and antihomophobic contribution to a feminist movement with which, nonetheless, I identified fairly unproblematically. Not that I think the transferential poetics of identification and address are *ever* simple; they aren't. But the undertows and opacities that perturbed the address of this book to a variety of women readers seemed, at the time, less weird than its phantasmic relation to a potential readership of gay men.

Michael Lynch, a long-time pioneer of gay studies whom I met a few years later, told me his first response to *Between Men* was "this woman has a lot of ideas about a lot of things, but she doesn't know much about gay men!" He was so right. During the writing of *Between Men,* I was very involved with lesbian-inflected feminist culture and critique, but I actually knew only one openly gay man. From the 1990s vantage of an elaborated and activist gay/lesbian studies scene in academia, a vocal and visible national gay/lesbian movement, and (for me and many other women and men of various dissident sexualities) an emerging, highly productive queer community whose explicit basis is the criss-crossing of the lines of identification and desire among genders, races, and sexual definitions, it's hard to remember what that distant country felt like. Rereading the book now, I'm brought up short, often, with dismay at the thinness of the experience on which many of its analyses and generalizations are based. Yet I'm also relieved, and proud, that its main motives and imperatives still seem so recognizable.

A growing gay and lesbian studies movement already existed in American academia at the time (a look back at the *Gay Studies Newsletter,* under Lynch's editorship, shows how active, as well as how precarious it was); an intensely vital gay liberation culture was also being created in any number of urban spaces. So I don't know how to account for the dependence of this book on much more distant traditions of gay thought, mostly British or European: the work of Jeffrey Weeks, Guy Hocquenghem, Paul Hoch, Mario Mieli, Alan Bray. Already published in books and translated into if not written in English, these texts appear in *Between Men* as canonical or established secondary sources by authors who might—for any sense *Between Men* gives of their contemporaneity—have been dead for a century. They function in the book as objects of an almost theologically speculative meditation, rather than as evidence of lives and communities actually, presently inhabited. That there was something (in this sense) irrepressibly *provincial* about the young author of this book is manifest. But will it make sense if I describe that provinciality as not only a measure of her distance from the scenes of gay male creativity, whose utopian invocation tacitly motivates the book, but also a ground of her passionate, queer, and fairly uncanny identification with it?

The more than Balzacian founding narrative of a certain modern identity for Euro-American gay men, after all, vibrates along a chord that stretches from provincial origins to metropolitan destinies. As each individual story begins in the isolation of queer childhood, we compulsorily and excruciatingly misrecognize ourselves in the available mirror of the atomized, procreative, so-called heterosexual pre- or ex-urban nuclear family of origin, whose bruisingly inappropriate interpellations may wound us—those resilient or lucky enough to survive them—into life, life of a different kind. The site of that second and belated life, those newly constituted and denaturalized "families," those tardy, wondering chances at transformed and transforming self- and other-recognition, is the metropolis. But a metropolis continually recruited and reconstituted by having folded into it the incredulous energies of the provincial. Or—I might better say—the provincial energies of incredulity itself.

There's a way in which the author of this book seems not quite to have been able to believe in the reality of the gay male communities toward whose readership the book so palpably yearns. The yearning makes the incredulity. It makes, too, however, the force of a bond with at least some readers equally incredulous (in that distant moment) at the encounter with the book's own intimate, desiring, direct address, emanating from an unaccustomed and, to some degree, unspecified place on the map of cultural authority, of gender/sexuality, of disciplinarity.

Obsessions are the most durable form of intellectual capital. So perhaps it's folly to second-guess them, even though it seems patent that the intellectual enablements of this obsessionally motivated project were also interlined with profound blockages. Blockage and frozenness have seemed to characterize its address, in particular, to many of the women queer readers whose incredulous desire it has also solicited. In fact *Between Men* has evoked rage (perhaps among other responses) on a continuing basis from many readers. For that matter, virtually all the readers who have forcefully used it have drawn, I believe, on a hardly less heterogeneous and conflictual spectrum of responses to it. The proliferation, the re-markable creativity of so much subsequent work in the field may say something—I hope it does—for the direct or oblique energizing powers of an unconventional literary intervention like *Between Men*. But it has vastly more to say for the inveterate, gorgeous generativity, the specula-tive generosity, the daring, the permeability, and the activism that have long been lodged in the multiple histories of queer *reading*.

November 1992

ACKNOWLEDGMENTS

THIS book was completed in the especially conducive environment of the Mary Ingraham Bunting Institute of Radcliffe College, during the term of a fellowship funded by the Carnegie Foundation. Other important financial support for the project came in the form of research grants from Boston University, Hamilton College, and the Kirkland Endowment.

Between Men owes a lot to the personal participation of others. This is partly because I meant it to be interdisciplinary, partly because it is political and occurs within a framework of public language, and partly because its subject reaches deeply into my own experiences and those of many people I know. Three feminist women's groups—the Faculty for Women's Concerns at Hamilton College, and the ID 450 Collective and a nameless research group in Boston—have contributed most materially (not to mention, immaterially) to the book's progress. Many people have been generous with readings of chapters and with specific ideas. Gordon Braden advised me on Shakespeare's Sonnets, and Laura Brown on the economic context of *The Country Wife*. Henry Abelove encouraged me and discussed with me a variety of issues in eighteenth- and nineteenth-century English history. Coppélia Kahn, Richard Poirier, and Richard Vann were variously respondents to the essay on *Our Mutual Friend*. Jonathan Kamholtz, among his contributions of ideas and energy, convinced me that that essay ought to lead to a book. Michael McKeon gave an especially helpful reading of the material on historicism. David Kosofsky sent barrages of clippings, ideas, and encouragement in my direction from all over the world. Linda Gordon, Caroline Walker Bynum, Nancy K. Miller, Ellen Bassuk, and Marilyn Chapin Massey each read several chapters and offered irreplaceable responses from the perspective of her own discipline and sensibility.

Other kinds of intellectual and moral support that underpin a years-long project are even harder to categorize. Among the Usual Suspects are Laverne Berry, Cynthia Chase, Paul Farrell, Joseph Gordon, Madelyn Gutwirth, Elaine Tuttle Hansen, Neil Hertz, Marsha Hill, Nancy Sorkin Rabinowitz, Nancy Waring, Carolyn Williams, and Joshua Wilner. Rita Kosofsky and Leon Kosofsky each gave a stylistic scrubbing to several chapters, but it would be hardest of all to enumerate their true contributions—among them, language itself.

In addition to the sections of this book that have appeared in journals, several sections have been presented as talks, to groups that have included the MLA, the English Institute, Mid-Atlantic Women's Studies Association, Northeast Victorian Studies Association, an Ohio Shakespeare Conference, Wesleyan University, the University of Cincinnati, Hamilton College, Colgate University, Harvard University, Brooklyn College, Cornell University, Johns Hopkins University, Hebrew University, and the Center for the Study of Women at Wellesley College, among others. In each of these encounters, I learned from the comments of many more people than I could name here, including many whose names I never knew.

A version of chapter 9 appeared in *Raritan;* of the Coda, in *Delta;* and of chapters 3 and 4, in *Critical Inquiry*. Some material from chapter 5 appeared as part of a review in *Studies in Romanticism*. I am grateful to the editors of all these journals for their willingness to reassign me the necessary permissions.

INTRODUCTION

i. Homosocial Desire

THE subject of this book is a relatively short, recent, and accessible passage of English culture, chiefly as embodied in the mid-eighteenth- to mid-nineteenth-century novel. The attraction of the period to theorists of many disciplines is obvious: condensed, self-reflective, and widely influential change in economic, ideological, and gender arrangements. I will be arguing that concomitant changes in the structure of the continuum of male "homosocial desire" were tightly, often causally bound up with the other more visible changes; that the emerging pattern of male friendship, mentorship, entitlement, rivalry, and hetero- and homosexuality was in an intimate and shifting relation to class; and that no element of that pattern can be understood outside of its relation to women and the gender system as a whole.

"Male homosocial desire": the phrase in the title of this study is intended to mark both discriminations and paradoxes. "Homosocial desire," to begin with, is a kind of oxymoron. "Homosocial" is a word occasionally used in history and the social sciences, where it describes social bonds between persons of the same sex; it is a neologism, obviously formed by analogy with "homosexual," and just as obviously meant to be distinguished from "homosexual." In fact, it is applied to such activities as "male bonding," which may, as in our society, be characterized by intense homophobia, fear and hatred of homosexuality.[1] To draw the "homosocial" back into the orbit of "desire," of the potentially erotic, then, is to hypothesize the potential unbrokenness of a continuum between homosocial and homosexual—a continuum whose visibility, for men, in our society, is radically disrupted. It will become clear, in the course of my argument, that my hypothesis of the unbrokenness of this continuum is not a *genetic* one—I do not mean to discuss genital homosexual desire as "at the root of" other forms of male homosociality—but rather a strategy for making generalizations about, and marking historical differences in, the *structure* of men's relations with other men. "Male homosocial desire" is the name this book will give to the entire continuum.

I have chosen the word "desire" rather than "love" to mark the erotic emphasis because, in literary critical and related discourse, "love" is more easily used to name a particular emotion, and "desire" to name a structure; in this study, a series of arguments about the structural permutations of social impulses fuels the critical dialectic. For the most part, I will be using "desire" in a way analogous to the psychoanalytic use of "libido"—not for a particular affective state or emotion, but for the affective or social force, the glue, even when its manifestation is hostility or hatred or something less emotively charged, that shapes an important relationship. How far this force is properly sexual (what, historically, it means for something to be "sexual") will be an active question.

The title is specific about *male* homosocial desire partly in order to acknowledge from the beginning (and stress the seriousness of) a limitation of my subject; but there is a more positive and substantial reason, as well. It is one of the main projects of this study to explore the ways in which the shapes of sexuality, and what *counts* as sexuality, both depend on and affect historical power relationships.[2] A corollary is that in a society where men and women differ in their access to power, there will be important gender differences, as well, in the structure and constitution of sexuality.

For instance, the diacritical opposition between the "homosocial" and the "homosexual" seems to be much less thorough and dichotomous for women, in our society, than for men. At this particular historical moment, an intelligible continuum of aims, emotions, and valuations links lesbianism with the other forms of women's attention to women: the bond of mother and daughter, for instance, the bond of sister and sister, women's friendship, "networking," and the active struggles of feminism.[3] The continuum is crisscrossed with deep discontinuities—with much homophobia, with conflicts of race and class—but its intelligibility seems now a matter of simple common sense. However agonistic the politics, however conflicted the feelings, it seems at this moment to make an obvious kind of sense to say that women in our society who love women, women who teach, study, nurture, suckle, write about, march for, vote for, give jobs to, or otherwise promote the interests of other women, are pursuing congruent and closely related activities. Thus the adjective "homosocial" as applied to women's bonds (by, for example, historian Carroll Smith-Rosenberg)[4] need not be pointedly dichotomized as against "homosexual"; it can intelligibly denominate the entire continuum.

The apparent simplicity—the unity—of the continuum between "women loving women" and "women promoting the interests of women," extending over the erotic, social, familial, economic, and political realms, would not be so striking if it were not in strong contrast to the arrangement among males. When Ronald Reagan and Jesse Helms get down to serious logrolling on "family policy," they are men promoting men's interests. (In fact, they embody Heidi Hartmann's definition of patriarchy: "relations between men, which have a material base, and which, though hierarchical, establish or create interdependence and solidarity among men that enable them to dominate women.")[5] Is their bond in any way congruent with the bond of a loving gay male couple? Reagan and Helms would say no—disgustedly. Most gay couples would say no—disgustedly. But why not? Doesn't the continuum between "men-loving-men" and "men-promoting-the-interests-of-men" have the same intuitive force that it has for women?

Quite the contrary: much of the most useful recent writing about patriarchal structures suggests that "obligatory heterosexuality" is built into male-dominated kinship systems, or that homophobia is a *necessary* consequence of such patriarchal institutions as heterosexual marriage.[6] Clearly, however convenient it might be to group together all the bonds that link males to males, and by which males enhance the status of males—usefully symmetrical as it would be, that grouping meets with a prohibitive structural obstacle. From the vantage point of our own society, at any rate, it has apparently been impossible to imagine a form of patriarchy that was not homophobic. Gayle Rubin writes, for instance, "The suppression of the homosexual component of human sexuality, and by corollary, the oppression of homosexuals, is . . . a product of the same system whose rules and relations oppress women."[7]

The historical manifestations of this patriarchal oppression of homosexuals have been savage and nearly endless. Louis Crompton makes a detailed case for describing the history as genocidal.[8] Our own society is brutally homophobic; and the homophobia directed against both males and females is not arbitrary or gratuitous, but tightly knit into the texture of family, gender, age, class, and race relations. Our society could not cease to be homophobic and have its economic and political structures remain unchanged.

Nevertheless, it has yet to be demonstrated that, because most patriarchies structurally include homophobia, therefore patriarchy structurally *requires* homophobia. K. J. Dover's recent study, *Greek Homosexuality,* seems to give a strong counterexample in classical Greece. Male homosexuality, according to Dover's evidence, was a widespread, licit, and very influential part of the culture. Highly structured along lines of class, and within the citizen class along lines of age, the pursuit of the adolescent boy by the older man was described by stereotypes that we associate with romantic heterosexual love (conquest, surrender, the "cruel fair," the absence of desire in the love object), with the passive part going to the boy. At the same time, however, because the boy was destined in turn to grow into manhood, the assignment of roles was not permanent.[9] Thus the love relationship, while temporarily oppressive to the object, had a strongly educational function; Dover quotes Pausanias in Plato's *Symposium* as saying "that it would be right for him [the boy] to perform any service for one who improves him in mind and character."[10] Along with its erotic component, then, this was a bond of mentorship; the boys were apprentices in the ways and virtues of Athenian citizenship, whose privileges they inherited. These privileges included the power to command the labor of slaves of both sexes, and of women of any class including their own. "Women and slaves belonged and lived together," Hannah Arendt writes. The system of sharp class and gender subordination was a necessary part of what the male culture valued most in itself: "Contempt for laboring originally [arose] out of a passionate striving for freedom from necessity and a no less passionate impatience with every effort that left no trace, no monument, no great work worthy to remembrance";[11] so the contemptible labor was left to women and slaves.

The example of the Greeks demonstrates, I think, that while heterosexuality is necessary for the maintenance of any patriarchy, homophobia, against males at any rate, is not. In fact, for the Greeks, the continuum between "men loving men" and "men promoting the interests of men" appears to have been quite seamless. It is as if, in our terms, there were no perceived discontinuity between the male bonds at the Continental Baths and the male bonds at the Bohemian Grove[12] or in the board room or Senate cloakroom.

It is clear, then, that there is an asymmetry in our present society between, on the one hand, the relatively continuous relation of female homosocial and homosexual bonds, and, on the other hand, the radically discontinuous relation of male homosocial and homosexual bonds. The example of the Greeks (and of other, tribal cultures, such as the New Guinea "Sambia" studied by G. H. Herdt) shows, in addition, that the structure of homosocial continuums is culturally contingent, not an innate feature of either "maleness" or "femaleness." Indeed, closely tied though it obviously is to questions of male vs. female power, the explanation will require a more exact mode of historical categorization than "patriarchy," as well, since patriarchal power structures (in Hartmann's sense) characterize both Athenian and American societies. Nevertheless, we may take as an explicit axiom that the historically differential shapes of male and female homosociality—much as they themselves may vary over time—will always be articulations and mechanisms of the enduring inequality of power between women and men.

Why should the different shapes of the homosocial continuum be an interesting question? Why should it be a *literary* question? Its importance for the practical politics of the gay movement as a minority rights movement is already obvious from the recent history of strategic and philosophical differences between lesbians and gay men. In addition, it is theoretically interesting partly as a way of approaching a larger question of "sexual politics": What does it mean—what difference does it make—when a social or political relationship is sexualized? If the relation of homosocial to homosexual bonds is so shifty, then what theoretical framework do we have for drawing any links between sexual and power relationships?

ii. Sexual Politics and Sexual Meaning

This question, in a variety of forms, is being posed importantly by and for the different gender-politics movements right now. Feminist along with gay male theorists, for instance, are disagreeing actively about how direct the relation is between power domination and sexual sadomasochism. Start with two arresting images: the naked, beefy motorcyclist on the front cover, or the shockingly battered nude male corpse on the back cover, of the recent so-called "Polysexuality" issue of *Semiotext(e)* (4, no. 1 [1981])—which, for all the women in it, ought to have been called the semisexuality issue of *Polytext*. It seemed to be a purpose of that issue to insist,

and possibly not only for reasons of radical-chic titillation, that the violence imaged in sadomasochism is not mainly theatrical, but is fully continuous with violence in the real world. Women Against Pornography
and the framers of the 1980 NOW Resolution on Lesbian and Gay Rights
share the same view, but without the celebratory glamor: to them too it
seems intuitively clear that to sexualize violence or an image of violence
is simply to extend, unchanged, its reach and force.[13] But, as other feminist writers have reminded us, another view is possible. For example: is
a woman's masochistic sexual fantasy really only an internalization and
endorsement, if not a cause, of her more general powerlessness and sense
of worthlessness? Or may not the sexual drama stand in some more oblique,
or even oppositional, relation to her political experience of oppression?[14]

The debate in the gay male community and elsewhere over "man-boy
love" asks a cognate question: can an adult's sexual relationship with a
child be simply a continuous part of a more general relationship of education and nurturance? Or must the inclusion of sex qualitatively alter the
relationship, for instance in the direction of exploitiveness? In this case,
the same NOW communiqué that had assumed an unbroken continuity
between sexualized violence and real, social violence, came to the opposite conclusion on pedophilia: that the injection of the sexual charge *would*
alter (would corrupt) the very substance of the relationship. Thus, in
moving from the question of sadomasochism to the question of pedophilia, the "permissive" argument and the "puritanical" argument have
essentially exchanged their assumptions about how the sexual relates to
the social.

So the answer to the question "what difference does the inclusion of
sex make" to a social or political relationship, is—it varies: just as, for
different groups in different political circumstances, homosexual activity
can be either supportive of or oppositional to homosocial bonding. From
this and the other examples I have mentioned, it is clear that there is not
some ahistorical *Stoff* of sexuality, some sexual charge that can be simply
added to a social relationship to "sexualize" it in a constant and predictable direction, or that splits off from it unchanged. Nor does it make sense
to *assume* that the sexualized form epitomizes or simply condenses a broader
relationship. (As, for instance, Kathleen Barry, in *Female Sexual Slavery*,
places the Marquis de Sade at the very center of all forms of female
oppression, including traditional genital mutilation, incest, and the economic as well as the sexual exploitation of prostitutes.)

Instead, an examination of the relation of sexual desire to political power must move along two axes. First, of course, it needs to make use of whatever forms of analysis are most potent for describing historically variable power asymmetries, such as those of class and race, as well as gender. But in conjunction with that, an analysis of representation itself is necessary. Only the model of representation will let us do justice to the (broad but not infinite or random) range of ways in which sexuality functions as a signifier for power relations. The importance of the rhetorical model in this case is not to make the problems of sexuality or of violence or oppression sound less immediate and urgent; it is to help us analyze and use the really very disparate intuitions of political immediacy that come to us from the sexual realm.

For instance, a dazzling recent article by Catherine MacKinnon, attempting to go carefully over and clear out the grounds of disagreement between different streams of feminist thought, arrives at the following summary of the centrality of sexuality per se for every issue of gender:

> Each element of the female *gender* stereotype is revealed as, in fact, *sexual*. Vulnerability means the appearance/reality of easy sexual access; passivity means receptivity and disabled resistance. . . ; softness means pregnability by something hard. . . . Woman's infantilization evokes pedophilia; fixation on dismembered body parts . . . evokes fetishism; idolization of vapidity, necrophilia. Narcissism insures that woman identifies with that image of herself that man holds up. . . . Masochism means that pleasure in violation becomes her sensuality.

And MacKinnon sums up this part of her argument: "Socially, femaleness means femininity, which means attractiveness to men, which means sexual attractiveness, which means sexual availability on male terms."[15]

There's a whole lot of "mean"-ing going on. MacKinnon manages to make every manifestation of sexuality mean the same thing, by making every instance of "meaning" mean something different. A trait can "mean" as an element in a semiotic system such as fashion ("softness means pregnability"); or anaclitically, it can "mean" its complementary opposite ("Woman's infantilization evokes pedophilia"); or across time, it can "mean" the consequence that it enforces ("Narcissism insures that woman identifies. . . . Masochism means that pleasure in violation becomes her sensuality"). MacKinnon concludes, "What defines woman as such is what turns men on." But what defines "defines"? That every node of sexual experience is in *some* signifying relation to the whole fabric of gender oppression, and vice versa, is true and important, but insufficiently exact to be of analytic use on specific political issues. The danger lies, of course, in the illusion that we do know from such a totalistic analysis where to look for our sexuality and how to protect it from expropriation when we find it.

On the other hand, one value of MacKinnon's piece was as a contribution to the increasing deftness with which, over the last twenty years, the question has been posed, "Who or what is the subject of the sexuality we (as women) enact?" It has been posed in terms more or less antic or frontal, phallic or gyno-, angry or frantic—in short, perhaps, Anglic or Franco-. But in different terms it is this same question that has animated the complaint of the American "sex object" of the 1960s, the claim since the 70s for "women's control of our own bodies," and the recently imported "critique of the subject" as it is used by French feminists.

Let me take an example from the great ideological blockbuster of white bourgeois feminism, its apotheosis, the fictional work that has most resonantly thematized for successive generations of American women the constraints of the "feminine" role, the obstacles to and the ravenous urgency of female ambition, the importance of the economic motive, the compulsiveness and destructiveness of romantic love, and (what Mac-Kinnon would underline) the centrality and the total alienation of female sexuality. Of course, I am referring to *Gone with the Wind*. As Mac-Kinnon's paradigm would predict, in the life of Scarlett O'Hara, it is expressly clear that to be born female is to be defined entirely in relation to the role of "lady," a role that does take its shape and meaning from a sexuality of which she is not the subject but the object. For Scarlett, to survive as a woman does mean learning to see sexuality, male power domination, and her traditional gender role as all meaning the same dangerous thing. To absent herself silently from each of them alike, and learn to manipulate them from behind this screen as objects or pure signifiers, as men do, is the numbing but effective lesson of her life.

However, it is *only* a white bourgeois feminism that this view apotheosizes. As in one of those trick rooms where water appears to run uphill and little children look taller than their parents, it is only when viewed from one fixed vantage in any society that sexuality, gender roles, and power domination can seem to line up in this perfect chain of echoic meaning. From an even slightly more ec-centric or disempowered perspective, the *dis*placements and *dis*continuities of the signifying chain come to seem increasingly definitive. For instance, if it is true in this novel that all the women characters exist in some meaning-ful relation to the role of "lady," the signifying relation grows more tortuous—though at the same time, in the novel's white bourgeois view, more totally determining—as the women's social and racial distance from that role grows. Melanie is a woman as she is a lady; Scarlett is a woman as she is required to be and pretends to be a lady; but Belle Watling, the Atlanta prostitute, is a woman not in relation to her own role of "lady," which is exiguous, but only negatively, in a compensatory and at the same time parodic relation to Melanie's and Scarlett's. And as for Mammy, her mind and life, in this view, are *totally* in thrall to the ideal of the "lady," but in a relation that excludes herself entirely: she is the template, the support, the enforcement, of Scarlett's "lady" role, to the degree that her personal femaleness loses any meaning whatever that is not in relation to Scarlett's role. Whose mother is Mammy?

At the precise intersection of domination and sexuality is the issue of rape. *Gone with the Wind*—both book and movie—leaves in the memory a most graphic image of rape:

> As the negro came running to the buggy, his black face twisted in a leering grin, she fired point-blank at him. . . . The negro was beside her, so close that she could smell the rank odor of him as he tried to drag her over the buggy side. With her own free hand she fought madly, clawing at his face, and then she felt his big hand at her throat and, with a ripping noise, her basque was torn open from breast to waist. Then the black hand fumbled between her breasts, and terror and revulsion such as she had never known came over her and she screamed like an insane woman.[16]

In the wake of this attack, the entire machinery by which "rape" is signified in this culture rolls into action. Scarlett's menfolk and their friends in the Ku Klux Klan set out after dark to kill the assailants and "wipe out that whole Shantytown settlement," with the predictable carnage on both sides. The question of how much Scarlett is to blame for the deaths of the white men is widely mooted, with Belle Watling speaking for the "lady" role—"She caused it all, prancin' bout Atlanta by herself, enticin' niggers and trash"—and Rhett Butler, as so often, speaking from the central vision of the novel's bourgeois feminism, assuring her that her desperate sense of guilt is purely superstitious (chs. 46, 47). In preparation for this central incident, the novel had even raised the issue of the legal treatment of rape victims (ch. 42). And the effect of that earlier case, the classic effect of rape, had already been to abridge Scarlett's own mobility and, hence, personal and economic power: it was to expedite her business that she had needed to ride by Shantytown in the first place.

The attack on Scarlett, in short, fully means rape, both *to her* and to all the forces in her culture that produce and circulate powerful meanings. It makes no difference at all that one constituent element of rape is missing; but the missing constituent is simply sex. The attack on Scarlett had been for money; the black hands had fumbled between the white breasts because the man had been told that was where she kept her money; Scarlett knew that; there is no mention of any other motive; but it does not matter in the least, the absent sexuality leaves no gap in the character's, the novel's, or the society's discourse of rape.

Nevertheless, *Gone with the Wind* is not a novel that omits enforced sexuality. We are shown one actual rape in fairly graphic detail; but when it is white hands that scrabble on white skin, its ideological name is "blissful marriage." "[Rhett] had humbled her, used her brutally through a wild mad night and she had gloried in it" (ch. 54). The sexual predations of white men on Black women are also a presence in the novel, but the issue of force vs. consent is never raised there; the white male alienation of a Black woman's sexuality is shaped differently from the alienation of the white woman's, to the degree that rape ceases to be a meaningful term at all. And if forcible sex ever did occur between a Black male and female character in this world, the sexual event itself would have no signifying power, since Black sexuality "means" here only as a grammatic transformation of a sentence whose true implicit subject and object are white.

We have in this protofeminist novel, then, in this ideological microcosm, a symbolic economy in which both the meaning of rape and rape itself are insistently circulated. Because of the racial fracture of the society, however, *rape and its meaning circulate in precisely opposite directions.* It is an extreme case; the racial fracture is, in America, more sharply dichotomized than others except perhaps for gender. Still, other symbolic fractures such as class (and by fractures I mean the lines along which quantitative differentials of power may in a given society be read as qualitative differentials with some other name) are abundant and actively disruptive in every social constitution. The signifying relation of sex to power, of sexual alienation to political oppression, is not the most stable, but precisely the most volatile of social nodes, under this pressure.

Thus, it is of serious political importance that our tools for examining the signifying relation be subtle and discriminate ones, and that our literary knowledge of the most crabbed or oblique paths of meaning not be oversimplified in the face of panic-inducing images of real violence, especially the violence of, around, and to sexuality. To assume that sex signifies power in a flat, unvarying relation of metaphor or synecdoche will always entail a blindness, not to the rhetorical and pyrotechnic, but to such historical categories as class and race. Before we can fully achieve and use our intuitive grasp of the leverage that sexual relations seem to offer on the relations of oppression, we need more—more different, more complicated, more diachronically apt, more off-centered—more daring and prehensile applications of our present understanding of what it may mean for one thing to signify another.

iii. Sex or History?

It will be clear by this point that the centrality of sexual questions in this study is important to its methodological ambitions, as well. I am going to be recurring to the subject of sex as an especially charged leverage-point, or point for the exchange of meanings, *between* gender and class (and in many societies, race), the sets of categories by which we ordinarily try to describe the divisions of human labor. And methodologically, I want to situate these readings as a contribution to a dialectic within feminist theory between more and less historicizing views of the oppression of women.

In a rough way, we can label the extremes on this theoretical spectrum "Marxist feminism" for the most historicizing analysis, "radical feminism" for the least. Of course, "radical feminism" is so called not because it occupies the farthest "left" space on a conventional political map, but because it takes gender itself, gender alone, to be the most radical division of human experience, and a relatively unchanging one.

For the purposes of the present argument, in addition, and for reasons that I will explain more fully later, I am going to be assimilating "French" feminism—deconstructive and/or Lacanian-oriented feminism—to the radical-feminist end of this spectrum. "French" and "radical" feminism differ on very many very important issues, such as how much respect they give to the brute fact that everyone gets categorized as either female or male; but they are alike in seeing all human culture, language, and life as structured in the first place—structured radically, transhistorically, and essentially *similarly,* however coarsely or finely—by a drama of gender difference. (Chapter 1 discusses more fully the particular terms by which this structuralist motive will be represented in the present study.) French-feminist and radical-feminist prose tend to share the same vatic, and perhaps imperialistic, uses of the present tense. In a sense, the polemical energy behind my arguments will be a desire, through the rhetorically volatile subject of sex, to recruit the representational finesse of deconstructive feminism in the service of a more historically discriminate mode of analysis.

The choice of sexuality as a thematic emphasis of this study makes salient and problematical a division of thematic emphasis between Marxist-feminist and radical-feminist theory as they are now practiced. Specifically, Marxist feminism, the study of the deep interconnections between on the one hand historical and economic change, and on the other hand the vicissitudes of gender division, has typically proceeded in the absence of a theory of sexuality and without much interest in the meaning or experience of sexuality. Or more accurately, it has held implicitly to a view of female sexuality as something that is essentially of a piece with reproduction, and hence appropriately studied with the tools of demography; or else essentially of a piece with a simple, prescriptive hegemonic ideology, and hence appropriately studied through intellectual or legal history. Where important advances have been made by Marxist-feminist-oriented research into sexuality, it has been in areas that were already explicitly distinguished as deviant by the society's legal discourse: signally, homosexuality for men and prostitution for women. Marxist feminism has been of little help in unpacking the historical meanings of women's experience of heterosexuality, or even, until it becomes legally and medically visible in this century, of lesbianism.[17]

Radical feminism, on the other hand, in the many different forms I am classing under that head, has been relatively successful in placing sexuality in a prominent and interrogative position, one that often allows scope for the decentered and the contradictory. Kathleen Barry's *Female Sexual Slavery,* Susan Griffin's *Pornography and Silence,* Gilbert and Gubar's *The Madwoman in the Attic,* Jane Gallop's *The Daughter's Seduction,* and Andrea Dworkin's *Pornography: Men Possessing Women* make up an exceedingly heterogeneous group of texts in many respects—in style, in urgency, in explicit feminist identification, in French or American affiliation, in "brow"-elevation level. They have in common, however, a view that sexuality is centrally problematical in the formation of women's experience. And in more or less sophisticated formulations, the subject as well as the ultimate object of female heterosexuality within what is called patriarchal culture are seen as male. Whether in literal interpersonal terms or in internalized psychological and linguistic terms, this approach privileges sexuality and often sees it within the context of the structure that Lévi-Strauss analyzes as "the male traffic in women."

This family of approaches has, however, shared with other forms of structuralism a difficulty in dealing with the diachronic. It is the essence of structures viewed as such to reproduce themselves; and historical change from this point of view appears as something outside of structure and threatening—or worse, *not* threatening—to it, rather than in a formative and dialectical relation with it. History tends thus to be either invisible or viewed in an impoverishingly glaring and contrastive light.[18] Implicitly or explicitly, radical feminism tends to deny that the meaning of gender or sexuality has ever significantly changed; and more damagingly, it can make future change appear impossible, or necessarily apocalyptic, even though desirable. Alternatively, it can radically oversimplify the prerequisites for significant change. In addition, history even in the residual, synchronic form of class or racial difference and conflict becomes invisible or excessively coarsened and dichotomized in the universalizing structuralist view.

As feminist readers, then, we seem poised for the moment between reading sex and reading history, at a choice that appears (though, it must be, wrongly) to be between the synchronic and the diachronic. We know that it must be wrongly viewed in this way, not only because in the abstract the synchronic and the diachronic must ultimately be considered in relation to one another, but because specifically in the disciplines we are considering they are so mutually inscribed: the narrative of Marxist history is so graphic, and the schematics of structuralist sexuality so narrative.

I will be trying in this study to activate and use some of the potential congruences of the two approaches. Part of the underpinning of this attempt will be a continuing meditation on ways in which the category *ideology* can be used as part of an analysis of *sexuality*. The two categories seem comparable in several important ways: each mediates between the material and the representational, for instance; ideology, like sexuality as we have discussed it, *both* epitomizes *and* itself influences broader social relations of power; and each, I shall be arguing, mediates similarly between diachronic, narrative structures of social experience and synchronic, graphic ones. If commonsense suggests that we can roughly group historicizing, "Marxist" feminism with the diachronic and the narrative, and "radical," structuralist, deconstructive, and "French" feminisms with the synchronic and the graphic, then the methodological promise of these two mediating categories will be understandable.

In *The German Ideology,* Marx suggests that the function of ideology is to conceal contradictions in the status quo by, for instance, recasting them into a diachronic narrative of origins. Corresponding to that function, one important structure of ideology is an idealizing appeal to the outdated values of an earlier system, in defense of a later system that in practice undermines the material basis of those values.[19]

For instance, Juliet Mitchell analyzes the importance of the family in ideologically justifying the shift to capitalism, in these terms:

> The peasant masses of feudal society had individual private property; their ideal was simply more of it. Capitalist society seemed to offer more because it stressed the *idea* of individual private property in a new context (or in a context of new ideas). Thus it offered individualism (an old value) plus the apparently new means for its greater realization—freedom and equality (values that are conspicuously absent from feudalism). However, the only place where this ideal could be given an apparently concrete base was in the maintenance of an old institution: the family. Thus the family changed from being the economic basis of individual private property under feudalism to being the focal point of the *idea* of individual private property under a system that banished such an economic form from its central mode of production—capitalism. . . . The working class work socially in production for the private property of a few capitalists *in the hope of* individual private property for themselves and their families.[20]

The phrase "A man's home is his castle" offers a nicely condensed example of ideological construction in this sense. It reaches *back* to an emptied-out image of mastery and integration under feudalism in order to propel the male wage-worker *forward* to further feats of alienated labor, in the service of a now atomized and embattled, but all the more intensively idealized home. The man who has this home is a different person from the lord who has a castle; and the forms of property implied in the two possessives (his [mortgaged] home/ his [inherited] castle) are not only different but, as Mitchell points out, mutually contradictory. The contradiction is assuaged and filled in by transferring the lord's political and economic control over the *environs* of his castle to an image of the father's personal control over the *inmates* of his house. The ideological formulation thus permits a criss-crossing of agency, temporality, and space. It is important that ideology in this sense, even when its form is flatly declarative ("A man's home is his castle"), is always at least implicitly narrative, and that, in order for the reweaving of ideology to be truly invisible, the narrative is necessarily chiasmic in structure: that is, that the subject of the beginning of the narrative is different from the subject at the end, and that the two subjects cross each other in a rhetorical figure that conceals their discontinuity.

It is also important that the sutures of contradiction in these ideological narratives become most visible under the disassembling eye of an alternative narrative, ideological as that narrative may itself be. In addition, the diachronic opening-out of contradictions within the status quo, even when the project of that diachronic recasting is to conceal those very contradictions, can have just the opposite effect of making them newly visible, offering a new leverage for critique. For these reasons, distinguishing between the construction and the critique of ideological narrative is not always even a theoretical possibility, even with relatively flat texts; with the fat rich texts we are taking for examples in this project, no such attempt will be made.

Sexuality, like ideology, depends on the mutual redefinition and occlusion of synchronic and diachronic formulations. The developmental fact that, as Freud among others has shown, even the naming of sexuality as such is always retroactive in relation to most of the sensations and emotions that constitute it,[21] is *historically* important. What *counts* as the sexual is, as we shall see, variable and itself political. The exact, contingent space of indeterminacy—the place of shifting over time—of the mutual boundaries between the political and the sexual is, in fact, the most fertile space of ideological formation. This is true because ideological formation, like sexuality, depends on retroactive change in the naming or labelling of the subject.[22]

The two sides, the political and the erotic, necessarily obscure and misrepresent each other—but in ways that offer important and shifting affordances to all parties in historical gender and class struggle.

iv. What This Book Does

The difficult but potentially productive tension between historical and structuralist forms of feminism, in the theoretical grounding of this book, is echoed by a tension in the book between historical and more properly literary organization, methodologies, and emphases. Necessarily because of my particular aptitudes and training, if for no better reason, the historical argument almost throughout is embodied in and guided by the readings of the literary texts. For better and for worse, the large historical narrative has an off-centering effect on the discrete readings, as the introversive techniques of literary analysis have in turn on the historical argument. The resulting structure represents a continuing negotiation between the book's historicizing and dehistoricizing motives. The two ways in which I have described to myself the purpose of this book express a similar tension: first, to make it easier for readers to focus intelligently on male homosocial bonds throughout the heterosexual European erotic ethos; but secondly, to use the subject of sexuality to show the usefulness of certain Marxist-feminist historical categories for literary criticism, where they have so far had relatively little impact.

Chapter 1 of the book, "Gender Asymmetry and Erotic Triangles," locates the book's focus on male homosocial desire within the structural context of triangular, heterosexual desire. René Girard, Freud, and Lévi-Strauss, especially as he is interpreted by Gayle Rubin, offer the basic paradigm of "male traffic in women" that will underlie the entire book. In the next three chapters a historically deracinated reading of Shakespeare's Sonnets, a partially historical reading of Wycherley's *The Country Wife,* and a reading of Sterne's *A Sentimental Journey* in relation to the inextricable gender, class, and national anxieties of mid-eighteenth-century English men both establish some persistent paradigms for discussion, and begin to locate them specifically in the terms of modern England.

Chapters 5 and 6, on homophobia and the Romantic Gothic, discuss the paranoid Gothic tradition in the novel as an exploration of the changing meaning and importance of homophobia in England during and after the eighteenth century. A reading of James Hogg's *Confessions of a Justified Sinner* treats homophobia not most immediately as an oppression of homosexual men, but as a tool for manipulating the entire spectrum of male bonds, and hence the gender system as a whole.

Chapters 7 and 8 focus on more "mainstream," public Victorian ideological fictions, and on the fate of the women who are caught up in male homosocial exchange. This section treats three Victorian texts, historical or mock-historical, that claim to offer accounts of changes in women's relation to male bonds: Tennyson's *The Princess,* Thackeray's *Henry Esmond,* and Eliot's *Adam Bede;* it approaches most explicitly the different explanatory claims of structuralist and historical approaches to sex and gender.

Chapters 9 and 10, on Dickens' Victorian Gothic, show how Dickens' last two novels delineate the interactions of homophobia with nineteenth-century class and racial as well as gender division.

Finally, a Coda, "Toward the Twentieth Century: English Readers of Whitman," uses an account of some influential English (mis-)understandings of Whitman's poetry, to sketch in the links between mid-Victorian English sexual politics and the familiar modern Anglo-American landscape of male homosexuality, heterosexuality, and homophobia as (we think) we know them.

The choices I have made of texts through which to embody the argument of the book are specifically *not* meant to begin to delineate a separate male-homosocial literary canon. In fact, it will be essential to my argument to claim that the European canon as it exists is already such a canon, and most so when it is most heterosexual. In this sense, it would perhaps be easiest to describe this book (as will be done more explicitly in chapter 1) as a recasting of, and a refocusing on, René Girard's triangular schematization of the existing European canon in *Deceit, Desire, and the Novel*. In fact, I have simply chosen texts at pleasure from within or alongside the English canon that represented particularly interesting interpretive problems, or particularly symptomatic historical and ideological nodes, for understanding the politics of male homosociality.

I hope it is obvious by this point that I mean to situate this book in a dialectically usable, rather than an authoritative, relation to the rapidly developing discourse of feminist theory. Of course, the readings and interpretations are as careful in their own terms as I have known how to make them; but at the same time I am aware of having privileged certain arresting (and hence achronic) or potentially generalizable formulations, in the hope of making interpretations like these dialectically available to readers of other texts, as well. The formal models I have had in mind for this book are two very different books, Girard's *Deceit, Desire, and the Novel* and Dorothy Dinnerstein's *The Mermaid and the Minotaur*: not in this instance because of an agreement with the substance of their arguments, but because each in a relatively short study with an apparently idiosyncratic focus nevertheless conveys a complex of ideas forcefully enough—even, repetitiously enough—to make it a usable part of any reader's repertoire of approaches to her or his personal experience and future reading. *From* that position in the repertoire each can be—must be—criticized and changed. To take such a position has been my ambition for this book. Among the directions of critique and alteration that seem to me most called for, but which I have been unable so far to in-corporate properly in the argument itself, are the following:

First, the violence done by my historicizing narrative to the literary readings proper shows perhaps most glaringly in the overriding of dis-tinctions and structural considerations of genre. And in general, the number and the *different*ness of the many different mechanisms of mediation be-tween history and text—mechanisms with names like, for instance, "lit-erary convention," "literary history"—need to be reasserted in newly applicable formulations.

At the same time, the violences done to a historical argument by em-bodying it in a series of readings of works of literature are probably even more numerous and damaging. Aside from issues of ideological conden-sation and displacement that will be discussed in chapters 7 and 8, the form of violence most obvious to me is simply the limitation of my ar-gument *to* the "book-writing classes"—a group that is distinctive in more than merely socioeconomic terms, but importantly in those terms as well.

Next, the isolation, not to mention the absolute subordination, of women, in the structural paradigm on which this study is based (see chapter 1 for more on this) is a distortion that necessarily fails to do justice to women's own powers, bonds, and struggles.[23] The absence of lesbianism from the book was an early and, I think, necessary decision, since my argument is structured around the distinctive relation of the male ho-mosocial spectrum to the transmission of unequally distributed power. Nevertheless, the exclusively heterosexual perspective of the book's atten-tion to women is seriously impoverishing in itself, and also an index of the larger distortion. The reading of *Henry Esmond* is the only one that explicitly considers the bond of woman with woman in the context of male homosocial exchange; but much better analyses are needed of the relations between female-homosocial and male-homosocial structures.

The book's almost exclusive focus on male authors is, I think, similarly justified for this early stage of this particular inquiry; but it has a similar effect of impoverishing our sense of women's own cultural resources of resistance, adaptation, revision, and survival. My reluctance to distin-guish between "ideologizing" and "de-ideologizing" narratives may have had, paradoxically, a similar effect of presenting the "canonical" cultural discourse in an excessively protean and inescapable (*because* internally contradictory) form. In addition, the relation between the traffic-in-women paradigm used here and hypotheses, such as Dinnerstein's, Chodorow's, and Kristeva's in *Powers of Horror*, of a primary fear in men and women of the maternal power of women, is yet to be analyzed.

Again, the lack of entirely usable paradigms, at this early moment in feminist theory, for the complicated relations among violence, sexual violence, and the sadomasochistic sexualization of violence,[24] has led me in this book to a perhaps inappropriately gentle emphasis on modes of gender oppression that could be (more or less metaphorically) described in economic terms.

At the same time, the erotic and individualistic bias of literature itself, and the relative ease—not to mention the genuine pleasure—of using feminist theoretical paradigms to write about eros and sex, have led to a relative deemphasis of the many, crucially important male homosocial bonds that are less glamorous to talk about—such as the institutional, bureaucratic, and military.

Finally, and I think most importantly, the focus of this study on specifically English social structures, combined with the hegemonic claim for "universality" that has historically been implicit in the entire discourse of European social and psychological analysis, leave the relation of my discussion to non-European cultures and people entirely unspecified, and at present, perhaps, to some extent unspecifiable. A running subtext of comparisons between English sexual ideology and some ideologies of American racism is not a token attempt to conceal that gap in the book's coverage, but an attempt to make clear to other American readers some of the points of reference in white America that I have used in thinking about English ideology. Perhaps what one can most appropriately ask of readers who find this book's formulations useful is simply to remember that, important as it is that they be criticized at every step of even European applications, any attempt to treat them as cross-cultural or (far more) as universal ought to involve the most searching and particular analysis.

As a woman and a feminist writing (in part) about male homosexuality, I feel I must be especially explicit about the political groundings, assumptions, and ambitions of this study in that regard, as well. My intention throughout has been to conduct an antihomophobic as well as feminist inquiry. However, most of the (little) published analysis up to now of the relation between women and male homosexuality has been at a lower level of sophistication and care than either feminist or gay male analysis separately. In the absence of workable formulations about the male homosocial spectrum, this literature has, with only a few recent exceptions,[25] subscribed to one of two assumptions: either that gay men and all women share a "natural," transhistorical alliance and an essential identity of interests (e.g., in breaking down gender stereotypes);[26] or else that male homosexuality is an epitome, a personification, an effect, or perhaps a primary cause of woman-hating.[27] I do not believe either of these assumptions to be true. Especially because this study discusses a continuum, a potential structural congruence, and a (shifting) relation of meaning between male homosexual relationships and the male patriarchal relations by which women are oppressed, it is important to emphasize that I am not assuming or arguing either that patriarchal power is primarily or necessarily homosexual (as distinct from homosocial), or that male homosexual desire has a primary or necessary relationship to misogyny. Either of those arguments would be homophobic and, I believe, inaccurate. I will, however, be arguing that homophobia directed by men against men is misogynistic, and perhaps transhistorically so. (By "misogynistic" I mean not only that it is oppressive of the so-called feminine in men, but that it is oppressive of women.) The greatest potential for misinterpretation lies here. Because "homosexuality" and "homophobia" are, in any of their avatars, historical constructions, because they are likely to concern themselves intensely with each other and to assume interlocking or mirroring shapes, because the theater of their struggle is likely to be intrapsychic or intra-institutional as well as public, it is not always easy (sometimes barely possible) to distinguish them from each other. Thus, for instance, Freud's study of Dr. Schreber shows clearly that *the repression of homosexual desire* in a man who by any commonsense standard was heterosexual, occasioned paranoid psychosis; the psychoanalytic use that has been made of this perception, however, has been, not against *homophobia* and its schizogenic force, but against *homosexuality*—against homosexuals—on account of an association between "homosexuality" and mental illness.[28] Similar confusions have marked discussions of the relation between "homosexuality" and fascism. As the historically constructed nature of "homosexuality" as an institution becomes more fully understood, it should become possible to understand these distinctions in a more exact and less prejudicious theoretical context.

Thus, profound and intuitable as the bonds between feminism and antihomophobia often are in our society, the two forces are not the same. As the alliance between them is not automatic or transhistorical, it will be most fruitful if it is analytic and unpresuming. To shed light on the grounds and implications of that alliance, as well as, through these issues, on formative literary texts, is an aim of the readings that follow.

CHAPTER ONE

Gender Asymmetry and
Erotic Triangles

THE graphic schema on which I am going to be drawing most heavily in the readings that follow is the triangle. The triangle is useful
as a figure by which the "commonsense" of our intellectual tradition
schematizes erotic relations, and because it allows us to condense into a
juxtaposition with that folk-perception several somewhat different streams
of recent thought.

René Girard's early book, *Deceit, Desire, and the Novel,* was itself something of a schematization of the folk-wisdom of erotic triangles. Through
readings of major European fictions, Girard traced a calculus of power
that was structured by the relation of rivalry between the two active
members of an erotic triangle. What is most interesting for our purposes
in his study is its insistence that, in any erotic rivalry, the bond that links
the two rivals is as intense and potent as the bond that links either of the
rivals to the beloved: that the bonds of "rivalry" and "love," differently
as they are experienced, are equally powerful and in many senses equivalent. For instance, Girard finds many examples in which the choice of
the beloved is determined in the first place, not by the qualities of the
beloved, but by the beloved's already being the choice of the person who
has been chosen as a rival. In fact, Girard seems to see the bond between
rivals in an erotic triangle as being even stronger, more heavily determinant of actions and choices, than anything in the bond between either of
the lovers and the beloved. And within the male-centered novelistic tradition of European high culture, the triangles Girard traces are most often
those in which two males are rivals for a female; it is the bond between
males that he most assiduously uncovers.

The index to Girard's book gives only two citations for "homosexuality" per se, and it is one of the strengths of his formulation not to depend on how homosexuality as an entity was perceived or experienced—indeed, on what was or was not considered sexual—at any given historical moment. As a matter of fact, the symmetry of his formulation always depends on *suppressing* the subjective, historically determined account of which feelings are or are not part of the body of "sexuality." The transhistorical clarity gained by this organizing move naturally has a cost, however. Psychoanalysis, the recent work of Foucault, and feminist historical scholarship all suggest that the place of drawing the boundary between the sexual and the not-sexual, like the place of drawing the boundary between the realms of the two genders, *is* variable, but is *not* arbitrary. That is (as the example of *Gone with the Wind* suggests), the placement of the boundaries in a particular society affects not merely the definitions of those terms themselves—sexual/nonsexual, masculine/feminine—but also the apportionment of forms of power that are not obviously sexual. These include control over the means of production and reproduction of goods, persons, and meanings. So that Girard's account, which thinks it is describing a dialectic of power abstracted from either the male/female or the sexual/nonsexual dichotomies, is leaving out of consideration categories that in fact preside over the distribution of power in every known society. And because the distribution of power according to these dichotomies is not and possibly cannot be symmetrical, the hidden symmetries that Girard's triangle helps us discover will always in turn discover hidden obliquities. At the same time, even to bear in mind the lurking possibility of the Girardian symmetry is to be possessed of a graphic tool for historical measure. It will make it easier for us to perceive and discuss the mutual inscription in these texts of male homosocial and heterosocial desire, and the resistances to them.

Girard's argument is of course heavily dependent, not only on a brilliant intuition for taking seriously the received wisdom of sexual folklore, but also on a schematization from Freud: the Oedipal triangle, the situation of the young child that is attempting to situate itself with respect to a powerful father and a beloved mother. Freud's discussions of the etiology of "homosexuality" (which current research seems to be rendering questionable as a set of generalizations about personal histories of "homosexuals")[1] suggest homo- and heterosexual outcomes in adults to be the result of a complicated play of desire for and identification with the parent of each gender: the child routes its desire/identification through the mother to arrive at a role like the father's, or vice versa. Richard Klein summarizes this argument as follows:

> In the normal development of the little boy's progress towards heterosexuality, he must pass, as Freud says with increasing insistence in late essays like "Terminable and Interminable Analysis," through the stage of the "positive" Oedipus, a homoerotic identification with his father, a position of effeminized subordination to the father, as a condition of finding a model for his own heterosexual role. Conversely, in this theory, the development of the male homosexual requires the postulation of the father's absence or distance and an abnormally strong identification by the child with the mother, in which the child takes the place of the father. There results from this scheme a surprising neutralization of polarities: heterosexuality in the male . . . presupposes a homosexual phase as the condition of its normal possibility: homosexuality, obversely, requires that the child experience a powerful heterosexual identification.[2]

I have mentioned that Girard's reading presents itself as one whose symmetry is undisturbed by such differences as gender; although the triangles that most shape his view tend, in the European tradition, to involve bonds of "rivalry" between males "over" a woman, in his view *any* relation of rivalry is structured by the same play of emulation and identification, whether the entities occupying the corners of the triangle be heroes, heroines, gods, books, or whatever. In describing the Oedipal drama, Freud notoriously tended to place a male in the generic position of "child" and treat the case of the female as being more or less the same, "mutatis mutandis"; at any rate, as Freud is interpreted by conventional American psychoanalysis, the enormous difference in the degree and kind of female and male power enters psychoanalytic view, when at all, as a result rather than as an active determinant of familial and intrapsychic structures of development. Thus, both Girard and Freud (or at least the Freud of this interpretive tradition) treat the erotic triangle as symmetrical—in the sense that its structure would be relatively unaffected by the power difference that would be introduced by a change in the gender of one of the participants.

In addition, the asymmetry I spoke of in section i of the Introduction—the radically disrupted continuum, in our society, between sexual and nonsexual male bonds, as against the relatively smooth and palpable continuum of female homosocial desire—might be expected to alter the structure of erotic triangles in ways that depended on gender, and for which neither Freud nor Girard would offer an account. Both Freud and

Girard, in other words, treat erotic triangles under the Platonic light that perceives no discontinuity in the homosocial continuum—none, at any rate, that makes much difference—even in modern Western society. There is a kind of bravery about the proceeding of each in this respect, but a historical blindness, as well.

Recent rereadings and reinterpretations of Freud have gone much farther in taking into account the asymmetries of gender. In France, recent psychoanalytic discourse impelled by Jacques Lacan identifies power, language, and the Law itself with the phallus and the "name of the father." It goes without saying that such a discourse has the potential for setting in motion both feminist and virulently misogynistic analyses; it does, at any rate, offer tools, though not (so far) historically sensitive ones, for describing the mechanisms of patriarchal power in terms that are at once intrapsychic (Oedipal conflict) and public (language and the Law). Moreover, by distinguishing (however incompletely) the phallus, the locus of power, from the actual anatomical penis,[3] Lacan's account creates a space in which anatomic sex and cultural gender may be distinguished from one another and in which the different paths of *men's* relations to male power might be explored (e.g. in terms of class). In addition, it suggests ways of talking about the relation between the individual male and the cultural institutions of masculine domination that fall usefully under the rubric of representation.

A further contribution of Lacanian psychoanalysis that will be important for our investigation is the subtlety with which it articulates the slippery relation—already adumbrated in Freud—between desire and identification. The schematic elegance with which Richard Klein, in the passage I have quoted, is able to summarize the feminizing potential of desire for a woman and the masculinizing potential of subordination to a man, owes at least something to a Lacanian grinding of the lenses through which Freud is being viewed. In Lacan and those who have learned from him, an elaborate meditation on introjection and incorporation forms the link between the apparently dissimilar processes of desire and identification.

Recent American feminist work by Dorothy Dinnerstein and Nancy Chodorow also revises Freud in the direction of greater attention to gender/power difference. Coppélia Kahn summarizes the common theme of their argument (which she applies to Shakespeare) as follows:

> Most children, male or female, in Shakespeare's time, Freud's, or ours, are not only borne but raised by women. And thus arises a crucial difference

between the girl's developing sense of identity and the boy's. For though she follows the same sequence of symbiotic union, separation and individuation, identification, and object love as the boy, her femininity arises in relation to a person of the *same* sex, while his masculinity arises in relation to a person of the *opposite* sex. Her femininity is reinforced by her original symbiotic union with her mother and by the identification with her that must precede identity, while his masculinity is threatened by the same union and the same identification. While the boy's sense of *self* begins in union with the feminine, his sense of *masculinity* arises against it.[4]

It should be clear, then, from what has gone before, on the one hand that there are many and thorough asymmetries between the sexual continuums of women and men, between female and male sexuality and homosociality, and most pointedly between homosocial and heterosocial object choices for males; and on the other hand that the status of women, and the whole question of arrangements between genders, is deeply and inescapably inscribed in the structure even of relationships that seem to exclude women—even in male homosocial/homosexual relationships. Heidi Hartmann's definition of patriarchy in terms of "relationships between men" (see Introduction i), in making the power relationships between men and women appear to be dependent on the power relationships between men and men, suggests that large-scale social structures are congruent with the male-male-female erotic triangles described most forcefully by Girard and articulated most thoughtfully by others. We can go further than that, to say that in any male-dominated society, there is a special relationship between male homosocial (*including* homosexual) desire and the structures for maintaining and transmitting patriarchal power: a relationship founded on an inherent and potentially active structural congruence. For historical reasons, this special relationship may take the form of ideological homophobia, ideological homosexuality, or some highly conflicted but intensively structured combination of the two. (Lesbianism also must always be in a special relation to patriarchy, but on different [sometimes opposite] grounds and working through different mechanisms.)

Perhaps the most powerful recent argument through (and against) a traditional discipline that bears on these issues has occurred within anthropology. Based on readings and critiques of Lévi-Strauss and Engels, in addition to Freud and Lacan, Gayle Rubin has argued in an influential essay that patriarchal heterosexuality can best be discussed in terms of one or another form of the traffic in women: it is the use of women as ex-

changeable, perhaps symbolic, property for the primary purpose of cementing the bonds of men with men. For example, Lévi-Strauss writes,
"The total relationship of exchange which constitutes marriage is not established between a man and a woman, but between two groups of men,
and the woman figures only as one of the objects in the exchange, not as
one of the partners."[5] Thus, like Freud's "heterosexual" in Richard Klein's
account, Lévi-Strauss's normative man uses a woman as a "conduit of a
relationship" in which the true *partner* is a man.[6] Rejecting Lévi-Strauss's
celebratory treatment of this relegation of women, Rubin offers, instead,
an array of tools for specifying and analyzing it.

Luce Irigaray has used the Lévi-Straussian description of the traffic in
women to make a resounding though expensive leap of register in her
discussion of the relation of heterosexual to male homosocial bonds. In
the reflections translated into English as "When the Goods Get Together," she concludes: "[Male] homosexuality is the law that regulates
the sociocultural order. Heterosexuality amounts to the assignment of roles
in the economy."[7] To begin to describe this relation as having the asymmetry of (to put it roughly) *parole* to *langue* is wonderfully pregnant; if
her use of it here is not a historically responsive one, still it has potential
for increasing our ability to register historical difference.

The expensiveness of Irigaray's vision of male homosexuality is, oddly,
in a sacrifice of sex itself: the male "homosexuality" discussed here turns
out to represent anything but actual sex beteen men, which—although it
is also, importantly, called "homosexuality"—has something like the same
invariable, tabooed status for her larger, "real" "homosexuality" that incest has in principle for Lévi-Straussian kinship in general. Even Irigaray's supple machinery of meaning has the effect of transfixing, then sublimating, the quicksilver of sex itself.

The loss of the diachronic in a formulation like Irigaray's is, again, most
significant, as well. Recent anthropology, as well as historical work by
Foucault, Sheila Rowbotham, Jeffrey Weeks, Alan Bray, K. J. Dover, John
Boswell, David Fernbach, and others, suggests that among the things that
have changed radically in Western culture over the centuries, and vary
across cultures, about men's genital activity with men are its frequency,
its exclusivity, its class associations, its relation to the dominant culture,
its ethical status, the degree to which it is seen as defining nongenital
aspects of the lives of those who practice it, and, perhaps most radically,
its association with femininity or masculinity in societies where gender is
a profound determinant of power. The virility of the homosexual orien-

tation of male desire seemed as self-evident to the ancient Spartans, and perhaps to Whitman, as its effeminacy seems in contemporary popular culture. The importance of women (not merely of "the feminine," but of actual women as well) in the etiology and the continuing experience of male homosexuality seems to be historically volatile (across time, across class) to a similar degree. Its changes are inextricable from the changing shapes of the institutions by which gender and class inequality are structured.

Thus, Lacan, Chodorow and Dinnerstein, Rubin, Irigaray, and others, making critiques from within their multiple traditions, offer analytical tools for treating the erotic triangle not as an ahistorical, Platonic form, a deadly symmetry from which the historical accidents of gender, language, class, and power detract, but as a sensitive register precisely for delineating relationships of power and meaning, and for making graphically intelligible the play of desire and identification by which individuals negotiate with their societies for empowerment.

CHAPTER TWO

Swan in Love: The Example of Shakespeare's Sonnets

"A man is not feminized because he is inverted but because he is in love."
Barthes[1]

TO illustrate the suppleness and organizing power of the triangular schema, even within a dehistoricizing context, I would like to look briefly at Shakespeare's Sonnets. They are one of the two nonnovelistic texts that will frame this study (*Leaves of Grass* is the other), and I was attracted to them for similar reasons: both texts have figured importantly in the formation of a specifically homosexual (not just homosocial) male intertextuality. Whitman—visiting Whitman, liking Whitman, giving gifts of "Whitman"—was of course a Victorian homosexual shibboleth, and much more than that, a step in the consciousness and self-formation of many members of that new Victorian class, the bourgeois homosexual.[2] Shakespeare's Sonnets, similarly, have been a kind of floating decimal in male homosexual discourse; Wilde, Gide, Auden, Pasolini, and others have contributed to the way we understand them, while critics writing from outside that tradition have been forced by the Sonnets, as by few other pre-1895 texts, to confront its issues, speak its name, and at least formulate their working assumptions on the subject.

The Sonnets are different from *Leaves of Grass* in that their popularization, never mind their popularization as homosexual documents, did not occur until centuries had detached them from their original social, erotic, and narrative contexts. *The* tradition of the Sonnets is the tradition of reading them plucked from history and, indeed, from factual grounding. There are all the notorious mysteries of whether they are a sequence, when they were written, to whom and to how many people addressed, how autobiographical, how conventional, why published, etc., etc. To most readers of the sequence, this decontextualization has seemed to provide a license for interpreting the Sonnets as a relatively continuous erotic narrative played out, economically, by the smallest number of characters—in this case four, the poet, a fair youth, a rival poet, and a dark lady. I am going to take this reductive interpretive tradition (which represents the way I read the Sonnets, in fact) as a license in turn for using the Sonnets to illustrate, in a simplified because synchronic and ahistorical form, what I take to be some of the patterns traced by male homosocial desire. Marx's warning about the "developed, or stunted, or caricatured form etc." in which historically decontextualized abstractions are apt to appear should be prominently posted at the entrance.[3]

The Sonnets make good illustrative material because both the symmetry of the sexual triangle and the asymmetry of gender assignment are startlingly crisp in them. The Girardian point that the speaker cares as much about the fair youth as about the dark lady for whom, in the last group of sonnets, they are rivals, is Shakespeare's point, and no critic is likely to be more obsessive about the orderliness of the symmetry than the poet is himself.

> That thou hast her, it is not all my grief,
> And yet it may be said I loved her dearly;
> That she hath thee is of my wailing chief,
> A loss in love that touches me more nearly.
> Loving offenders, thus I will excuse ye:
> Thou dost love her, because thou know'st I love her,
> And for my sake ev'n so doth she abuse me,
> Suff'ring my friend for my sake to approve her.
> If I lose thee, my loss is my love's gain,
> And losing her, my friend hath found that loss;
> Both find each other, and I lose both twain,
> And both for my sake lay on me this cross. . . .[4]

It is easy to see from such a sonnet how a critic like Murray Krieger could insist that the sex of the beloved is irrelevant to the meaning of the Sonnets—at least of sonnets 1–126 (the ones usually thought to be addressed to a man). "In view of the chaste character of the neo-Platonic love [Shakespeare] speaks of . . . I must maintain that, whatever the truth, my case would not be altered by it."[5] Sonnet 42 is not strikingly neo-Platonic or even platonic, but even here the rhetorical effacement of "accidental" differences between lovers, between loves, in the service of a wishful recuperative ideal of symmetry and balance, is remarkably thorough.

Another, more famous example of the structural imperative in the Sonnets is more revealing about the interplay of this crystalline symmetry with the destabilizing force of gender difference.

> Two loves I have of comfort and despair,
> Which like two spirits do suggest me still;
> The better angel is a man right fair,
> The worser spirit a woman coloured ill.
> To win me soon to hell, my female evil
> Tempteth my better angel from my side,
> And would corrupt my saint to be a devil,
> Wooing his purity with her foul pride.
> And whether that my angel be turn'd fiend
> Suspect I may, yet not directly tell,
> But being both from me both to each friend,
> I guess one angel in another's hell.
> > Yet this shall I ne'er know, but live in doubt,
> > Till my bad angel fire my good one out. (144)

This sonnet creates and operates within a table of pairings that are syntactically arranged to be seen as always equal or exactly opposite:

love #1	love #2
comfort	despair
better	worser
MAN	WOMAN
right fair	coloured ill
angel	evil
saint	devil
purity	foul pride
angel	fiend
from me #1	from me #2
friend #1	friend #2.
. . .	. . .

The dominant syntactic structure, then, is highly symmetrical. Even within the list above, however, which is taken from the sonnet's first nine lines, and more strongly in the last five lines, semantic differences eddy about and finally wash over the sonnet's syntactic formality. By the end, even the syntactic symmetry is gone: the female has mastered three active verbs, while the male has only one, passive verb; and more importantly, the female has an attribute (a "hell") to which it is not syntactically clear whether the male has a counterpart.

Semantically, of course, the unequal valuations of male and female are blisteringly clear. Aside from the stark *opposition* of values (simply, good vs. evil), there is a related *asymmetry* of powers and energies. The female is the character who desires and acts; the male, at most, potentially resists. There is also the suggestion of a one-way route from point to point on this triangle: angels may turn fiend, but there is no suggestion that fiends may turn angel. The entire plot seems to depend on the initiative of one of the two supposedly corresponding spirits.

The question of "hell," again, is very slippery. In line five, where it first occurs, we arrive at it prepared for a tableau of a Herculean choice: two spirits, one at each hand, luring the speaker—to hell? to heaven? But it is just here that the poem's promise of symmetry starts to derail. (1) There is no mention of heaven, no active wooing by the better angel. (This sends us back to note that "comfort" is, after all, a rather oblique and undynamic role for a "better angel" in this tableau.) (2) More disruptively, the worser spirit is too sly, or too impatient, to engage the better angel in a brute, symmetrical tug-of-war over the speaker, deciding instead to suborn the good angel first. For the rest of the poem she ignores the poet altogether. And in fact, the shape of the poem after line five presents an importantly rearranged tableau: the better angel in the central, Herculean spot, flanked by the worser spirit soliciting at one side and the poet, dumbstruck but hoping for the best, at the other. Presumably the elided final tableau that the worser spirit is supposed to have in mind would be conclusively asymmetrical: good angel turned to a fiend, and both of them tugging at the poet from the same side, certain of overpowering him. On the other hand, everyone seems to have forgotten by line 14 that that was ever the point. The coolness with which the possibility of a "heaven" for the poet (and, indeed, the question of the poet's destiny at all, even the centrality of the poet) is made to evaporate from the poem is rather breathtaking; surely that, more than particular suspicions about the two spirits, makes the poem so disconcerted and moving.

By line 12, the question about the symmetry of "hell" is not whether the good angel has a heaven to compete with the fiend's hell, but whether or not the good angel himself has a hell: after the symmetrical symmetries of the preceding line, "I guess one angel in another's hell" could be indeterminate. Of course, the determination might be semantic, depending on whether one reads "hell" generally as the torment of erotic obsession (which could pertain to either) or pointedly as vagina (which must pertain to the worser spirit). The final line certainly settles the question of whose hell is being discussed, and at least inclines the question of how to interpret "hell" in the direction of the vagina, as well.

If we now stop abstracting the issues of this sonnet into "symmetry" and "asymmetry," what do we find? A distribution of traits between a man and a woman in which the woman finds grouped with her femaleness an overwhelmingly, eschatologically negative moral valuation, a monopoly on initiative, desire, and power, and a strain of syntax and word choice suggesting that she is the container and others are the thing contained. The connection between the negative moral valuation and the negative (concave) space is not surprising as a treatment of femaleness; neither is the connection between negative male valuation and active female desire; but that "hell's" hunger, implicit and undescribed, should be the *only* active force in a domain that includes, besides the woman, two men, seems distinctive and from a post-Romantic vantage surprising. (Barthes for instance, in his useful compendium of received ideas, associates woman with absence but it is on account of her passivity: "Woman is faithful (she waits), man is fickle (he sails away, he cruises). It is Woman who gives shape to absence, elaborates its fiction, for she has time to do so."[6] It would be anachronistic to associate the Dark Lady with that particular, otiose, bourgeois Eternal Feminine.)

The male who is paired with/against this female has, at the most, one trait (if "fair" means beautiful here and not just not "coloured"), and no energy. Even to be "tempted" or "corrupted" does not seem to be a dynamic, internal process for him, as far as this sonnet shows; he seems to be stolidly, unitarily, purely either angel or fiend, in hell or out of hell.

The third member of the triangle, the second male, syntactically unpaired, the first person, has something in common with each of the others. Like the worser spirit, he is actually the subject of active verbs, the locus rather than merely the object of happenings. On the other hand, the verbs are not *very* active—verbs not even of knowing, but of not knowing. Conscious, self-divided, and even to some degree sharing a de-

sire with "my female evil," the narrator is nevertheless more closely identified (as passive, as object, as male) with "my saint."

The basic configuration here, then, includes a stylized female who
functions as a subject of action but not of thought; a stylized male who
functions as pure object; and a less stylized male speaker who functions
as a subject of thought but not of action. Uncommonsensical as it may
be, this conformation is very characteristic of the Sonnets as a whole, and
is recurrent in the plays. What interests me here is not the devastating
thoroughness with which the Sonnets record and thematize misogyny and
gynephobia, but rather the ways in which that plays off against the range
of male bonds and the speaker's programmatic assertions of symmetry.

Really, in the Sonnets, we are dealing with *two* possible strong symmetries. The one I have been discussing in Sonnet 144, and to which we
shall return, is the asserted and subverted symmetry between the fair youth
and the dark lady as objects of the speaker's desire. This symmetry is most
forcefully presented in the sonnets that are directly about the triangular
love among the three of them, but it is also suggested by comparisons
between early sonnets addressed to the youth alone and later sonnets addressed to the lady. The other symmetry, which is writ so large in the
Sonnets as to be almost invisible, is between the first group, where the
speaker is pleading with the fair youth to put an end to his celibacy and
enter the heterosexual order, and the last group, where the speaker is
plunged into torment by the fair youth's heterosexual involvement with
the speaker's mistress. To what extent does the final configuration of
poet/youth/lady supply an echoing answer, even if a cruelly ironic or accurate one, to the demands the poet makes of the fair youth in the first
group of sonnets?

Part of the difficulty of superimposing the heterosexuality that the poet
prescribes for the youth in the early sonnets onto the heterosexuality by
which the youth and the lady torment the poet in the last sonnets is that
the first group of sonnets is notable for the almost complete absence of
mention of women; women are merely the vehicles by which men breed
more men, for the gratification of other men:

> Make thee another self for love of me,
> That beauty still may live in thine or thee. (10)

Women are introduced into these early sonnets mostly as suggesting possible obstacles, which are then discounted:

> For where is she so fair whose uneared womb
> Disdains the tillage of thy husbandry? (3)

> Is it for fear to wet a widow's eye
> That thou consum'st thyself in single life?
> Ah, if thou issueless shalt hap to die,
> The world will wail thee like a makeless wife. (9)

On the whole, the project of instilling in the fair youth a socialized, heterosexual identity is conducted firmly under the aspect of male relationships and solicitations. If any one attitude toward women is presumed in the youth, it is indifference, or perhaps active repulsion, suggested in Sonnet 8:

> If the true concord of well tuned sounds,
> By unions married, do offend thine ear
> They do but sweetly chide thee, who con-
>   founds
> In singleness the parts that thou shouldst bear.

("Thou single wilt prove none," the poem concludes, prefiguring the "none" and "nothing" of Sonnet 136, and meaning essentially the same thing as the brutal highschool-boy axiom, "Use it or lose it.") Neither desire for women nor even mastery seems to be an explicit issue; what is at stake is preserving the continuity of an existing dominant culture.

· The argumentative trajectory of these early sonnets is via the heterosexual, the manly, toward the homosocial, or men. Actual women are so far from the center of consciousness that even to be womanlike, *in relation to men,* is not very dangerous. Sonnet 20, which begins famously

> A woman's face, with nature's own hand painted
> Hast thou, the master mistress of my passion—

seems in the context of those earlier poems to be part of the heterosexualizing campaign. You can have women and *still* keep loving me, the speaker seems to say:

> Mine be thy love, and thy love's use their treasure.

Even the speaker's apparent disclaimer of any active, genital sexual interest in the youth, in this sonnet, suggests a light-hearted equivocation: the boy's penis is "one thing to my purpose nothing"; but here again as else-where in the Sonnets, "nothing" denotes, among other things, female genitals. (I do not make this point in order to assert that the Sonnets *say* that there was a genital sexual relationship between these men; to the best of my understanding, the sexual context of that period is too far irrecov-erable for us to be able to disentangle boasts, confessions, undertones, overtones, jokes, the unthinkable, the taken-for-granted, the unmention-able-but-often-done-anyway, etc.) What can be said is that the speaker in this sonnet can, for one reason or another, afford to be relaxed and ur-bane (in what may not have been intended to be a public text) on the subject of sexual interchangeability of males and females—as long as he is addressing a male. And this closeness between males, to which a reader from outside the culture finds it difficult to perceive the boundaries, seems to occur unproblematically within a suasive context of heterosexual so-cialization.

My persistence in referring to the fair youth sonnets as heterosexual may require more explanation. If all this is heterosexual, the common-sensical reader may ask, then what on earth does it take to be homosex-ual? One thing that it takes is a cultural context that defines the homosexual as against the heterosexual. My point is obviously not to deny or de-em-phasize the love between men in the Sonnets, the intense and often gen-itally oriented language that describes that love, or even the possibility that the love described may have been genitally acted out. Nor do I mean to argue that the bond between the speaker and his male beloved is less strong, less central, or, certainly, less valued ethically than the bond with the desired female. However, I am saying that within the world sketched in these sonnets, there is not an equal opposition or a choice posited be-tween two such institutions as homosexuality (under whatever name) and heterosexuality. The Sonnets present a male-male love that, like the love of the Greeks, is set firmly within a structure of institutionalized social relations that are carried out via women: marriage, name, family, loyalty to progenitors and to posterity, all depend on the youth's making a par-ticular use of women that is not, in the abstract, seen as opposing, de-nying, or detracting from his bond to the speaker.

When we turn from the heterosexuality of the early poems to that of the final poems, on the other hand, we find threat and chaos. The most obvious difference is that this is a heterosexuality that includes women. (Precisely, it includes *a* woman; how different this world would look through a frame that encompassed relations among women is moot in this intensively focused series.) As we saw in "Two loves I have," to say that a woman is present is not to say that her point of view is expressed, that we are in a position to know anything about her, or that she is a subject of consciousness; although she is a subject of action. (It is easy to fail to perceive how little the Sonnets present the lady—and, for that matter, the youth—as characters, and that failure of readerly perspective occurs for a particular reason: since the nineteenth century it has been easiest to read the Sonnets as a novel, but the novel had made the claim that its main characters were knowable. Thus Oscar Wilde feels free to extend his authoritative insight into the speaker, toward the lady, as well, as if they were knowable in the same way: for instance he is confident that Richard Burbage "was not the sort of man who would have fascinated" her.[7] It remained, probably, for novel-readers educated by Proust, to recover the radical partiality of desiring vision (different from the mere play of point-of-view, as in James) that had seemed natural to prenovelistic readers of the Sonnets-as-lyric.) The dark lady is, for the most part, perceptible only as a pair of eyes and a vagina, but even in such a fragmentary form she disrupts that earlier vision of heterosexuality in which it had denoted mainly a broad avenue of patrimonial continuity among males. The irruption of an actual female onto the scene coincides with the disappearance of the children, miniature fathers, who were to have been the object of the sexual union in the early sonnets; and it also coincides with the end of the rhetoric urging the youth to keep the paternal roof in good repair.

The heterosexuality that succeeded in eclipsing women was also, as we have seen, relatively unthreatened by the feminization of one man in relation to another. To be feminized or suffer gender confusion within a framework that includes a woman is, however, dire; and, as we shall see, *any* erotic involvement with an actual woman threatens to be unmanning. Lust itself (meaning, in this context, desire for women) is a machine for depriving males of self-identity (Sonnet 129).

The inclusion of a woman alters not only heterosexual but specifically homosocial relations, as well. The speaker's early relationship with the fair youth is like his later relationship with the dark lady in that he can commune with other men through the beloved. Either love brings its male subject into relation with other males, but that relation may confirm or subvert the position of the subject.

Even concerning the dark lady, the response to sharing sexual territory with other men may be unexpectedly, if briefly, exhilarated. It is a way of participating in a supraindividual male power over women, and of being close to more fully entitled males. Two consecutive sonnets make an especially important example of the mechanisms of and internal threats to this exhilaration.

> Whoever hath her wish, thou hast thy will,
> And will to boot, and will in overplus;
> More than enough am I that vex thee still,
> To thy sweet will making addition thus.
> Wilt thou, whose will is large and spacious,
> Not once vouchsafe to hide my will in thine?
> Shall will in others seem right gracious,
> And in my will no fair acceptance shine?
> The sea, all water, yet receives rain still,
> And in abundance addeth to his store;
> So thou being rich in will add to thy will
> One will of mine, to make thy large will more.
>> Let no unkind, no fair beseechers kill;
>> Think all but one, and me in that one will.
>
> If thy soul check thee that I come so near,
> Swear to thy blind soul that I was thy will,
> And will thy soul knows is admitted there;
> Thus far for love my love-suit sweet fulfil.
> Will will fulfill the treasure of thy love,
> Ay fill it full with wills, and my will one.
> In things of great receipt with ease we prove,
> Among a number one is reckoned none.
> Then in the number let me pass untold,
> Though in thy store's account I one must be,
> For nothing hold me, so it please thee hold
> That nothing me, a something sweet to thee.
>> Make but my name thy love, and love that still,
>> And then thou lov'st me, for my name is Will. (135,136)

The cutely boyish speaker in these sonnets ("More than enough am I that vex thee still") seems to feel that more is merrier; it is funny, even as it is very insulting, to court someone on the basis simply that she will not know you are there. (It is insulting even aside from the attribution of promiscuity, insulting through an image that some women might also find appealing: female sexuality as a great sociable melting-pot, accommodating without fuss the creatures it has admitted through sheer inattention.) Whereas in "Two loves I have" (and characteristically in the

Sonnets) it seems that sexual pleasure is something that belongs only to women, in these obscene and pleasurable sonnets it seems oddly that no one is in a position to feel anything very sexual, at least until the last four lines of 136: the men, or their "wills," seem to be reduced to the scale of homunculi, almost plankton, in a warm but unobservant sea. What are the pleasures that our "Will" promises himself? To hide, or more pleasurably, to be hidden, a delight of toddlerhood; but more importantly and adultly, the pleasure of giving his name (Will) to a woman (or part of a woman); the pleasure of being mistaken for a man or men who have some proprietary rights in the woman; perhaps the pleasure of being mistaken for a younger and more energetic male; and in general, the pleasure of amalgamation, not in the first place with the receptive woman but with the other men received ("Think all but one, and me in that one will"). Here is a man who is serious about rolling *all* his strength and *all* his sweetness up into one ball.

My point is of course again not that we are here in the presence of homosexuality (which would be anachronistic) but rather (risking anachronism) that we are in the presence of male heterosexual desire, in the form of a desire to consolidate partnership with authoritative males in and through the bodies of females.

But the path of heterosexual desire is never simple. In the short moment of playful exhilaration dangers are invoked that will not be blandished away at line 14. The sonnet after these two is one of the most wretchedly bitter of the series, though tied to the happier ones by strong thematic links. How can we trace the potential for disaster and the disaster's nascent form in the "will" sonnets?

It is too unexplanatory to say that jealousy is lying in wait. Perhaps a rhetorical sidestep would be more helpful. Notice, among the pleasures of 135–136, the satisfaction of naming genitals, the odd career of these obscene periphrases. Stephen Booth gives evidence that these syllables were used by other writers with the same meanings (as what was not), but in the case of "will" (for instance) no erudition is necessary. The nonsensical iteration (14 "will"s in Sonnet 135) tells the whole story: it has to point to a double entendre, and double entendre, by definition, can mean only one thing. But this double entendre means too many things; it is the name of at least one, probably two, and possibly three of the men involved; it is an auxiliary verb with the future tense; it is a common noun meaning (roughly) desire; it means penis; it means vagina. Its gender bearings are, far from neutral, but wildly and, as it turns out, dangerously scattered.

What seems most striking in the poem's treatment of "will" is the extension of the word (as, really, its main meaning) to the female genitals, considering that its first meaning on this particular stage must have been as a male name, the poet's own and perhaps his beloved's. Why should he do this? The genital names in 136 are also shifty in gender. Booth glosses "nothing" in Sonnet 20, "(1) worthless; (2) no-thing, a non-thing. 'Nothing' and 'naught' were popular cant terms for 'vulva' (perhaps because of the shape of a zero)" (p. 164). The speaker, momentarily sanguine enough to be renunciatory, is willing (for privileges) to be "reckoned none"—"For nothing hold me," as long as you hold me, "hold/ That nothing me, a something sweet to thee." This last nothing, the one that is to be held "to thee," seems most distinctly to be a penis; in fact these are the only lines in the two sonnets that sound like actual genital sensation, as opposed to the gargantuan, distracted catholicity of the dark lady's "will." But the speaker's sensate "nothing" is only barely not a female organ or no-thing. The dark lady's pleasure in holding him is finally meant to be masked, not by her pleasure in some other Will, but by her pleasure in holding her own genitals—"For nothing hold me." Similarly in the couplet, "love" takes its place in the chain of names for ambisexual genitals. "Make but my name thy love," the poet instructs, and specifies which name: Will, the vagina/penis. (If he had focused on his other name, the gender ambiguities would have been over-balanced.) "And love that still,/ And then thou lov'st me . . . ."

To attribute masturbatory pleasure to the woman is unusual in these poems—unusually benign and empathetic, I would say. What is not unusual is the rhythm in which, plunging into heterosexual adventure with an eye to confirming his identification with other men, the speaker finds himself unexpectedly entrapped in, not quite an identification, but a confusion of identities with the woman, instead. The moment when sexual pleasure, as opposed to bravado and joky insult, enters the poem is the moment when the speaker risks being held for "nothing"; when, as he gives his name to the woman's "love," the name itself is feminized. The very next sonnet begins with a furious adjuration:

> *Thou blind fool love,* what dost thou to mine eyes,
> That they behold and see not what they see?
> They know what beauty is, see where it lies,
> Yet what the best is take the worst to be.
>
> (137; emphasis mine)

Leslie Fiedler, discussing some closely related issues in Shakespeare's poetry, makes a wonderfully apt use of Ovid's treatment of Hermaphroditus, a man in flight from women who, plunging into a pool, is transformed into a half-man half-woman. His curse:

> . . . O father and mother, grant me this!
> May every one hereafter, who comes diving
> Into this pool, emerge half man, made weaker
> By the touch of this evil water![8]

In the Sonnets, the pool in which this transformation takes place is the female Hell. Only women have the power to make men less than men within this world. At the same time, to be fully a man requires having obtained the instrumental use of a woman, having *risked* transformation by her.

To have contact with other men through a rivalry for a male beloved has structural similarities to the rivalries for the dark lady, but it is less radically threatening. Just as it is possible for the "large and spacious" lady to think all her lovers "but one, and me in that one," so the fair youth, too, is a place where the elite meet. "All love's loving parts," the "trophies of my lovers gone," live "hung," "buried," "hidden" in the fair youth;

> Their images I loved I view in thee,
> And thou, all they, hast all the all of me. (31)

The value of the youth is increased by his power to attract and concentrate the love of other men; it is attractive, not incriminating, for a man to possess a "lovely gaze where every eye doth dwell" (5). The hating lines about the dark lady in 137, in the catastrophic denouement after the "Will" sonnets, are a damned and damning echo of that bland "lovely gaze where every eye doth dwell," however:

> If eyes corrupt by over-partial looks
> Be anchored in the bay where all men ride,
> Why of eyes' falsehood hast thou forged hooks,
> Whereto the judgement of my heart is tied?
> Why should my heart think that a several plot,
> Which my heart knows the wide world's common place?

"The bay where all men ride" of course is the dysphoric transformation of the spermatic community of 135 ("The sea, all water, yet receives rain still,/ And in abundance addeth to his store;/ So thou, being rich in 'Will' . . ."). A humbler, less hysterical seamanship is applied to the youth and his relation to the rival poet.

> . . . since your worth, wide as the ocean is,
> The humble as the proudest sail doth bear,
> My saucy bark, inferior far to his,
> On your broad main doth wilfully appear.
> Your shallowest help will hold me up afloat,
> Whilst he upon your soundless deep doth ride;
> Or, being wracked, I am a worthless boat,
> He of tall building and of goodly pride. (80)

It would be quite wrong to say that the speaker never expresses jealousy over the fair youth (in the pre-dark-lady sonnets) to correspond to the jealousy he expresses over the dark lady. As the example of the beloved-as-ocean metaphor suggests, the thematic and so to speak generic parallels between the two loves are fairly complete. Corresponding occasions for celebration, disquiet, accusation, self-torment, epic simile, and so forth, occur in the two relationships, a correspondence that is knotted into a threatening unity in the final triangle. But the affective, structural, and stylistic differences in treatment are, for the most part, only barely not enough to conceal the thematic correspondences.

Let me take as an example—because it is especially interesting on gender grounds—the question of self-division and self-identity in the youth and the lady. To the extent that the Sonnets say anything "factual" about this, they say that both the youth and the lady have the ability to deceive the speaker, and that he at least sometimes suspects each of them of doing so. Nevertheless, the Sonnets' poetic goes to almost any length to treat the youth as a moral monolith; while the very definition of the lady seems to be doubleness and deceit. What changes, in order to compose such different pictures around essentially similar elements, is the position—the self-definition—of the speaker.

In the sonnets addressed to the fair youth, there is plenty of dissonance, doubleness, and self-division, but it is all described as located outside the youth himself, and whenever possible, within the speaker. The relation of the youth's deceits to himself is that of clouds—at most, eclipses—to the sun; but their effect on the speaker is to divide him against himself in the very effort to understand and excuse the supposedly simpler, pastoral youth,

Authorizing thy trespass with compare,
Myself corrupting salving thy amiss,
Excusing thy sins more than thy sins are;
For to thy sensual fault I bring in sense—
Thy adverse party is thy advocate—
And 'gainst myself a lawful plea commence. (35)

So shall those blots that do with me remain,
Without thy help by me be borne alone. (36)

Against that time [when you cease to love me] do I ensconce me here
Within the knowledge of mine own desert,
And this my hand against myself uprear
To guard the lawful reasons on thy part— (49)

When thou shalt be disposed to set me light,
And place my merit in the eye of scorn,
Upon thy side against myself I'll fight,
And prove thee virtuous, though thou art forsworn. (88)

Say that thou didst forsake me for some fault,
And I will comment upon that offense.
Speak of my lameness, and I straight will halt. . . . (89)

Incapable of more, replete with you,
My most true mind thus maketh m'eyne untrue. (113)

The youth's very indivisibleness can seem sinister: if he were to betray the speaker, it would be impossible to detect,

For there can live no hatred in thine eye,
Therefore in that I cannot know thy change.
In many's looks, the false heart's history
Is writ in moods and frowns and wrinkles strange;
But heav'n in thy creation did decree,
That in thy face sweet love should ever dwell,
Whate'er thy thoughts or thy heart's workings be,
Thy looks should nothing thence but sweetness tell. (93)

The notorious difficulties of Sonnet 94, "They that have pow'r to hurt, and will do none," are at least partly traceable to this interplay between the (apparent) monolithicness of the youth and the self-divisive effect he has on the man who loves him. When the youth does change, an imperious and punitive external agent—Time—is called into play to effect the alteration.

All this is very different from the speaker's treatment of the dark lady, but it is oddly familiar as *a* style of addressing—of objectifying—women. The Sonnets present fair youth-as-ingenue, as the prerational, premoral, essentially prehuman creature that it is not possible to resist, to understand, or to blame. Like Marilyn Monroe, the youth makes the man viewing him feel old, vitiated, and responsible, even as the man luxuriates in the presence (the almost promise) of youth and self-possession. The cognitive division of labor set by the speaker is perfectly clear: you are sensuality, I am sense; you are animal ease and sweetness and authenticity, I am adult guilt and self-subversion and ambivalence. The corollary of this division of labor is that you can do anything to me—reject me, torment me, exhaust me, make me crazy—anything except surprise me. For there is a strong anticipatory self-protectiveness in the speaker's attitude to the youth (anything you can do to me, I can do worse) that is one of the strongest links with the lovers in Proust, and one of the things that most prevents the fair youth from becoming visible in his own right. The speaker's best (at any rate, most characteristic) expression of love is a forestalling of disloyalty, or of a regret which there is no evidence that the youth proffers:

> No longer mourn for me when I am dead
> Than you shall hear the surly sullen bell . . .
> Nay, if you read this line, remember not
> The hand that writ it, for I love you so
> That I in your sweet thoughts would be forgot,
> If thinking on me then should make you woe. (71)
>
> After my death, dear love, forget me quite. . . . (72)
>
> No more be grieved at that which thou hast done. . . . (35)
>
> Take all my loves, my love, yea take them all. . . . (40)
>
> That god forbid, that made me first your slave,
> I should in thought control your times of pleasure. . . . (58)

The youth's changes, disloyalties, qualms, self-divisions, *arrières-pensées*, are so comprehensively anticipated and personified by his admirer—in order to preserve the image of the beloved as simple and single-hearted to a degree that, the speaker knows, no one *can* be—that the image of the youth himself is flattened and all but effaced. Readers' intuitive guesses about the youth swing wide: one reader's Alcibiades is another's Lord Alfred Douglas.

To say that the speaker treats the youth, rhetorically, as a dumb blonde, is not to say that the youth is effeminized in the sonnets. To the contrary, it is to emphasize how historically contingent even the most influentially oppressive images of women are: Marilyn Monroe, Hetty Sorrel, Bella Wilfer, even Milton's Eve are not part of Shakespeare's repertoire of damaging or exalting female portraits. (If anything, the fair youth, "woman's face" and all, is presented as exaggeratedly phallic—unitary, straightforward, unreflective, pink, and dense.) The youth has his womanlike features, but in the Gestalt of the Sonnets, he is a very touchstone of maleness: he represents the masculine as pure object. In fact, to the degree that self-division is seen as always displaced from him to take up residence in the speaker, it is the speaker who is, in this context, rendered more feminine.

For contagious self-division seems to be the definition of femininity in the Sonnets—or, more succinctly, "false plague," meaning plague of falseness. The extraordinarily dilative insistence on the "paradox" of a woman who is *dark* being perceived as *fair* (an otherwise not very telling pun that is the crux of at least ten of the dark lady sonnets) indicates that, in some way not so facilely expressed, to be a woman is already to be oxymoron militant, and to love or desire a woman is to be split with the same chisel.

> My thoughts and my discourse as madmen's are,
> At random from the truth vainly expressed:
>> For I have sworn thee fair, and thought thee bright,
>> Who art as black as hell, as dark as night. (147)

The implicit homology fair:dark::fair:foul, the association of foulness with contagious illness on the one hand, and of darkness with hell and with female genitals on the other, lead to a clustering together of the woman's dark coloring, the "falseness" of its being perceived as fair, her sexual promiscuity (one kind of contagion of falseness), and the speaker's alienation from himself (another kind of contagion of falseness).

The speaker's psychic strategy in his relationship with the fair youth had been to voluntarily absorb the shock of any self-division in the youth;

for the youth to be "fair" meant to be unified and static, at the expense of the person in whose eyes he was "fair." The relationship with the dark lady is not all that different; but in this case the self-division is seen as originally lodged in her, and as communicated to the speaker in a manner over which he can exert no control. The speaker's exercises in anticipatory forgiveness, the forestalling of betrayal by self-betrayal, are not applicable to the woman as they had been to the man; instead, the speaker is hystericized, reduced to the voice of his resistance and his hating submission to her.

One useful way of putting the difference between the male-male bond and the male-female bond seems to be that the tensions implicit in the male-male bond are spatially conceived (you are this way, I am that way) and hence imagined as stable; while the tensions of the male-female bond are temporally conceived (as you are, so shall I be) and hence obviously volatile. Thus, to be self-divided in loving the fair youth feels like being stoical, while to be self-divided in loving the dark lady feels like becoming ruined. Differently put, for a man to undergo even a humiliating change in the course of a relationship with a man still feels like preserving or participating in a sum of male power, while for a man to undergo any change in the course of a relationship with a woman feels like a radical degeneration of substance.

This difference also helps describe the impression of sexlessness that persists in the relation of speaker to fair youth, even in the face of any amount of naughtiness, genital allusion, minute personal attention, frustration, and just plain love. Sexuality itself seems to be defined in the Sonnets, not primarily in terms of any of those things, but as a principle of irreversible change, as the diachronic itself,

> A bliss in proof, and proved, a very woe,
> Before, a joy proposed, behind, a dream (129)

in *opposition* to love, the "ever-fixed mark" (116). (Thus the mutilating, ravenous male figure, Time, in the fair youth sonnets, may be on the side of what will later turn out to be (female) sexuality—but is to be *opposed* by the institutions of marriage and family, as well as by poetry.) We have seen that in the most direct description of the supposedly symmetrical triangle, in Sonnet 144, both action and sexuality are exclusively female prerogatives, but both happen only through altering men, through taking them on the one-way journey from angel to fiend, from heaven (or, in some other versions, via heaven) to hell.

From this point, several different theoretical strategies might take over. Most readily, the genital allegory suggested above for the transfer of power between males and females could be made more explicit and complex, and, I think profitably, could be extended in the direction of the implicit and extremely volatile image of the family, of childhood and motherhood and perhaps most interestingly of fatherhood, that lurks among the Sonnets.

An even more interesting line of discussion, however, and one that would help give the question of family some specificity and grounding, would require us to pluralize and specify the notion of power, which I have had to treat so far as reified and even quantitative. It is here that one most wishes the Sonnets were a novel, that readers have most treated it as a novel, and that we are, instead, going to bring the Sonnets' preoccupations to bear on real novels. Not to know whether the youth's "power to hurt" represents the nobleman's power of patronage, or the actor's power over the playwright, even though each could be embodied in a bond of love; not to know how far "that beauteous roof . . . Which to repair should be thy chief desire" (10) represents the youth's stewardship of a pre-established house and name, or his narcissistic adventurism with an individualistic capital of looks and virility; not to know in what senses the pervasive language of law, of capital and usury, of food and need, may really have been knitting together these relationships; not to know in the specificity of a class, a gender, a historical moment, what a person dares who breaks her "bed-vow" (152) or endangers who "rob[s] others' beds' revenues of their rents" (142); not to know how pivotally sardonic the underlying taunt may be when a given man asks a given woman,

> What need'st thou wound with cunning when thy might
> Is more than my o'erpressed defence can bide? (139)

—not, in short, to have even a primer to the language of worldliness in this work *except* insofar as it is purely self-reflexive—what we lose in these great blanks is not "the man Shakespeare," or his age, but much of the texture, the proportions, the syntax, the rhetoric, of a mercurial and obsessive meditation on sexual politics. Moreover, our reading across the great blanks drives us to wider misprision—specifically, to universalizing and essentializing, in defense against our age's and class's anxieties, certain of the few particulars that happen powerfully to remain from the discourse of a different age and class (e.g., the genital allegory). Gender and genitals we have always with us; but "family," "sexuality," "masculine," "feminine," "power," "career," "privacy," "desire," the meanings and substance of gender and genitals, are embodied in times and institutions, literature among them.

At the same time, the following are among the tentative generalizations offered by this deracinated reading of the Sonnets to the more filiated, novelistic readings ahead:

An erotic triangle is likely to be experienced in terms of an explicit or implicit assertion of symmetry between genders and between homo- and hetero-social or -sexual bonds.

That symmetry will be factitious or distorted both because of the raw differences in the amount and kinds of male and female power, and because in the discourse of most cultures, beneath a rhetoric of "opposites" and "counterparts" and "complementarity," one gender is treated as a marginalized subset rather than as an equal alternative to the other. As a corollary, bonds between members of the same sex will not be directly comparable with bonds to members of the other sex (and same-sex bonds between men will have different meanings and bearings from same-sex bonds between women). Male homosexual bonds may have a subsumed and marginalized relation to male heterosexuality similar to the relation of femaleness to maleness, but different because carried out within an already dominantly male-homosocial sphere.

The assertion of symmetry will be made possible by a suppression of effectual gender differences or by a translation of them into factitiously comparable spatial and/or temporal rhetorical figures; the "comparable" figures will bear the mark of their asymmetrical origins but not in a way that will permit them to be retranslated into an intelligible version of their original condition.

The figure of a person who can be "halfway between" male and female will recur as an important topos for the fiction of gender symmetry, but in a form that finally reveals the tendentiousness of the assertion of symmetry. This has been a sticking point in even some very acute and daring criticism of the Sonnets; the rhetorical and political juggernaut toward symmetry has led, for instance, Wilde, Wyndham Lewis, and G. Wilson Knight to privilege the feminized male as a *shaman,* as the observer beyond gender: "Poetry is itself a bisexual awareness, or action"; "In any ordinary love-affair the male finds completion in the female. Here a completed unit, for at choice moments the poet attains to such a state, sees its soul-state reflected in a physical embodiment of its own unity [the fair youth]; and from that unique experience flower our supreme pieces."[9]

Finally, as I suggested in the Introduction, while genital sexuality is a good place to look for a concentration of language about power relationships, the relation of that language—and, in fact, of sexuality itself—to other power relationships is one of meaning, and hence intensively structured, highly contingent and variable, and often cryptic. Even the strength and shape of the bond by which "the sexual" is connected to the genital changes as extragenital bonds and forms of power change, and in turn the nature of that bond affects their distribution.

CHAPTER THREE

The Country Wife:
Anatomies of Male Homosocial Desire

S HAKESPEARE'S Sonnets seem to offer a single, discursive, deeply felt narrative of the dangers and vicissitudes of one male homosocial adventure. It includes a woman, but perhaps optionally: among the many uncertainties surrounding these historically deracinated lyrics is our ignorance of the range of shapes taken in Shakespeare's time and circle by nonheterosexually-routed male erotic relationships.[1] A text from the next century, William Wycherley's Restoration comedy *The Country Wife,* supplements the Sonnets: not by filling in the gaps in our knowledge of exclusively male relationships (a task begun by Alan Bray and others, using other sixteenth- and seventeenth-century texts), but in the opposite way, by examining a comprehensive range of responses to a social situation in which the routing of homosocial desire through women is clearly presented as compulsory. The play seems to offer a circulating library of different, vivid prototypes for this relationship, and I will use the next few pages to give darker outline to these prototypes so that we can use them as objects of reference throughout our readings of later texts, as well.

The given of *The Country Wife* is that cuckoldry is the main social engine of the aristocratic society depicted. "To cuckold" is by definition a sexual act, performed on a man, by another man. Its central position means that the play emphasizes heterosexual love chiefly as a strategy of homosocial desire. In the title of his study, David Vieth acutely calls the play an "anatomy of masculinity";[2] specifying further, I will discuss it as an analysis of several different paths by which men may attempt to arrive at satisfying relationships with other men. What I mean to show, of course, is that the men's heterosexual relationships in the play have as their raison d'être an ultimate bonding between men; and that this bonding, if successfully achieved, is not detrimental to "masculinity" but definitive of it.

The bond of cuckoldry differs from at least some social conformations of homosexuality in being *necessarily* hierarchical in structure, with an "active" participant who is clearly in the ascendancy over the "passive" one. Most characteristically, the difference of power occurs in the form of a difference of knowledge: the cuckold is not even supposed to know that he is in such a relationship. Thus, cuckoldry inscribes and institutionalizes what is only contingently a feature of male homosexual bonds—an impoverishment of horizontal or mutual ties in favor of an asymmetrical relation of cognitive transcendence. The most common image for a cuckolding relationship in *The Country Wife* is of one man cheating another at cards.

Obviously, "to cuckold" differs additionally from more directly sexual male homosocial bonds in that it requires a woman. And as Shakespeare's Sonnets showed, the male path through heterosexuality to homosocial satisfaction is a slippery and threatened one—although for most men, in at least most cultures, compulsory. To women, in addition, the heterosexual detour of male homosocial desire is potentially damaging almost regardless of whether it succeeds, although perhaps damaging in various ways depending on its "success."

The programmatic emphasis on cuckoldry in *The Country Wife* means that the triangular transaction between men of the possession of a woman—a transaction whose structuring presence in other texts it sometimes requires some inferential work to detect—is simply the most patent subject. The status of the women in this transaction is determiningly a problem in the play: not their status in the general political sense, but their status within the particular ambiguity of being at the same time objects of symbolic exchange and also, at least potentially, users of symbols and subjects in themselves. As Lévi-Strauss puts it, "woman could never become just a sign and nothing more, since even in a man's world she is still a person, and since insofar as she is defined as a sign she must be recognized as a generator of signs."[3] The play teaches that women are in important senses property, but—as in the Sonnets—property of a labile and dangerous sort. As in the Sonnets, too, there is something contagious about the ambiguities of femininity. To misunderstand the kind of property women are or the kind of transaction in which alone their value is realizable means, for a man, to endanger his own position as a subject in the relationship of exchange: to be permanently feminized or objectified in relation to other men. On the other hand, success in making this transaction requires a willingness and ability to temporarily risk, or assume, a feminized status. Only the man who can proceed through that stage, *while* remaining in cognitive control of the symbolic system that presides over sexual exchange, will be successful in achieving a relation of mastery to other men.

Sparkish and Pinchwife are the characters in the play who embody most clearly the cautionary comedy of those who misunderstand the rules of this symbolic circulation. They are complementary characters: each has the page from the rule-book that the other one is missing, and each thinks that his page is the whole rule-book.

Sparkish's distinctive humor is his puppyish eagerness to be a wit, a spark, one of the boys; the transparency of his desire makes it unachievable, but the play does not consistently undercut the value of what he desires. Sparkish understands correctly that, in the total scheme of things, men's bonds with women are meant to be in a subordinate, complementary, and instrumental relation to bonds with other men. Dorilant, who speaks for the play's worldly system, explains, "A mistress should be like a little country retreat near the town, not to dwell in constantly, but only for a night and away, to taste the town better when a man returns."[4] Sparkish likes the same gustatory metaphor: "It may be I love to have rivals in a wife," since "loving alone is as dull as eating alone" (III.ii).

> But, Harry, what, have I a rival in my wife already? But with all my heart, for he may be of use to me hereafter; for though my hunger is now my sauce, and I can fall on heartily without, but the time will come when a rival will be as good sauce for a married man to a wife as an orange to veal. (IV.iii)

Sparkish's behavior when he introduces his friend Harcourt to his fiancée Alithea makes clear that his strongest motive is really not even to use Harcourt as a sweetener for the marriage, but to use his wife, and Harcourt's approval of her, as an intensifier of his homosocial bond with Harcourt and the wits. He instructs Alithea, "Him you must bid welcome ever to what you and I have," while the anxious questions are reserved for Harcourt's verdict: "Do you approve my choice?" "Tell me, I say, Harcourt, how dost thou like her?" "Prithee, Frank, dost think my wife that shall be there a fine person?" Finally—"Go, go with her into a corner, and try if she has wit; talk to her anything; she's bashful before me." Thrusting friend and wife together is part of Sparkish's wishful sense of "what we wits do for one another." Pinchwife puts it more sourly and accurately: "Be a pander to your own wife, bring men to her, let 'em make love before your face, thrust 'em into a corner together, then leave 'em in private!" (II.i)

Sparkish says to Harcourt, "I'll be divorced from her sooner than from thee" (III.ii), and this is an accurate summary of his priorities. He imagines that a proper deployment (which he interprets as a lavish one) of his beautiful fiancée will help him secure not only a bond with but a certain mastery over the men he most admires. He does not fail to perceive Harcourt's desire for Alithea, but he is too quick and explicit in supposing that Harcourt's desire turns the man who is, after all, his own beau idéal, into "an humble, menial friend," whom he can fascinate and master with his valuable property. "It may be I have a pleasure in't, as I have to show fine clothes at a playhouse the first day, and count money before poor rogues" (III.ii), he says, would-be-condescendingly. He takes no pleasure in Alithea for her own sake. Walking with his men friends and glimpsing her, he tries to hide, worried that she will interrupt their manly communion and his later attendance on the King at Whitehall. And losing her, at the end of the play, he makes explicit,

> I never had any passion for you till now, for now I hate you. 'Tis true I might have married your portion, as other men of parts of the town do sometimes, and so your servant; and to show my unconcernedness, I'll come to your wedding, and resign you with as much joy as I would a stale wench to a new cully; nay, with as much joy as I would after the first night, if I had been married to you. (V.iii)

Even in this final situation which is—according to the programmatic arrangement of the plot—supposed to show Sparkish as finally "jealous," it is still only for his reputation among men as a particular kind of man that he is jealous: "Could you find out no easy country fool to abuse? none but me, a gentleman of wit and pleasure about the town? But it was your pride to be too hard for a man of parts, unworthy false woman!" (V.iii). So the best recuperation he can manage—and it may seem to him quite adequate—is the assertion that he has simply acted like "other men of parts of the town," and the fantasy that he is still passing Alithea on from (male) hand to hand, like the used currency she is.

In treating Alithea as currency that has no inherent value, but takes on value only in circulation among men, Sparkish seems to have access to half of the truth. After all, Pinchwife, his foil, becomes far more ridiculous, and in addition frighteningly violent, through his *failure* to see that a stable relation to a woman is impossible in the context of male transactive circulation. Sparkish is disastrously candid about the purely instrumental, symbolic value that Alithea has for him; Pinchwife, on the other hand, is forced to psychotic extremes of concealment in his unsuccessful attempt to withdraw his wife from circulation, to fix her value in herself and keep it for his own private use.

By Pinchwife as much as by Sparkish, the system of male traffic in women is treated as a given; the two men are only making different choices of relation to it. The primacy of the male-homosocial category "cuckold" determines every shred of Pinchwife's behavior as a husband—so much that his unworldly wife learns both to want to cuckold him and how to go about doing so, purely from his phantasmic and obsessional harping on the subject. His fetishization of women's value makes him as unable to perceive intrinsic value in a woman as does Sparkish's too-ready speculation in their transactive liquidity. "What is wit in a wife good for, but to make a man a cuckold?" (I.i). Pinchwife also joins Sparkish in describing women as potentially nauseating food that is to be made palatable only by triangular mystifications: "a woman masked, like a covered dish, gives a man curiosity and appetite, when, it may be, uncovered, 'twould turn his stomach" (III.i). The difference is that the seeming omnipotence of this triangular structure terrifies Pinchwife, while Sparkish over-relishes it.

Pinchwife speaks on the subject of cuckoldry and debauchery with the authority of experience, as well, having been "a whoremaster," "one that knew the town so much, and women so well." But, Horner asks him,

> was not the way you were in better? Is not keeping better than marriage?
> PINCHWIFE: A pox on't! The jades would jilt me; I could never keep a whore to myself.
> HORNER: So, then you only married to keep a whore to yourself. (I.i)

As this exchange makes clear, Pinchwife has felt undermined by the very flow of women as exchangeable property among men. Only an arrested and individualized version of this relation of collective ownership promises to assuage his jumpy, projective terror of male encroachment.

Like the dealers in gold and silver who claim that the value of cash is merely assigned by "economists," while the value of precious metals is inalienable, Pinchwife imagines that he can pick one element out of the larger stream of exchange and stamp it forever with the value that is really, however, lent to it only by its position in that stream. "Our sisters and daughters," he says, "like usurers' money, are safest when put out; but our wives, like their writings, never safe but in our closets under lock and key" (V.ii). As this remark also suggests, the ambiguously referential status of women, currency, and the written word are all alike intolerable to Pinchwife. Forcing his wife to write a letter dismissing Horner, he threatens her, in a shocking and crucial image: "Write as I bid you, or I will write 'whore' with this penknife in your face" (IV.ii). Wishing to physically mark this particular piece of currency as inalienably his own—which is to say, as with the example of gold and silver, wishing to locate its value in its inherent physical nature and possession, rather than in its position within a larger, symbolic economy—his only recourse, the one he threatens here, inevitably betrays him in two ways. First, it would physically spoil the very object whose physical possession he claims is valuable. And second, the imprint he threatens to make is the very one that names her public and circulable character, his own worst fear.

Again, when Pinchwife has finished dictating his wife's letter to Horner, having repressed her every expressive impulse ("Her style, I find, would be very soft")—"Come," he orders her, "wrap it up now, whilst I go fetch wax and a candle; and write on the backside, 'For Mr. Horner.' " Soft and impressible as wax, endorsed "whore" on the obverse and "For Mr. Horner" on the backside, Pinchwife's little parcel of desire goes promptly off to its destination, but containing exactly the opposite message from the one intended, since his wife, "now he has taught me to write letters," has substituted an affectionate one of her own. ("There's my letter going to Mr. Horner, since he'll needs have me send letters to folks.") The systems of symbolic exchange in this world have the property that every attempt to stabilize them in terms of either private or collective ownership, either the materiality or the transparency of the objects exchanged, either the heterosexual or the homosocial aim of desire, brings the countervailing, denied term instantly, uncontrollably, and as it were vengefully into play, orienting the entire symbolic system suddenly around the denied term itself, and transferring its value to the now feminized (cuckolded) person of the would-be manipulator of signs.

While Sparkish and Pinchwife make complementary mistakes in manipulating the symbolic economy as it relates to women, Horner has the whole rule book at his disposal. He holds on at the right moments and lets go at the right moments; he values women just enough but not too much; he moves back and forth acrobatically and effortlessly between a privatizing and a circulative relation to the female commodity. Given that the object of man's existence is to cuckold men, Horner is a master. As in Shakespeare's Sonnets, the fiction of male androgyny—of a symmetrical relation between men and women in which one person (a man) could place himself "halfway between" the two genders in order to view, and enjoy, them equally—is an important thematic possibility for this play, and for Horner within it. Also as in the Sonnets, though, male "androgyny" actually functions, instead, as a mask for a more efficient manipulation of women's *a*symmetrically marginal, subsumed, and objectified status.

At first glance, or in Horner's own rhetoric, his strategy of pretending to be sexually impotent, "as bad as a eunuch" (I.i), in order to make his sexual escapades easier and safer for himself and the women involved, seems to offer a critique of and an escape from the circuit of male homosocial desire. Horner claims that he, unlike the men around him, is actually interested in women, rather than in the opinions of other men:

> Vain fops but court, and dress, and keep a pother,
> To pass for women's men with one another;
> But he who aims by women to be priz'd,
> First by the men, you see, must be despis'd. (V.iv)

Certainly, Horner is withering on the subject of male friendship, even as it is represented by the attractive Harcourt and Dorilant, never mind the unappetizing Sparkish. He tries scornfully to egg Harcourt and Dorilant on into increasingly extravagant and misogynistic declarations about male bonding:

HORNER: Women serve but to keep a man from better company; though I can't enjoy them, I shall you the more. Good fellowship and friendship are lasting, rational, and manly pleasures.

> .   .   .

HARCOURT: [M]istresses are like books. If you pore upon them too much, they doze you and make you unfit for company; but if used discreetly, you are the fitter for conversation by 'em.

> .   .   .

HORNER: I tell you, 'tis as hard to be a good fellow, a good friend, and
a lover of women, as 'tis to be a good fellow, a good friend, and a
lover of money. You cannot follow both, then choose your side. Wine
gives you liberty, love takes it away.
DORILANT: Gad, he's in the right on't.

                    .   .   .

HORNER: Come, for my part I will have only those glorious, manly pleasures of being very drunk and very slovenly. (I.i)

Horner represents himself, and is perceived by some women, not only
as excepting himself from the male homosocial circuit, but as making a
sacrifice of his (homosocially defined) masculinity, in favor of the pleasure of women. Lady Fidget, for instance, wonders at him:

> But, poor gentleman, could you be so generous, so truly a man of honor, as
> for the sakes of us women of honor, to cause yourself to be reported no
> man? No man! And to suffer yourself the greatest shame that could fall upon
> a man, that none might fall upon us women by your conversation? (II.i)

Nevertheless, the play makes clear in many ways that, far from renouncing or subordinating the male-homosocial destination of desire,
Horner has actually elevated it to a newly transcendent status. If he gives
up the friendship and admiration of other men, it is only in order to come
into a more intimate and secret relation to them—a relation over which
his cognitive mastery is so complete that they will not even know that
such a bond exists. Horner's very name, to begin with, makes explicit
that the act of cuckolding a man, rather than of enjoying a woman, is his
first concern. His pursuit of Margery Pinchwife begins, not when he first
admires her beauty, but when he first learns that she is Pinchwife's jeal-
ously guarded bride. Most pointedly, the ending of the play makes clear
that a stable, nontriangular relationship with the hotly pursued woman
is the last thing in the world Horner wants. Margery Pinchwife's naive
assumption that because he wants to cuckold her husband, he must
therefore want *her,* threatens the very basis of his carefully constructed
strategy; and to protect that, to keep himself in circulation on the terms
he has chosen, Horner unhesitatingly packs her off back to her violent
and repressive husband. When she seems to threaten to be candid about
her fondness for Horner, he grumbles, "Well, a silly mistress is like a weak
place, soon got, soon lost, a man has scarce time for plunder" (V.iv); but
it is his desire, not hers, that makes their affair a transient one. "Next to

the pleasure of making a new mistress," he says, "is that of being rid of an old one" (I.i).

Sparkish and Pinchwife are finally feminized or immobilized by their denial or repression of the schism in women's status within the male-homosocial erotic economy. Horner's more successful strategy, on the other hand, is not to deny, repress, or project but to voluntarily embody and hence control that schism. Because he is willing, not to undergo, but himself to represent "castration," and because he takes on himself the role of passive and circulable commodity—because in one register he withdraws from the role of rival to that of object—he is able in another register to achieve an unrivaled power as an active subject. Only because he is a man, however, does his renunciation actually increase his mobility and power. These women are sometimes "free" to act out the contradictions of their status, as well, but, as we shall see, they never achieve the cognitive leverage, the mastery of their whole range of choices, that Horner's pseudofeminized masculinity allows him to achieve.

I have already suggested how Horner's supposedly castrated status lets him act out one aspect of the schism in women's status, between being ostensibly the objects of men's heterosexual desire and being more functionally the conduits of their homosocial desire toward other men. Horner is able to pretend, mockingly and opportunistically, to his men friends that he now can value only homosocial bonds; in relation to Sir Jasper Fidget, for instance, he consents to be treated as domestic property, essentially as a woman. He does this, however, actually in order to be brought near the women: at the same time as men mistakenly see him as entirely homosocial, he can convince the women that he alone among men is entirely heterosexual, more interested in them than in their husbands' opinion of him. In fact, however, his motivation *is,* as we have seen, homosocial, only at a higher than usual level of cognitive manipulativeness. Horner embodies the counterposed homosocial/heterosexual forces in women's erotic fates, but because he is a man and therefore an active subject of male homosocial desire—and because he alone realizes that men's homosocial and heterosexual desires need not be opposites but may be entirely complicit—he is able to use the apparent contradictions to his advantage against both men and women.

Similarly, Horner both acts out and exploits the schism between the private and public aspects of women's status as objects of possession and exchange. One manifestation of this, as we suggested in relation to Margery Pinchwife, is the apparently contradictory illusions of materiality and immateriality of the (symbolic) object of exchange. Horner carries out a brilliant parody of that tension in the famous "china" scene, where "china" arbitrarily becomes a signifier for the suddenly reified sex act: instead of sharing gestures, touches, and cutaneous sensations, the characters find themselves competing absurdly for quantities of a finite, material commodity.

MRS. SQUEAMISH: O Lord, I'll have some china too. Good Mr. Horner, don't think to give other people china, and me none; come in with me too.
HORNER: Upon my honor, I have none left now.
MRS. SQUEAMISH: Nay, nay, I have known you deny your china before now, but you shan't put me off so. Come.
HORNER: This lady had the last there.
LADY FIDGET: Yes, indeed, madam, to my certain knowledge he has no more left.
MRS. SQUEAMISH: Oh, but it may be he may have some you could not find.
LADY FIDGET: What, d'ye think if he had had any left, I would not have had it too? For we women of quality never think we have china enough.
HORNER: Do not take it ill, I cannot make china for you all, but I will have a roll-wagon for you too, another time. (IV.iii)

This scene shows Horner hapless, his sexual potency—great as it may be—publicly objectified, quantified, and judged, as women's bodies are. On the other hand, by submitting to and even furthering the objectifying, feminizing momentum of this scene, Horner as usual establishes ever more firmly his own secret control over the terms of the discourse.

LADY FIDGET (to Horner, aside): What do you mean by that promise?
HORNER (apart to Lady Fidget): Alas, she has an innocent, literal understanding. (IV.iii)

Horner's command of the broader schism in women's exchange status, between public circulation and privatization, is similarly participatory and deft. As he explains to Lady Fidget, the "secret" fact of his potency will function the better—the more secretly—the more widely he makes it known in action, since rather than [other women] shall prejudice your honor, I'll prejudice theirs; and to serve you, I'll lie with 'em all, make the secret their own, and then they'll keep it. . . . [T]he devil take me if censorious women are to be silenced in any other way. (IV.iii)

For Horner to circulate this "knowledge" means to circulate his own body, womanlike, as common property creating the illusion of private property. What is not womanlike is the control he is thus enabled to maintain over the terms of his sexual itinerary.

Horner's ploy is successful because, as I suggested, it allows him to split his erotic/political relations between two "registers." These registers are differentiated in more than one possible way. The most conventional way to describe the gap is between appearance and reality, or sign and signified.[5] In fact, the thematics and vocabulary of the play do make this gap a clamant subject. Again, however, we need to find a way of differentiating Horner's activist, volatilizing, and highly manipulative use of this gap from the more static uses of it available to the women. The play ranges its women carefully but simply along a continuum from truthful to mendacious. Alithea is exactly defined by her exact truthfulness, and the Fidget/Squeamish women by their exact (and often self-defeating) adherence to a system of hypocrisy about which they are very candid:

LADY FIDGET: Our virtue is like the statesman's religion, the Quaker's word, the gamester's oath, and the great man's honor: but to cheat those that trust us.

MRS. SQUEAMISH: And that demureness, coyness, and modesty that you see in our faces in the boxes at plays, is as much a sign of a kind woman as a vizard-mask in the pit. (V.iv.)

Margery Pinchwife moves in the course of the play from a truthful extreme of simplicity and literal-mindedness to an equally simple mendacity. Each of these women, while keeping her words and her actions in a different relation to each other, nevertheless accepts that their relation will be a *given* and univocal one. The "signs" of marriage and "honor," too, fall within this schema: the Fidget/Squeamish women are as compulsive and consistent in belying their social bonds as Alithea is in honoring hers; they are finally equally helpless to do anything but ratify (albeit by denial) the structures that define their social existence. (It is worth noting, too, that Alithea's truthfulness, which has at least a potential for subverting the system by which homosocial masquerades as heterosexual desire, is in fact permissible because her love relationship, with Harcourt, is the least triangular in the play: this in turn because she is, exceptionally, an orphan with (apparently) money of her own, and therefore comparatively free of patriarchal ownership. Her relatively nontriangular love is one of those cul-de-sacs in Wycherley's drama, a self-enclosed bubble that seems to have floated in from another genre, that features even more problematically in *The Plain Dealer.*)

Horner, on the other hand, unlike the women, from the start places himself in a commandingly, because knowingly, off-centered relation to the truth of representation. It is off-centered because it is different to men and women, but also because it involves the endurance and manipulation of a potentially painful temporal lag: "If I can but abuse the husbands," he says in a wittily and importantly off-balance formulation, "I'll soon disabuse the wives" (I.i). Because of his ability to submit to, gain momentum from, and thus expropriate the irrepressible and divisive power of gender representation, Horner constructs for himself an intelligible two-phase narrative of feminization followed by (rather than contradicted by) masculine recuperation.

Let me end with a few words about the exchange value in *The Country Wife* of wit, the commodity that comes closest to thematizing the generic status of the play itself. To begin with a biographical snippet, John Dennis reported in a letter

that the Correspondence between Mr. *Wycherley* and the foresaid Lady [Barbara Villiers, Duchess of Cleveland, who had also been the mistress of Charles II for a number of years previously] was the Occasion of bringing Mr. *Wycherley* into favour with *George* Duke of *Buckingham,* who was passionately in Love with that Lady, who was ill treated by her, and who believed Mr. *Wycherley* his happy *Rival.* After the duke had long sollicited her without obtaining any thing, whether the relation between them shock'd her, for she was his Cousin-Germain, or whether she apprehended that an Intrigue with a Person of his Rank and Character, a Person upon whom the eyes of all Men were fix'd, must of Necessity in a little time come to the King's Ears, whatever was the cause, she refus'd to admit of his Visits so long, that at last Indignation, Rage and Disdain took Place of his Love, and he resolv'd to ruin her. When he had takn this Resolution, he had her so narrowly watch'd by his Spies, that he soon came to the Knowledge of those whom he had reason to believe his Rivals. And after he knew them, he never fail'd to name them aloud, in order to expose the Lady, to all those who frequented him, and among others he us'd to name Mr. *Wycherley.* As soon as it came to the

Knowledge of the latter, who had all his Expectations from the Court, he apprehended the Consequence of such a Report, if it should reach the King. He applied himself therefore to *Wilmot* Lord *Rochester* and to Sir *Charles Sedley,* and entreated them to remonstrate to the Duke of *Buckingham* the Mischief which he was about to do to one who had not the Honour to be known to him, and who had never offended him. Upon their opening the Matter to the Duke, he cry'd out immediately, *that he did not blame* Wycherley, *he only accus'd his Cousin. Ay, but,* they reply'd, *by rendring him suspected of such an Intrigue, you are about to ruine him, that is, your Grace is about to ruine a Man with whose Conversation you would be pleas'd above all things.* Upon this Occasion they said so much of the shining Qualities of Mr. *Wycherley,* and of the Charms of the Conversation, that the Duke, who was as much in love with Wit, as he was with his Kinswoman, was impatient till he was brought to sup with him, which was in two or three Nights. After Supper Mr. *Wycherley,* who was then in the Height of his Vigor both of Body and Mind, thought himself oblig'd to exert himself, and the Duke was charm'd to that degree, that he cry'd out in a Transport, *By G———my Cousin is in the right of it;* and from that very Moment made a Friend of a Man whom he believ'd his happy Rival.

"It was but shortly after," Wycherley's biographer tells, "that Buckingham arranged for Wycherley to become Captain Lieutenant of the Company of Foot of which he was himself Captain."[6]

This anecdote confirms Freud's contention in *Jokes and their Relation to the Unconscious* that wit is an important mechanism for moving from an ostensible heterosexual object of desire to a true homosocial one.[7] What is also interesting in Wycherley's case—both in this biographical example and, more importantly, in the play—is the special position of wit as a token of class membership or mobility, expecially as these are associated with sexual status. In *The Country Wife,* to be a wit, a gamester (at the expense of "rooks" or "bubbles"), a spendthrift, and a cuckolder, are all associated with aristocratic gentlemen of the town. Lack of wit, conversely, goes with being a cuckold and with the urban bourgeoisie or the insufficiently urban gentry. Sir Jasper Fidget, for instance, the baronet who has gone into business in the City, is no wit, but "this grave man of business" (I.i), and hence a ready-made cuckold: his wife remarks,

> Who for his business from his wife will run,
> Takes the best care to have his business done. (II.i)

It is Sir Jasper's insistent, ostentatious, bourgeoislike acquisitiveness that impels him to attach Horner to his household in the first place: he loves to call Horner "my eunuch" (III.ii), and explains to his wife, "a lady should have a supernumerary gentleman-usher, as a supernumerary coach-horse, lest sometimes you should be forced to stay at home" (II.i).

Sparkish though wealthy is witless and untitled: hence he loves a Lord and "a wit to me is the greatest title in the world" (I.i). We have already seen how this affectation makes him vulnerable to cuckoldry; Horner says, "he is to be bubbled of his mistress, as of his money, the common mistress, by keeping him company" (III.ii). Pinchwife calls him "the flower of the true town fops, such as spend their estates before they come to 'em, and are cuckolds before they're married."

The dour Pinchwife, as usual, contrasts Sparkish's economic and sexual liquidity with his own conservatism, here seen as land-based: "But let me," he continues, "go look to my own freehold," meaning Margery (II.i). An aristocrat like Sir Jasper, Pinchwife becomes déclassé in the opposite way, in the play's urban-centered view—by retreating to his rural base and to a countrified fear of cash expenditure. He congratulates himself on having a country wife, who, though not wealthy, is "as rich as if she brought me twenty thousand pound out of this town; for she'll be as sure not to spend her moderate portion as a London baggage would be to spend hers, let it be what it would" (I.i). Both he and Sparkish consider wit and sexual possession exchangeable, though at different rates: "You may laugh at me, but you shall never lie with my wife," Pinchwife rumbles, while Sparkish feels just the opposite.

SPARKISH: Why, d'ye think I'll seem to be jealous, like a country bumpkin?
PINCHWIFE: No, rather be a cuckold, like a credulous cit. (II.i)

To be a wit and a cuckolder, then, is to be neither bumpkin nor cit, but a young, aristocratic man-about-town whose only visible relation to money is the playful (though predatory) one of gambling. Dorilant opines that "we they call spendthrifts" are indeed the only people who can be called wealthy, "who lay out [our] money upon daily new purchases of pleasure" (I.i).

The hidden, or uprooted, relation between these urbane yet noncommercial young men and their landed economic and political base is already rather precarious and slippery in capitalist Restoration England. (This may be why gambling is the economic image that captures their fancy.) One consequence of their sublimation of that relation—the sublimation that is signified in this play by "wit"—is that a share of the prestige that belongs to their economic and political position can also be achieved by men who cultivate the signifier "wit" even in the absence of its economic and political grounding.

The man who wishes to achieve his social position in this way, how-ever, must follow a discipline of transcendent renunciation as well as of ambition. As the examples of Pinchwife and Sir Jasper show, to appear to be concerned about material accumulation or conservation is fatal to the "wit" even of wealthy aristocrats. The man who, like Wycherley, without great wealth or unambiguous status sets out to live *by* his wits, and off the "wits," needs a strategy and skills that are rather like Hor-ner's. Deferring and sublimating his material need, disguising his ambi-tion through various forms of apparent feminization, being able to en-vision only a manipulative rather than a mutual relationship with the real "wits," such a figure, by giving a voice and body to real or apparent con-tradictions in the status of those he envies, may succeed in cleaving a path for himself to the ascendancy or even the material goods he desires. That such a career is dangerous and fails more often than it succeeds is clear from Wycherley's own life.

Some sexual bearings of this strategy are suggested in Wycherley's *"bil-let doux* dedicatory" to *The Plain Dealer.* Dedicating the play to Mother Bennet, a London procuress, in a shower of equivoques, Wycherley de-scribes her profession as analogous to that of the playwright-satirist:

> you have been a constant scourge to the old lecher, and often a terror to the young. You have made concupiscence its own punishment, and extinguished lust with lust, like blowing up of houses to stop the fire.[8]

Similarly, the prologue to *The Country Wife,* which Wycherley puts into the mouth of the man who plays Horner, compares the vulnerability of playwrights with the sexual availability of actresses, since both are be-trayed by the actors, handed over to the base appetites of the audience:

> But we, the actors, humbly will submit,
> Now, and at any time, to a full pit;
> Nay, often we anticipate your rage,
> And murder poets for you on our stage.
> We set no guards upon our tiring-room,
> But when with flying colors there you come,

We patiently, you see, give up to you
Our poets, virgins, nay, our matrons too. (p. 6)

The mixture here of the playwright's thematized dependency on actors
with his invisible control over "their" language—really, it is he who hands
them over to the audience—is cast in even more clearly sexual terms in
the "Epilogue, Spoken by Mrs. Knep [Lady Fidget]." Speaking as an ac-
tress and hence, inferentially, as a woman who is for sale on the sexual
market, she taunts the men in the audience for talking big for the sake of
homosocial prestige, but being unable to deliver in bed.

In fine, you essenc'd boys, both old and young,
Who would be thought so eager, brisk, and strong,
Yet do the ladies, not their husbands, wrong;

.   .   .

The world, which to no man his due will give,
You by experience know you can deceive,
And men may still believe you vigorous,
But then we women—there's no coz'ning us. (p. 142)

The play itself, like Horner, seems with this ending to identify itself with
the cause of women's pleasure, at the expense of appearances directed at
other men. The playwright himself seems to have undergone a metamor-
phosis. Prologue and Epilogue are the places where the artifice of the
drama—multiple bodies uttering as their own the words, and expressing
or misexpressing the intentions, of the playwright—is both underlined
and mediated; and the playwright here has gone from being embodied
as a man, a trans-actor in women, to being embodied as a woman, the
corrosive object transacted.

Once again, however, the context of the play's ending—in which Horner, to protect his own terms of negotiability, sends Margery Pinchwife
back to her abusive husband—combines with the larger context of Restoration theater-going, to make the apparent female identification of the
"Epilogue" seem merely a move in a larger male-homosocial strategy. The
very presence of female bodies on the stage at this period, speaking
"women"'s lines, was novel and remarkable enough to make an especially salient echo with the play's thematization of women's materiality or
transparency as objects of exchange. That is, the presumption goes un-
challenged in the play that women go on the stage to market their bodies

to men, as much as to embody the conceptions of male playwrights; even more, women in the audience, with the one exception of Alithea, are shown as being there for display and rental *rather* than as spectators.

Even insofar as it represents a woman's voice, "Mrs. Knep" 's Epilogue is a protest within this system rather than against it: "Mrs. Knep" merely makes a direct claim for the artifactual pleasures that are supposed to be a byproduct for women of the male-acted, male-prestige-enhancing theatrical traffic in whores and mistresses. Like "Molly Bloom" and many other female embodiments of men's voices, "Mrs. Knep" still speaks a sexual language that can embody only one message: variations on "yes." To receive the pleasure that she is claiming, would sweeten her position in the transactive sexual economy, but not change it: she is not trying to extend her vocabulary to "no." Even viewed as a strategy for prying apart the image and power of the patriarchal phallus from the frailties of the fallible individual penis (see chapter 1), the Epilogue offers no new social affordances to the female speaker: *her* relegation within the transactive economy is tied unambiguously to the phallus, however labile may be the career of the individual man within the space defined by penis and phallus.

In fact, the authorial male figure that consents to be embodied in this female voice and presence has much more to gain from "Mrs. Knep" 's tirade than "she" does. The hidden understanding of how men's heterosexual activity is both motivated and, potentially, sapped by its true homosocial object gives leverage to the ambitious, active man as it does not to the only peripherally existent woman. Once having undergone the apparent eclipse of taking on a female persona (as when Wycherley pleaded indirectly with the Duke of Buckingham not to "ruine" him), and hence gained command of the actual path of male desire ("that the Duke . . . was as much in love with Wit, as he was with his Kinswoman"), the satirist from his secret vantage can then more durably feminize his male object in relation to himself ("and the Duke was charm'd to that degree, that he cry'd out in a Transport, *By G———my cousin is in the right of it*").

In the next chapter, we will see this class and gender strategy more densely psychologized, and described in relation to a more densely populated social world, in Sterne's *Sentimental Journey.* In chapters 5 and 6, discussing the paranoiac Gothic novel, we will deal more explicitly with the ways in which the range of male homosocial bonds may have been fractured by homophobia or structured in relation to an emergent male homosexual role. For the purposes of this section, however, it is enough in that connection to re-stress three things in *The Country Wife:* the compulsory and double-edged involvement of women in all the male homosocial bonds, the absence of direct genital contact between men, and the cognitively hierarchical, authoritarian, "transcendent" nature of the homosocial bond signalized by cuckoldry. The homosociality of this world seems embodied fully in its heterosexuality; and its shape is not that of brotherhood, but of extreme, compulsory, and intensely volatile mastery and subordination.

CHAPTER FOUR

A Sentimental Journey:
Sexualism and the Citizen of the World

THE reading in this chapter, like those in the next two, records the
emergence in something close to modern terms of the social articulations of male homosocial desire. What is most foreign to the twentieth-century American reader, in *A Sentimental Journey,* is the relatively
crisp and differentiated treatment of class. What is most familiar to us,
and also newest in the period under discussion, is the automatic availability and salience, for the description of many different power transactions, of the image of the family—the family as psychoanalysis conceives
it, comprising one parent of each gender and, as subject, a single, male
child. The fantasy polarities of omnipotence and utter powerlessness, of
castration and phallic investiture, of maternal nurturance and depriva-
tion, form in *A Sentimental Journey* and in the Gothic, as in more recent
thought, the ground onto which other power transactions are mapped.
Within this warm space of pathos and the personal, however—a space
whose new distinctness and freightedness are described by Eli Zaretsky
and others as a kind of complementary artifact of developing capitalism[1]—
we can trace modern versions of Horner's cold-blooded, manipulative erotic
strategy as it moves into more psychologized and gemütlich-sounding in-
carnations. Although novels like *A Sentimental Journey* and the Gothic
spread a glamor of familial pathos over a complicated male strategy for
homosocial empowerment, they are also intricately, even appealingly candid about the worldly ties and meanings of their narrators' project. Like
psychoanalysis itself: imperialism with a baby face.

A conventional charge against psychoanalytic-like views of the family has been that they are bound by the perspective of the European bourgeoisie and do not extend their view beyond it. Part of my contention in the readings in this chapter and the next two, however, will be that this modern narrative of the male-homosocial subject was first and most influentially elaborated as part of a broad and very specific reading of class: that the clarity and breadth of class differentiation in these novels is most important to the emerging family narrative. To say that this narrative has (or originally had) a strong, conscious content about class is not exactly to celebrate it, however. The class awareness, acute and crucial as it is, *is* not only bourgeois-centered, but based on an aggressive pastoralization of working people, and an expropriation of the aristocracy, too, for the cognitive needs of elements of the middle class. In short, the struggle to control the newly potent terms[2] of the male-homosocial spectrum depended on mobilizing a new narrative of the "private," bourgeois family—a narrative that was socially powerful because it seemed itself able to make descriptive sense of relations across class.

> —They order, said I, this matter better in France—
> —You have been in France? said my gentleman, turning quick upon me with the most civil triumph in the world.[3]

When Laurence Sterne's Yorick sets his head toward Dover, he does it, like Gloucester in *King Lear,* as an unexamined response to the unmeant suggestion of others.[4] It is easy to see why the mysterious flows of the important people in his world might impel the blind and helpless Duke toward a goal that is not originally his; but the dandaic gentleman who ups with his portmanteau at a glance of civil triumph from his servant is a more modern type who merits a more sociological attention. Perhaps we are in the world of Wodehouse, with a gentleman's gentleman who happens, like Jeeves, to be the embodiment of all the prescriptive and opportunistic shrewdness necessary to maintain his master's castemark ingenuousness . . . but it is impossible to tell; the servant utters his five words, glances his glance, and disappears from the novel. The prestige that has lent force to his misprision (his sneer?) seems to belong not to a particular personality but to a position, a function (or lack of it), a bond between gentleman and gentleman's gentleman that, throughout this novel, makes up in affective and class significance what it lacks in utilitarian sense. Yorick's bond to another valet is the most sustained and one of the fondest in the novel; and for most of the novel, the bond is articulated through various forms of the conquest and exchange of women.

The underlying terms of Yorick's involvement with his French valet, LaFleur, are conventional in a way that the degree of his involvement is not. An unquestioning paternalism—an assumption that his own welfare is also LaFleur's; that LaFleur's urgent, personal desire to be of service both goes with the terms of employment and at the same time testifies to a special, personal rapport between them; that LaFleur's cares and involvements can be nothing but a miniaturized, comic version of his own—lies behind the condescension of the recurrent epithets, "honest" and "poor" LaFleur. LaFleur, like all the peasants Yorick encounters across the Channel, is seen as childlike—unqualified for any serious work, but ready for music, dance, and frolic at any hour of the day. Like the peasantry in general, LaFleur has a natural, untutored talent for music, and a natural joyousness of temper. On the other hand, he must, like a child, be protected from worry: when Yorick thinks he may be sent to the Bastille for lack of a passport,

> I could not find in my heart to torture LaFleur's with a serious look upon the subject of my embarrassment, which was the reason I . . . treated it so cavalierly: and to shew him how light it lay upon my mind, I dropt the subject entirely; and whilst he waited upon me at supper, talked to him with more than usual gaiety about Paris, and of the opera comique. . . . As soon as the honest creature had taken away, and gone down to sup himself, I then began to think a little seriously about my situation.

In short, LaFleur is ruefully acknowledged to be an encumbrance, though a cheering one—a child himself, in relation to whom Yorick can seem a merely attractively childlike adult. Yorick is unusual in acknowledging how fluctuous and uncertain his own grasp on "adult" responsibilities is. He is entirely conventional, though, in assigning LaFleur an *un*changingly childlike relation to them. The resulting imbalance is structured like the gender roles in *The Country Wife:* Yorick, like Horner, has a free and potentially manipulative choice of roles, which is displayed as both attractive and somehow renunciatory in relation to the more rigid role assignments of others. Working people in Sterne, like the women in Wycherley, are offered no such flexibility, however. A difference is that Horner's personal control—even his compulsiveness about it—is visible to the play's audience, while the manipulative potential of Yorick's position, even when he exerts and profits by it, is presented to the reader as well as to the other characters as a form of vulnerability and helplessness.

Yorick's articulateness about the way he thinks of LaFleur—his need to describe and justify, under the guise of celebrating, the particular shape of the bond between them—is, like the very degree of his emotional investment in LaFleur, a sign not of a stable, hereditary, traditional, paternalistic bond to a servant, but of an anxious and ideologically threatened one. Or more precisely: rather than being a sign of a traditional bond, it is an explicit, ideologizing narrative *about* such a bond, and hence suggests Yorick's belated and anxious relation to the earlier, stabler relationship. As we discussed in section iii of the Introduction, one useful view of ideology is precisely as a narrative that makes explicit, in idealizing and apparently contemporaneous terms, the outdated or obsolescent values of an earlier system, in the service of a newer system that in practice undermines the basis of those values. Thus, Yorick not only is not used to, but is acutely anxious about, this master-servant bond whose "naturalness" he is so busy in justifying. For instance, when LaFleur asks for a day off *"pour faire le galant vis-à-vis de sa maitresse,"* Yorick is highly discommoded ("Now it was the very thing I intended to do myself"); appealing to his own feelings, his reservoir of received ideas, however, he finds there a modern, capitalist version of Nature and the social contract that actually undermines his ability to exact service from his own servant:

> —the sons and daughters of service part with Liberty, but not with Nature, in their contracts; they are flesh and blood, and have their little vanities and wishes in the midst of the house of bondage, as well as their task-masters— no doubt they have set their self-denials at a price—and their expectations are so unreasonable, that I would often disappoint them, but that their condition puts it so much in my power to do it.
>
> *Behold—Behold, I am thy servant*—disarms me at once of the power of a master— (pp. 124)

No wonder it is necessary for Yorick, as it had not been for the employers of personal servants in *The Country Wife,* to make explicit to himself the countervailing, "natural" grounds that make it appropriate for one person to surrender liberty to another—and to couch them, not in the crudely rationalistic, potentially egalitarian modern terms of economic power and want, but in the reassuringly backward-looking ones of quasifamilial obligation. If LaFleur is like a child, he belongs (not to, but) with someone who is a little like an adult: his employer.

The respect in which LaFleur is more or other than a child is, again, nothing new in the annals of paternalism: it is the sexual. For a servant to have the assignment of sexual knowing and acting-out in relation to a more refined, inhibited, or inexperienced master is a usual topos. Again, all that is perhaps unusual here are the emotional intensity and the dense, novelistic texture and specificity with which this part of the servant-master bond is rendered and rationalized. The free crossing, too, between propria-persona conquests and triangulated conquests between the two men is a bit dizzying. La Fleur is seen as busy *both* in making his own conquests—which are always effortless and multiple, and most often aimed at the servants of the women in whom Yorick is interested, *ad majorem Yorick gloriam—and* in prospecting and courting on behalf of his master. For instance, "the officious zeal of a well-meaning creature for my honour"—La Fleur's puppyish eagerness to show Yorick in his best light to an artistocratic woman, a potential patroness (or lover?)—creates a situation where Yorick needs to produce an instant billet-doux to her. Yorick finds himself pen-tied, but— No problem: LaFleur, having created the opportunistic space, then fills it by offering with "a thousand apologies for the liberty he was going to take . . . a letter in his pocket wrote by a drummer in his regiment to a corporal's wife, which, he durst say, would suit the occasion." "I had a mind to let the poor fellow have his humour . . ." (69), Yorick says, and reads the tawdry document:

> It was but changing the corporal into the Count—and saying nothing about mounting guard on Wednesday—and the letter was neither right or wrong—so to gratify the poor fellow, who stood trembling for my honour, his own, and the honour of his letter,—I took the cream gently off it, and whipping it up in my own way—I sealed it up and sent him with it to Madame de L***—. (p. 70)

With this characteristically insouciant move, Yorick is playing the peasant man and the aristocratic woman off against one another through a powerful set of "fanciful" identifications. Without releasing LaFleur from his infantilized role of "poor" incompetent, Yorick is nevertheless at the same time submitting to his erotic advisement, making LaFleur his mentor/father in a complicit relation to the capture of the desired woman. By involving LaFleur in the plot, not bracketing his lower-class associations but emphasizing and insisting on them, Yorick is also implicitly reducing—even insulting—Madame de L***, of whom he has till now been rather frightened. Toward LaFleur, then, Yorick's bourgeois and male-homosocial needs lead him to adopt a pastoral, split view: LaFleur can be cast as both feckless, dependent child and sexually expert fa-

ther/advisor. (Neither of these can be mistaken for an equal; the pastor-
alizing split might be compared to the one in white Southern ideology
between Negro viewed as child and Negro viewed as Mammy.) The masculine complicities built into this split relationship then permit Yorick to
make double use of Madame de L***: Yorick's bond to her is a guaran-
tee of his right to condescend to "poor" LaFleur, but the as it were locker-
room, specifically lower-class-attributed nature of his confidential bond
with LaFleur, and their ability to relegate Mme de L*** between them
through "universal" male wisdom about how to deal with women, lets
Yorick place her, too, firmly in the category of those whom he deserves
to master.

   This incident is only one example of Yorick's facility for creating instant, supportive, apparently egalitarian "families" around himself by his
deftness in playing gender and class attribution off against one another.
How thoroughly gender divides the pie of class—how thoroughly class
divides the pie of gender—our hero is aware, and the new male type he
personifies is a deft broker of these differences. Not the least deft of his
strategies, as we have suggested, is the casting of a veil of nostalgic pathos, linked to the traffic in women within an idealized "classless" nuclear
family, over his power negotiations with men.[5] Rather than read Yorick
psychoanalytically, that is, I would like to read him as pioneering in the
ideological use of male "androgyny" and of ostensibly universal psychoanalytic perceptions to express and assuage the specific homosocial anxieties of the male middle-class intellectual.

   What features of the social landscape in *A Sentimental Journey* facilitate
Yorick's manipulations? To begin with, class difference, although one of
the main dimensions along which the social landscape is mapped, is described in particularly stylized terms. I am not referring here merely to
the pastoralization of the servant/peasant class, but to the absence of any
working class (especially of men) *except* for servants and peasants. Servants are personally responsible to, and in the paternalistic care of, persons of Yorick's class or higher; while peasants, in the novel's pastoral,
distant view, are easily perceived as decorative, animating projections on
a distant prospect of the picturesque. Each group is viewed in a way that
makes it singularly susceptible to being read through a fantasy of the personal, a fantasy of the middle-class male person. Women of the working
classes are even more available for this imaginative expropriation: if not
personal servants, they are vendors of personal linen, or of gloves, or precisely of sexual services. Thus, far from presenting a cross-grained world

of work that might occasionally frustrate, be indifferent to, or even fundamentally oppose the desires of the leisured gentleman, the novel edits and amends the working classes in the image of the gentleman and his desires. Similarly, the powers of the aristocracy and even of royalty do not, in this novel, seem either to arise from or to result in interests that are fundamentally different from those of the middle-class intellectual. The difference between Yorick and his aristocratic patrons is causeless, a given, a difference as vast as species difference but as easily sublimated as mercury. It is pure mystique; any material differences are expressive of the true difference but not causally involved with it. Accordingly, familial-style techniques of ingratiation, personal submission, swagger, sweetness, seductiveness—techniques that are purely individualistic, based on no explicit perception of class or group interest—are the appropriate ones for dealing upward across class difference, as well.

The fact that *A Sentimental Journey* is, by definition, a novel of travel, is probably important in permitting it to present such a wishful, seductive, impoverished social map with such an influential degree of conviction. For an Englishman (or in our century, an American) to travel for pleasure—especially to poor areas or countries—is to requisition whole societies in the service of fantasy needs. This is perhaps especially true of sexual fantasy. A present-day traveler I know reports that among the English-language tee-shirts that are popular in Japan (e.g., "Let's Sports Furiously All Day and Sweat"), by far the most common is one that says simply "SEXUALISM." This insinuating use of a literary reification of sexual desire, in the service of mobility and cosmopolitanism, is close to the strategy that appears in Sterne.

In our discussion of Wycherley, we isolated "wit" as a seventeenth-century name for the circulable social solvent, the sign that both represented political power in the male-homosocial framework, and could through sublimation (through shedding its relation as sign to a material signified) come to be a supposedly classless commodity in its own right. In Sterne, "wit" continues to be a name for that solvent. For instance, Yorick finally equips himself with a passport by (inadvertently) convincing a complete stranger, the Count de B****, that he is *the* Yorick, the one in *Hamlet: "Un homme qui rit . . . ne sera jamais dangereux.*—Had it been for anyone but the king's jester, added the Count, I could not have got it these two hours" (p. 111). In addition to wit, however, sex itself, sexual desire, in this late-eighteenth-century psychological novel, takes on the same representational volatility, the same readiness to represent every form of mobility and claim to power. Where in *The Country Wife* sex, however commodified and circulable, was still implicit in only one kind of situation—that of cuckoldry—in *A Sentimental Journey* every touch, every relationship, every exchange, seems to beg to be translated into sexual language—into the language of blood engorgement, of pulsing dilation, of the sexual fungibility of women. The predictability of this translation is, needless to say, one of the things that makes the novel sound so "psychoanalytic."

In the first few paragraphs of the novel, some important terms of Yorick's class/gender strategy are set. The whirlwind sown by his English servant's remark lands him in France by the middle of the second paragraph, but he is arrested there—not by the King of France, but by a fantasy about the King of France: he recollects the *Droits d'aubaine,* by which the property of foreigners who die in France is seized by the King, and he feels helpless and bereft, then reproachful ("Ungenerous! . . . Sire, it is not well done; and much does it grieve me. . . ."), then, after his dinner, generous, forgiving, disinterested, transcendent, finally blissful—"Now, was I a king of France, cried I—what a moment for an orphan to have begged his father's portmanteau of me!"

Yorick is alone during these paragraphs, but his expansiveness conjures up for him, not only a King of France to be reproached, forgiven, and finally displaced, but also, instrumentally, a female presence, that comes to him in order to facilitate, define, divert, and absorb the excitement aroused in him by the train of his homosocial/economic/nationalistic reflections. The excitement, characteristically for him, takes the physical form of an intensely heightened sensation of blood circulating in veins, which, beginning with thoughts of the King's lineage ("The Bourbon is by no means a cruel race . . . there is a mildness in their blood"), is then compared to a flush from drinking wine—a comparison that is rejected—then interpreted as a flush of disinterestedness and superiority to money considerations, and only then extended, inexplicitly, in the direction of sexual excitement:

> When man is at peace with man, how much lighter than a feather is the heaviest of metals in his hand! he pulls out his purse, and holding it airily and uncompressed, looks round him, as if he sought for an object to share it with.—In doing this, I felt every vessel in my frame dilate—the arteries beat all chearily together, and every power which sustained life, performed it with so little friction, that 'twould have confounded the most *physical precieuse* in France: with all her materialism, she could scarce have called me a machine—

I'm confident, said I to myself, I should have overset her creed.

The accession of that idea, carried nature, at that time, as high as she could go—I was at peace with the world before, and this finished the treaty with myself—

—Now, was I a king of France. . . . (p. 28)

The route from male orphan to male king, for Yorick, is to pull out his purse and imagine giving away money and overcoming a woman; and, if necessary, the phantom woman will arise unbidden at the "uncompression" of the purse. The initial imaginative transaction in property and cash between males has, "as if he sought for an object to share it with," been circulated through an aristocratic woman's absorbed interest in the motions of the traveler's blood.

This small, inner drama, once established as Yorick's imaginative property, is then played out in larger, literal, intersubjective terms for the next sixteen short chapters. The first thing we learn is that, absent the image of woman, Yorick's relation to his money is a much less urbane one. Approached directly by a distinguished-looking Franciscan monk, Yorick is overcome by a fit of money anxiety: not only does he refuse the monk, against all his principle and sentiment ("I was bewitched"), but he reproaches him for his mendicancy. The grounds of his reproach are that there are already *"great claims"* on the world's small stock of charity, and that priority ought to be given to the, so to speak, truly needy; that "the unfortunate of our own country, surely, have the first rights"; and that the Franciscan's order is not active in works of mercy, but "have no other plan in life, but to get through it in sloth and ignorance, *for the love of God"* (pp. 30–31).

These puritanical, nationalistic, constricted sentiments represent a repressed Yorick of whom the manifest, expressive Yorick is deeply ashamed. In contrast to the dilative style he prefers, he has "put my purse into my pocket—buttoned it up—set myself a little more up on my centre" (p. 29). His first impulse is to blame another imaginary woman, the moon, for "the ebbs and flows of our humours":

In many a case I should be more highly satisfied, to have it said by the world, "I had had an affair with the moon, in which there was neither sin nor shame," than have it pass altogether as my own act and deed, wherein there was so much of both. (p. 29)

An immediate result of Yorick's desire to exculpate himself for his ungenerous behavior is yet another female personification. He seeks out the landlord of the inn and begins to talk himself into making a very bad bargain for a chaise; and though the profit of the bad bargain will be entirely to the landlord, Yorick describes the transaction as a chivalrous act on behalf of a vehicle seen as female: "Much indeed was not to be said for [the chaise]—but something might—and when a few words will rescue misery out of her distress, I hate the man who can be a churl of them" (p. 37). The landlord, he insists, must take the same generous view of the matter. But in fact the small transaction via (fantasied) female distress ends satisfactorily, not in a resolution about the chaise, but in a tableau of the two men, the landlord affirming Yorick as "a man of honour, and . . . *un homme d'esprit*" (p. 38).

The scene wherein male rivals unite, refreshed in mutual support and definition, over the ruined carcase of a woman, will occur seriously again and again in the novels to be discussed, but it is cheering to have it appear *first* in the sketchy and parodic form that Sterne assigns it here. Like the imaginary overthrow of the imaginary *physical precieuse,* the spectacle of the ruin of a woman—apparently almost regardless of what counts as "ruin," or what counts as "woman"—is just the right lubricant for an adjustment of differentials of power between landlord and tenant, master and servant, tradesman and customer, or even king and subject.

It is not, in fact, just any female figure who can perform this role, however. Imaginary women can; "female" wheeled vehicles can; madwomen, peasant women, the moon, working-class women, prostitutes, all, as we shall see, equally can. But at this point in the novel a flesh-and-blood woman appears, an aristocrat, and it begins to become clear that another structural division as pivotal as that of gender is at work: that certain divisions of class have an extraordinary power of differentiation, and that the structural force of the particle "de" in a name is as strong as, and changes the meaning of, the structural force of gender difference.

The presence of the aristocratic woman who is announced at this point in the text is already retroactive; as an unannounced presence she has, we are told, already been at work in silently shaping Yorick's consciousness and actions:

When I told the reader that I did not care to get out of the *Desobligeant,* because I saw the monk in close conference with a lady just arrived at the inn—I told him the truth; but I did not tell him the whole truth; for I was full as much restrained by the appearance and figure of the lady he was talking to. Suspicion crossed my brain, and said, he was telling her what had passed [Yorick's refusal of money to the monk]: something jarred upon it within me—I wished him at his convent. (p. 40)

All that Yorick has noticed or inferred of this lady so far is that she "was of a better order of beings," but this social placement has already been enough to project into the thin air about him a three-dimensional family romance, in which any man may be his father, any powerful woman his mother, as soon as they are seen in an intercourse that could be fantasied to have himself as its subject. The primal scene imagined here would have as its euphoric version the child creeping to its parents' bedroom door at night, and the parents overheard, not at sex, but in whispered conversation: "Did you hear the cute thing little Yorick said today?" Its dysphoric version is the present one, where the father has the child's badness to report; but even in this painful version, the child is spared the consciousness that his parents have any business or pleasure to transact whose subject is not himself.

In the event, Yorick's placement in the center of this imagined family is an occasion of exquisite pleasure and success. By the time the lady is explicitly introduced into the narrative, Yorick has already hold of her hand, and under this empowering aegis, he finally brings his intercourse with the monk to the desired, legitimating conclusion. A choir of Yorick's self-accusation and monk's and lady's praise and reassurance of him—"I knew not that contention could be rendered so sweet and pleasurable a thing to the nerves as I then felt it" (p. 44)—culminates in the ceremonious exchange, between the two men, of their snuff-boxes. That this is or has been an Oedipal drama of masculine constitution through feminization is explicit in the two paragraphs that usher the monk out of the novel: Yorick has kept the monk's snuffbox always with him, he says, in order to regulate his own spirit through "the courteous spirit of its owner," the monk who had "upon some military services ill requited, and meeting at the same time with a disappointment in the tenderest of passions, . . . abandoned the sword and the sex together" (p. 44). On Father Lorenzo's death, visiting his grave, Yorick himself succeeds to the monk's strategy of freedom through renunciation: "I burst into a flood of tears—but I am as weak as a woman; and I beg the world not to smile, but to pity me" (p. 45).

However fully Yorick goes in for renunciation, though, he never lets go of the thematics—the "universal" currency—of sexual desire. In fact, as in the psychoanalytic allegory, the idea of reuncation makes sense *only*

in a space of the highest ambient sexual charge; no other form of renunciation seems imaginable. The aristocratic severities of Madame de L***
are expressed by a withdrawal of touch ("I was mortified with the loss of
her hand, and the manner in which I had lost it carried neither oil nor
wine to the wound: I never felt the pain of a sheepish inferiority so mi-
serably in my life" [p. 42]); her leniencies come with the returning touch,
and Yorick's education in the bovarystic techniques of social mobility is
an education in handholding:

> The pulsations of the arteries along my fingers pressing across hers, told her
> what was passing within me: she looked down—a silence of some moments
> followed.
>   I fear, in this interval, I must have made some slight efforts towards a closer
> compression of her hand, from a subtle sensation I felt in the palm of my
> own—not as if she was going to withdraw hers—but, as if she thought about
> it—and I had infallibly lost it a second time, had not instinct more than rea-
> son directed me to the last resource in these dangers—to hold it loosely, and
> in a manner as if I was every moment going to release it, of myself . . . and
> in the mean time I set myself to consider how I should undo the ill impres-
> sions which the poor monk's story, in case he had told it her, must have planted
> in her breast against me. (pp. 42–43)

Yorick's dealings with women who are below him in class are, if anything, only the more one-sidedly sexualized. Since only an aristocratic
woman seems able to express reproach, severity, or sexual refusal, the only
question between Yorick and lower-class women appears to be whether
he will succumb to temptation. At moments when he is not inclined to
do so, he is pruriently, insistently, insultingly moralistic, unable to look
at a pretty face without conjuring up an imaginary man, "some faithless
shepherd" (p. 90), to violate its innocence: the coin he gives a *fille de
chambre* "was a small tribute, I told her, which I could not avoid paying
to virtue, and would not be mistaken in the person I had been rendering
it to for the world—but I see innocence, my dear, in your face—and foul
befal the man who ever lays a snare in its way!" (p. 91). Yorick justifies
his interference in her private life by thinking of her as an (unspecified)
member of the family. "I felt the conviction of consanguinity so strongly,
that I could not help turning half round to look in her face, and see if I
could trace out anything in it of a family likeness—Tut! said I, are we
not all relations?" (p. 92).

The conviction of consanguinity is no obstacle—perhaps, indeed, a
stimulant, a necessary spark to the atmosphere—when Yorick next sees

the *fille de chambre*. They wind up tumbling about on the bed together, the climax (if any) of their contact obscured by a chapter break ("—and then— "). In the recitative with which the narrative voice resumes after the break ("Yes—and then—"), it becomes clear that however warmly Yorick had appeared to be concerned about the *fille de chambre*'s character in his earlier fantasies about the "faithless shepherd," the *fille de chambre* herself—always nameless, like all the working women in the book—is really present only as a kind of character exercise for Yorick's soul.

> If nature has so wove her web of kindness, that some threads of love and desire are entangled with the piece, must the whole web be rent in drawing them out?—Whip me such stoics, great governor of nature! said I to myself—Wherever thy providence shall place me for *the trials of my virtue*— whatever is *my danger*—whatever is *my situation*—*let me feel the movements* which rise out of it, and which *belong to me as a man*, and if I govern them as a good one, I will trust the issues to thy justice—for thou hast made us, and not we ourselves. (p. 118; emphasis mine)

The integrity of the *fille de chambre,* so fervently moralized by Yorick and so vividly thematized by his play with her little satin purse, has much less to do with any attribution of psychological processes to her than with Yorick's fantasy opposition-to/identification-with a fantasied male betrayer and a fantasied paternal "governor of nature." As for the woman herself, she is, like all the working women here, imagined at will as both pastorally innocent, and at the same time sexually "always all ready."

To anyone who has an appreciation of the astonishing plangency and elasticity of the narrative voice and form in *A Sentimental Journey,* explications like the ones above will sound plonking, churlish, literal-minded, irrelevant to the special pleasures of this book. In fact, it is one of the distinctions of the book—and one of its main ideological techniques, as well—that to say anything about it is necessarily to plonk; so protean, so mercurial are its tones and generic choices that the critic finds it more than usually impossible to paraphrase, to isolate "representative" incidents, or to make assumptions about a "normative" readerly response.

What makes it worth plonking ahead with this book—not leaving it untouched as an article of aesthetic appreciation, of sheer seductive virtuosity—is, I think, that the techniques by which it disarms analysis are themselves in the very closest relation to its sexual-political meaning. The creation of a warm, pseudo-egalitarian space of familial pathos, for instance, is not the work merely of the novel's thematics: the insinuating

nervous interruptive style tugs the reader into a complex, mirrorlike play
of identifications in her or his very effort to lend continuity to the successive sentences. An apparently trivial matter of punctuation, the lack of
any system to signal the frequent change of speakers, is, I think, particularly important. Appearing to open up the narrative as it were demo-
cratically to the permeation of different voices from the society, it also
assimilates those voices to elements of Yorick's consciousness—and, at the
same time, gives the same kind of "reality" to his fantasy-interlocutors,
his fantasy foils, his slightest mental projections, that it gives to the people around him. The project of mapping a large-scale sociology of class
and gender onto a private narrative of individual development within the
family becomes easier—becomes invisible, a matter of course—through
such techniques, which render the intersubjective transparent to the
intrapsychic.

The claim for universality made by Yorick's plural, inviting narrative
voice is not exactly belied by the precision with which the novel shows
him to be a male, unpropertied English valetudinarian intellectual of middle
age. Instead, the claim seems to be that *only* the person so specified *can*
achieve a universal consciousness. Perhaps, also, as we have seen in Wycherley, it is the unpropertied intellectual male who has the most to gain
during this century from the literary assertion of any "universal" value.
At any rate, like Horner's power, Yorick's is presented in the form of
noncommutative equations of "identification" and "desire" that are specified by both gender and class: he is mobile, encompassing, universal;
others are fixed, static, limited. That these *are* forms of power Horner
conceals from others; Yorick, through the image of the family, mystifies
it to himself.

In a sense, the lambency of Yorick's eros makes it especially difficult to
isolate homosocial elements as distinct from heterosexual ones. Again,
however, this perceptual difficulty—this transparency of the subject—is
not a sign only of a particular author's skill, but also of a newly emerging
"universal" literary consensus based on the normative figure of the pseudo-
androgynous, sexually highly valent male intellectual within the context
of an increasingly erotized and family-dominated public discourse.

I suggested earlier that Yorick's insistent explanations of the "naturalness" of the servant-master relation gave support in backward-looking,
ideological terms to a relation that was really more modern and less stable than the rationalizations would suggest. Similarly, the centrality of
the image of the family in *A Sentimental Journey* coincides with a loss in

the material stability of the families themselves. The image of the family that is most explicitly valorized is the reactionary one of the patriarchal peasant family, consisting of "an old grey-headed man and his wife, with five or six sons and sons-in-law, and their several wives, and a joyous genealogy out of 'em" (p. 142). Indeed, poverty, deference, and joy are the trademarks of this generic peasant family, as of all the peasants Yorick sees in his harvest-time Continental journey, "a journey through each step of which music beats time to *Labour,* and all her children are rejoicing as they carry in their clusters" (pp. 136–37). The peasant family we see in most detail merely literalizes this image: the old patriarch "all his life long . . . had made it a rule, after supper was over, to call out his family to dance and rejoice; believing, he said, that a cheerful and contented mind was the best sort of thanks to heaven that an illiterate peasant could pay—"; the man presiding on the "vielle," while "[h]is wife sung now and then a little to the tune—then intermitted—and joined her old man again as their children and grandchildren danced before them" (pp. 143–44).

The idyllic, the idealized and scenic, family described in this passage seems to recede when Yorick's own life and concerns loom larger in the novel, however. This image of the family is not dissipated then—in fact, it is far more powerful—but it is, so to speak, diffused. In place of the clear, literal generational layers of grandparents, children, and grandchildren, Yorick uses the charged image of the patriarchal family as a ready and enabling, but unspecifiable, image of "consanguinity" to legitimate his sexual exploitation of the *fille de chambre.* Similarly, in his fantasies about the mad, betrayed peasant Maria, Yorick does not distinguish between the relations of mistress and of daughter:

> affliction had touch'd her looks with something that was scarce earthly—still she was feminine—and so much was there about her of all that the heart wishes, or the eye looks for in woman, that could the traces ever be worn out of her brain, and those of Eliza's out of mine, she should *not only eat of my bread and drink of my own cup,* but Maria should lay in my bosom, and be unto me as a daughter. (p. 140)

We have discussed how influentially and at the same time shiftingly the image of the family presides over the view of class presented in this novel, especially as class and gender concerns intersect through Oedipal and male-homosocial narratives. What remains to be made explicit is perhaps chiefly the simple absence from the novel of any shred of a literal family for Yorick. As in modern European thought on the larger scale, the ideological force of the concept of "the family" strengthens as the jurisdiction and the private material basis of the family itself become weaker and more internally contradictory, under the atomizing effects of early capitalism. That the blossoming—or at least, the broadcast pollination—of a lambent and abstractible consciousness of "sexuality" itself, was also concommitant with the ideological sublation of the family, is one of the points of Foucault's *History of Sexuality.*

In the readings in the next two chapters, a term will be reintroduced that has been latent or missing in *A Sentimental Journey*—indeed in all three of these premodern works where the detour of male homosocial desire through the woman is simply assumed as the obligatory norm, however risky. That term is "homophobia." In the English Gothic novel, the possibility—the attraction, the danger—of simply dropping the female middle term becomes an explicit, indeed an obsessional literary subject. With it comes a much more tightly organized, openly proscriptive approach to sexuality and homosocial bonding. The move toward the familial location of this drama, implicit in Sterne, is literalized in the Gothic. At the same time, the Gothic holds on to the eighteenth-century novelistic interest in relations across classes as well as genders; it experiments further with the mutual mapping of class and family, but experiments with other readings of class relations as well.

CHAPTER FIVE

Toward the Gothic:
Terrorism and Homosexual Panic

THE century and a half after *The Country Wife* seems to have been a crucial one for the crystallization in modern terms of the male homosocial spectrum. In *Homosexuality in Renaissance England,* the most sophisticated work so far in prenineteenth-century gay male historiography, Alan Bray dates two related, important developments at around the time of the Restoration: first, the emergence of a distinct gay male subculture; second and more importantly for our purposes here, the formulation of a homophobic ideology in terms that were secular and descriptive enough to seem to offer the English public a usable set of cognitive categories for their day-to-day experience. In Bray's account, the oppression of male homosexuality before the late seventeenth century occurred primarily in anathematic theological terms that, absolute and apocalyptic as they were, were difficult for people to apply to the acts they ordinarily performed and perceived. Only after the last quarter of the seventeenth century does he find evidence of (what he calls) legal "pogroms" against whole groups of men, based on their recognized homosexual identity.

> It is not that homosexuality was more fiercely disapproved of. There is no evidence whatsoever of any absolute increase in hostility to homosexuality. . . . The change is not absolute but rather in the extent to which people actually came up against that hostility; and the reason for the change is not in the hostility but in its object. There was now a continuing culture to be fixed on and an extension of the area in which homosexuality could be expressed and therefore recognised; clothes, gestures, language, particular buildings and particular public places—all could be identified as having specifically homosexual connotations.[1]

Although the actual number of men caught up in the "pogroms" was small compared to the number of men who were probably involved in the new homosexual subculture, Bray describes the legal persecutions as having a disproportionate effect, chilling yet consolidating, on the emergent homosexual identity. The institutional locus of this identity he places in the "molly houses," taverns and places for socializing for gay men. Although the legal "pogroms" had a terroristic intent and effect against the houses, Bray also tries to account for the long stretches during which the houses *were* allowed to remain open and relatively unmolested.

> Effectively, they were tolerated, although in a tense and hostile atmosphere; and that accords ill with the violence and downright savagery of the periodic pogroms. For all the protestations to the contrary, one cannot avoid the conclusion that they served a function wider than the needs of those who took refuge in them: that society, however ambivalent its attitudes, had an interest in them. . . . [T]hey served, in effect, a dual purpose, for they must have restricted the spread of homosexuality at the same time as they secured its presence. To take on a new identity of this kind was a formidable prospect; for some altogether too much. If homosexuality had implications as broad as this, then for many it was not to be. Is the hostile but tangible toleration then so surprising? For the same reason that for some the molly houses provided a solution and a means of escape, for others they effectively closed the door: too much was involved. They thus served the needs of persecutor and persecuted alike.[2]

Although Bray sees that the society's (limited and marginalizing) tolerance of the molly houses is as important a theoretical question as its (sporadic) persecution of them, his argument is, I think, circumscribed by an implicit assumption that male homosexuality and the European social order are incompatible in essence: that if the regulation of male homosexuality proceeded through the selectivity of terrorism rather than through genocide, that was because the numbers of men involved were simply too great, and because the persecutions tended themselves to solidify the homosexual culture they were aimed at eradicating.

> [The molly houses] were not difficult to find; and they were vulnerable. Why then be content with containment? Why not pull them up by the roots and have done with them once and for all? That plausible chain of thought was the element of instability, and the result was an uneasy balance between two contradictory responses. It was at just this point that the Societies for the Reformation of Manners had their place; their role was to tip the balance, when they were able, from containment to the pogrom and genocide. Yet

ultimately it was a hopeless task. There are times when, if your right hand does offend you, it is not possible to cut it off. This was one of these; for the molly houses were not a finite entity within society that could be cut out: they were a function of society itself. *And so when the bloodletting was over, the pressures that had produced the molly houses in the first place began their work again;* and once more they appeared and gained a precarious stability until another attempt was made to suppress them. Not only did the intermittent persecutions ultimately fail in their objective; ironically *they added steam to the very pressures which were to recreate the molly houses* after the overt persecutions had ceased, for it was just such manifest and unavoidable animus that made the molly houses *so pressing a necessity.*[3] [Emphasis mine]

Bray claims to be describing how the molly houses and the emerging male homosexual culture "were a function of society itself." In effect, though, he is describing them in hydraulic terms as alien and inimical "pressures" on the society, or at most as its mere gaseous byproducts, whose impact the society in its own, conservative interests must by definition minimize as much as possible—whether through eradication (impracticable), suppression (counterproductive), or channelization (relatively effective). Bray's argument at this point is not only less supple than it might be but also somewhat circular, since the "pressures" in Bray's account can only come from a somehow already-constituted homosexual entity, whether social or intrapsychic, while it is just the formation of that entity that he is concerned to describe. He seems to recognize and deprecate this circularity, but his conceptual model does not quite let him dismantle it. In what senses *are* the molly houses "a function of society itself"?

Bray's argument at this point is similar to an argument Jeffrey Weeks elaborates from Mary McIntosh: that the modern "homosexual role"

> has two effects: it first helps to provide a clear-cut threshold between permissible and impermissible behaviour; and secondly, it helps to segregate those labelled as "deviants" from others, and thus contains and limits their behaviour pattern.[4]

Our discussion so far of the importance of male homosocial desire—the spectrum of male bonds that includes but is not limited to the "homosexual"—offers, I think, the beginnings of a rather different and more fully dialectical answer to Bray's important question about how the "molly houses" do perform a function for society as a whole. For while male genital homosexuality may or may not be "a function of society itself"—that is to say, a necessary, noncontingent element in the structure of social continuity and exchange—it should be clear that the larger category of male homosocial desire does have that signal importance.

Obviously, it is crucial to every aspect of social structure within the exchange-of-women framework *that* heavily freighted bonds between men exist, as the backbone of social form or forms. At the same time, a consequence of this structure is that any ideological purchase on the male homosocial spectrum—a (perhaps necessarily arbitrary) set of discriminations for defining, controlling, and manipulating these male bonds—will be a disproportionately powerful instrument of social control. The importance—an importance—of the category "homosexual," I am suggesting, comes not necessarily from its regulatory relation to a nascent or already-constituted minority of homosexual people or desires, but from its potential for giving whoever wields it a structuring definitional leverage over the whole range of male bonds that shape the social constitution.

That said, let me back up a little to clarify. One of the liabilities that goes with Bray's inadvertent reification of "the homosexual" as an already-constituted entity is a set of premature assumptions about the interest that "society" or "the status quo" has in suppressing or controlling it. Thus, even prior to a reification of "the homosexual" there goes a necessary reification of "society" as against it/him. This has a disturbingly functionalist effect on Bray's argument. The molly houses, he says, "served the needs of persecutor and persecuted alike"; but since by "persecutor" he evidently does not mean the Societies for the Prevention of Vice, it is not clear what he can mean, except for some tautologically founded entity that comprises the-interests-that-are-served-by-the-containment-of-homosexuality. It is clear, however, that we are meant to read this entity as coextensive with "the powers that be," "the status quo," or some similarly static and totalizing description of the social constitution. And how could such an entity, described in such a way, not have *some* purposes that could be served by the containment of male homosexuality?

The pull toward functionalist tautology is probably inevitable in history written from the point of view of oppressed groups—not least in the present study. We can, however, at least specify, for the formulation above, that the power of cognitively dividing and hence manipulating the male homosocial spectrum must itself always be understood to be an object of struggle, not something that resides passively in a reified "status quo." Within any "status quo," even among the more privileged constituents of it, a competition of interests will lead to competing models and formulations of ideologically important social nodes. And while the consequences of the entire process can therefore not be what any single interest "had in mind," the resultant space of power—perhaps even the vacuum of power—then powerfully invites appropriation by interests that are themselves consequently reshaped by their inclusion of it.

Thus, to describe a repressive recuperation of new social or technological developments does not require a conspiracy theory, a fantasy of omniscience or omnipotence about a particular party or interest. Neither, though, does it require an equally totalizing refusal to consider the separate interests of separate constituencies. Bray follows Foucault in, as it were, anthropomorphizing as a single organism the entire body of society (excluding, in Bray's case, the objects of homophobic oppression), as an alternative to the vulgar plural anthropomorphizations of conspiracy theory. Foucault, perhaps unlike Bray, realizes that the functionalist tautologies of explanation are not to be opened out through this strategy, and so to a large extent simply suspends the category of "explanation." Bray rightly declines to follow Foucault in such an expensive move; but by acceding to a premature and narrowed-down view of the scope of the social effects of homophobia, he perpetuates rather than dismantles the not-very-explanatory opposition of "society" as against "the homosexual."

In fact, once the secularization of terms that Bray incisively traces began to make "the homosexual" available as a descriptive category of lived experience, what had happened was not only that the terms of a newly effective minority oppression had been set, but that a new and immensely potent tool had become available for the manipulation of every form of power that was refracted through the gender system—that is, in European society, of virtually every form of power. Not being the creation of any one agency in the society, this tool—the ability to set proscriptive and descriptive limits to the forms of male homosocial desire—became the object of competition among those who wished to wield it, as well as an implement of oppression against those whose practices it at a given time proscribed. What modern European-style homophobia delineates is thus a space, and perhaps a mechanism, of domination, rather than the agency or motivation or political thrust of that domination. So far as it is possible to do so without minimizing the specificity and gravity of European homosexual oppression and identity, it is analytically important to remember that the domination offered by this strategy is not only over a minority population, but over the bonds that structure all social form.

If we see homophobia as a mechanism for regulating the behavior of the many by the specific oppression of a few, then we are in a better position to consider the question set by Bray. How, he asks, *given* a virulently homophobic public ideology, are we to account for the many episodes of calm, for the relative continuity, actually enjoyed by most of the molly houses most of the time? Or to extend the question to a broader one about modern European-style homophobia: what does it mean— whom may it benefit—when the oppression of homosexual men has a marginal, terroristic, synecdochic structure rather than a wholesale, genocidal, literalizing one?

In linking the descriptions "terroristic" and "synecdochic" here, I am describing a relation of part to whole that is, constitutively, unstable and unascertainable. The terrorism of the lynch mob would not have been a potent weapon if the Black Americans claiming their rights and freedoms had known, not only that some proportion of them would be murdered, but which ones. The genocidal "solution" was never possible in the American South because the struggle was, precisely, over the control of labor power: only the specifically *disproportionate* effect of terrorism, made possible by the randomness of the violence, gave the needed leverage without destroying the body on which it was to work.

European society may or may not have actually "needed" for there to be homosexual men. What it did need—or, to put it less functionalistically, what its constituent interests found many ways to use—was a disproportionate leverage over the channels of bonding between all pairs of men. To maintain such a disproportionate leverage, however, requires that shows of power be unpredictable and in an unstable relation to the "crime" that is ostensibly being regulated. (For example, even though rape was the pretext for the lynchings of Black men in the American South, fewer than a third of the men lynched were even accused of rape. And this gap between the rationalization of terrorist acts and their actual execution was not an obstacle to, but an important part of, their efficacy as terrorism.)

For the elaboration of secular power over male bonds, then, it made sense that the molly-house persecutions be pogromlike in nature, that the distinctly homosexual man not know whether or not to expect to be an object of legalized violence. But a subtler, answering strategy was also called for, complementary to this one, to consolidate control over the bonds of men who were not part of the distinctly homosexual subculture. Not only must homosexual men be unable to ascertain whether they are to be the objects of "random" homophobic violence, but no man must be able to ascertain that he is not (that his bonds are not) homosexual. In this way, a relatively small exertion of physical or legal compulsion potentially rules great reaches of behavior and filiation.

The repeated verb "must" in the last paragraph flirts in a now-familiar fashion with the functionalism we just discussed. (It is a more forceful form of the shadowy, ominous "It is no accident. . . .") Again, though, what we are describing is a space or mechanism of potential power; to activate it does require a manipulation of the pincers movement sketched in the last paragraph; this activation has been performed or attempted repeatedly in different interests in the last three centuries of European and American culture; and, ideological processes being as past-dependent and structurally conservative as they are (see Introduction iii), the result has been a structural residue of terrorist potential, of *blackmailability*, of Western maleness through the leverage of homophobia.

So-called "homosexual panic" is the most private, psychologized form in which many twentieth-century western men experience their vulnerability to the social pressure of homophobic blackmail; even for them, however, that is only one path of control, complementary to public sanctions through the institutions described by Foucault and others as defining and regulating the amorphous territory of "the sexual." (As we have seen, and will discuss further in chapter 8, the exact amorphousness of the body of "the sexual" is where its political power resides, in a sexually repressive modern context.)

From this point of view, another phenomenon that begins to make sense in a new way is the tendency toward important correspondences and similarities between the most sanctioned forms of male-homosocial bonding, and the most reprobated expressions of male homosexual sociality. To put it in twentieth-century American terms, the fact that what goes on at football games, in fraternities, at the Bohemian Grove, and at climactic moments in war novels can look, with only a slight shift of optic, quite startlingly "homosexual," is not most importantly an expression of the psychic origin of these institutions in a repressed or sublimated homosexual genitality.[5] Instead, it is the coming to visibility of the normally implicit terms of a coercive double bind.[6] (It might be compared to the double bind surrounding rape that imprisons American women: to dress and behave "attractively," i.e., as prescribed, is always also to be "asking for it.") For a man to be a man's man is separated only by an invisible, carefully blurred, always-already-crossed line from being "interested in men." Those terms, those congruences are by now endemic and perhaps ineradicable in our culture. The question of who is to be free to define, manipulate, and profit from the resultant double bind is no less a site of struggle today than in the eighteenth century, however.

It is perhaps a truism by now that a major thrust of the male gay movement throughout its history has been, not so much to redefine "the homosexual," but to assume or resume some control over the uses and consequences of historically residual definitions. (Consider, for instance, the controversial position of drag, of camp, of outrageousness, in gay politics since Stonewall.[7]) The struggle within "conservative" politics—say, within the Republican party, between its "moral majority" and capitalist constituencies—over how, how pointedly, and for what ends to exploit the residual shapes of American homophobia and homosociality is equally agonistic, but less public.

The present study is concerned, not distinctively with homosexual experience, but with the shape of the entire male homosocial spectrum, and its effects on women. Historiographers of male homosexuality are, as we have seen, already exploring the nature, development, and effects of the active persecutions directed against institutions and members of the emergent subculture; our own emphasis will be on the mechanisms, the ideological tentacles into their own lives, by which nonhomosexual-identified men were subject to control through homophobic blackmailability.

This chapter and the next will discuss the Gothic novel as an important locus for the working-out of some of the terms by which nineteenth- and twentieth-century European culture has used homophobia to divide and manipulate the male-homosocial spectrum. To view the Gothic in this light is to some extent consistent with the "commonsense" of modern criticism of the Gothic, which typically views it as an exploration of "the perverse." When I began to read Gothic novels, as an undergraduate, it was because they had an alluring reputation for decadence. Decadence is a notably shifty idea,[8] but clearly its allure to the middle-class adolescent lies in its promise of initiatory shortcuts to the secret truths of adulthood. The secrets of sexuality are represented by practices (most explicitly, incest and rape) that run counter to the official version. In a close relation with these, the secrets of class are represented in decadent literature by elements of the bourgeoisie that can dissociate themselves from the productive modes of their class and, by learning to articulate an outdated version of aristocratic values, can seem to offer some critique of—some ready leverage on—the bourgeois official culture.

Even beyond the allure of decadence to the naive and ambitious reader, though, the Gothic makes a teasing proffer of insight into important historical questions. Within the historical frame of the Industrial Revolution, the Gothic is preoccupied with dramatizing versions of the mutual reappraisal of the middle and upper classes. The ties of the Gothic novel to an emergent female authorship and readership have been a constant for two centuries, and there has been a history of useful critical attempts to look to the Gothic for explorations of the position of women in relation to the changing shapes of patriarchal domination.[9] A less obvious point has to do with the reputation for "decadence": the Gothic was the first novelistic form in England to have close, relatively visible links to male homosexuality, at a time when styles of homosexuality, and even its visibility and distinctness, were markers of division and tension between classes as much as between genders.

Notoriously, as well, the Gothic seems to offer a privileged view of individual and family psychology. Certain features of the Oedipal family are insistently foregrounded there: absolutes of license and prohibition, for instance; a preoccupation with possibilities of incest; a fascinated proscription of sexual activity; an atmosphere dominated by the threat of violence between generations. Even the reader who does not accept the Oedipal family as a transhistorical given can learn a lot from the Gothic about the terms and conditions under which it came to be enforced as a norm for bourgeois society. Indeed, traces of the Gothic are ubiquitous in Freud's writing, and not only in literary studies like "The 'Uncanny' " or "Delusion and Dream"; it is not surprising, though maybe circular, that psychoanalysis should be used as a tool for explicating these texts that provided many of its structuring metaphors.

Particularly relevant for the Gothic novel is the perception Freud arrived at in the case of Dr. Schreber: that paranoia is the psychosis that makes graphic the mechanisms of homophobia. In our argument about the Gothic in the next chapter, we will not take Freud's analysis on faith, but examine its grounds and workings closely in a single novel. To begin with, however, it is true that the limited group of fictions that represent the "classic" early Gothic contains a large subgroup—*Caleb Williams, Frankenstein, Confessions of a Justified Sinner,* probably *Melmoth,* possibly *The Italian*—whose plots might be mapped almost point for point onto the case of Dr. Schreber: most saliently, each is about one or more males who not only is persecuted by, but considers himself transparent to and often under the compulsion of, another male. If we follow Freud in hypothesizing that such a sense of persecution represents the fearful, phan-

tasmic rejection by recasting of an original homosexual (or even merely
homosocial) desire, then it would make sense to think of this group of
novels as embodying strongly homophobic mechanisms. (This is not to
say that either the authors [as distinct from the characters], or the overall
cultural effects of the novels, were necessarily homophobic, but merely
that through these novels a tradition of homophobic thematics was a force
in the development of the Gothic.)

At the same time, for a group of authors (Walpole, Beckford, Lewis)
of other classic early Gothic novels, not novels of paranoia in this rigid
sense, a case can be made about each that he was in some significant sense
homosexual—Beckford notoriously, Lewis probably, Walpole iffily.
Beckford was hounded out of England in 1785 over charges involving a
younger man, and had other more readily verifiable passions for young
men as well. Different writers about "Monk" Lewis attach different de-
grees of belief to reports (such as Byron's) that Lewis had "male-loves";
Louis F. Peck, a careful, conservative biographer, seems to find Byron's
account plausible although "impossible to confirm or disprove," and else-
where in the biography includes apparently supporting evidence without
comment. About Walpole, his archivist Wilmarth Lewis simply concludes that no "proof" of " 'overt behavior' " "has come to light." [10] A
stigma, sometimes an honorific one, of "decadence" and "obliquity" that
settled over the genre owed much more to these three figures than to the
other five, at any rate. The Gothic novel crystallized for English audi-
ences the terms of a dialectic between male homosexuality and homophobia, in which homophobia appeared thematically in paranoid plots. Not
until the late-Victorian Gothic did a comparable body of homosexual
thematics emerge clearly, however. In earlier Gothic fiction, the associations with male homosexuality were grounded most visibly in the lives of
a few authors, and only rather sketchily in their works.

One of the concerns of Bray's *Homosexuality in Renaissance England* is
to dispute the stereotype—conveyed by historians such as Lawrence Stone [11]
as well as by popular literature—linking English male homosexuality, or
at any rate the emergence of a male homosexual subculture, to the aristocracy. On Bray's evidence, the molly houses were frequented by a strikingly wide social spectrum of Englishmen. On the other hand, it seems
to be true that the line between the aristocracy and the bourgeoisie, practically undermined and yet ideologically hypostasized as it was at the end
of the eighteenth century, was an important faultline for, among other
things, the apportionment of knowledge and perceptions about the shape

of the male homosocial spectrum. For example, the conservative uses of visibility and invisibility differ strikingly across class lines: of Walpole, whose life was staggeringly well-documented, we cannot tell how far he was homosexual, because of the close protective coloration given by the aristocratic milieu. Of Beckford we know on the whole much less, but his homosexuality was a public scandal—a scandal created, and periodically revived, to keep his newly rich family from a peerage!

At the same time, creators of ideological meanings for the bourgeoisie were, as we saw in the last chapter, busily constructing a view of the social world in which the English class system was shaped like an Oedipal family, with the aristocracy acting the role of parents whose fate it was to be both overthrown and subsumed. An important, recurrent, wishful gesture of this ideological construction was the feminization of the aristocracy as a whole, by which not only aristocratic women (as in Sterne), but the abstract image of the entire class, came to be seen as ethereal, decorative, and otiose in relation to the vigorous and productive values of the middle class. (As I will discuss in chapters 7 and 8, this mapping of the "feminine" onto the "aristocratic" represented a distinctive moment in the ideology of femininity, as well; it is important to keep emphasizing, in this discussion of the mutual mapping of gender and class ideologies, that the meanings of the gender and familial terms are as historically contingent as those of the class terms.)

If we look at the history of distinctively homosexual roles in England, we find that something recognizably related to one modern stereotype of male homosexuality has existed since at least the seventeenth century—at least for aristocrats. The cluster of associations about this role (the King James Version?) include effeminacy, connoisseurship, high religion, and an interest in Catholic Europe—all links to the Gothic. (If this culture is distinct from, or only partially overlaps with, the homosexual culture associated by Bray with the molly houses, that may be accounted for by the English focus of his inquiry; mobility and internationalism being among the things that most readily distinguished the English aristocracy from their compatriots.) This stereotype is not very different, of course, from a more broadly applicable aristocratic stereotype, at least as viewed by the bourgeoisie. The stylistic links between Lord Alfred Douglas and a heterosexual Regency rake would have been much stronger than those between Douglas and nineteenth-century middle-class homosexuals like the Housmans, or Edward Carpenter, who, relatively untouched by this aristocratic tradition, turned toward a homosexual role that would emphasize the virile over the effeminate, the classical over the continental. (See chapter 9 and the Coda for more on the class stratification of late-Victorian styles of male homosexuality.)

It was part of the strange fate of the early Gothic that the genre as a whole, conflicted as it was, came in the nineteenth century to seem a crystallization of the aristocratic homosexual role, even as the aristocracy was losing its normative force in English society more generally. And by the turn of the twentieth century, after the trials of Oscar Wilde, the "aristocratic" role had become the dominant one available for homosexual men of both the upper and middle classes. Among the other consequences of this shift was probably the political isolation of gay men until the 1960s, at the same time as there seems to have been considerable, tacit, and in many respects conservative male homosexual influence over English high culture.[12] The structural importance of this shift for the emergent middle-class homophobic culture of "male bonding," as well as on women and the perception of women, was thorough and richly complicated.

One of the most distinctive of Gothic tropes, the "unspeakable," had a symptomatic role in this series of shifts. Sexuality between men had, throughout the Judaeo-Christian tradition, been famous among those who knew about it at all precisely for having no name—"unspeakable," "unmentionable," "not to be named among Christian men," are among the terms recorded by Louis Crompton.[13] Of course, its very namelessness, its secrecy, was a form of social control. Many critics of the Gothic mention, and I have discussed at length elsewhere,[14] the defining pervasiveness in Gothic novels of language about the unspeakable. In the paranoiac novel *Melmoth,* for instance, when Melmoth the persecutor finally wears down his victims into something like receptiveness, he then tells them what he wants from them; but this information is never clearly communicated to the reader. The manuscripts crumble at this point or are "wholly illegible," the speaker is strangled by the unutterable word, or the proposition is preterited as "one so full of horror and impiety, that, even to listen to it, is scarce less a crime than to comply with it!"[15]

The trope of the "unspeakable" here seems to have a double function. Its more obvious referent is a Faustian pact, for Melmoth practices "that [nameless] art, which is held in just abomination by all 'who name the name of Christ.' "[16] The other half of the double meaning—the sexual half—excluded the exoteric portion of Maturin's audience (possibly including Maturin himself?). Certainly, however, it meant something to

Maturin's great-nephew, Oscar Wilde. Seventy years later, forced to leave England after his disgrace and imprisonment for homosexual offenses, Wilde was to change his name to Melmoth.

But although in the Romantic period the Gothic unspeakable was a near-impenetrable shibboleth for a particular conjunction of class and male sexuality, its role had changed markedly by the turn of the twentieth century. Partly through Wilde's own voluntary and involuntary influence ("I am the Love that dare not speak its name"), what had been a shibboleth became a byword. What had been the style of homosexuality attributed to the aristocracy, and to some degree its accompanying style of homophobia, now washed through the middle classes, with, as I have said, complicated political effects. The Gothic, too, changed: homosexual implications in *Melmoth* or *Vathek* had been esoteric; parts of *Dorian Gray* were, or were used as, a handbook of gay style and behavior.

A story, Gothic in its own right, from Beverley Nichols' twentieth-century autobiography, *Father Figure,* will illustrate the particular comic, educative, and terrorizing potential that the Gothic novel and the "unspeakable" had realized by the first decades of this century. Nichols' middle-class parents had a higher-class male friend who rouged, acted effeminate, and would to a knowing observer have seemed from the first glance to be telegraphing his homosexuality. The elder Nicholses, reactionary but unworldly, saw none of this. They were simply delighted that their friend took such a keen interest in their young son. One night, though, Beverley's father came into the boy's room drunk and found him with a copy of *Dorian Gray*—a present from the friend. The father nearly choked. He hurled the book at his son. He spat on it over and over, frothing at the mouth. Finally he began ripping the book to shreds—with his teeth.

Beverly was terrified and puzzled: why was his father so angry? The father couldn't believe he didn't know, but finally the boy's obvious puzzlement convinced him. "What did Wilde do?" The father couldn't utter the words that would explain it. Instead, he stole into the bedroom again at daybreak, and left a slip of paper on which he had written down, he said, the man's crime. As his father left, Beverley, now delirious with anticipation, tiptoed across the room to where the paper lay.

On it was written: "ILLUM CRIMEN HORRIBILE QUOD NON NOMINANDUM EST."[17]

It is hard to imagine today that a Gothic novel and a Gothic trope could have such a pivotal and mystifying force. For the Nichols circle, the Gothic acted as an electrified barrier between generations, between classes, between sexual choices; for the middle-class reader today it is something to pass up at the supermarket. In the following discussion of Hogg's *Confessions,* and in the discussions in chapters 9 and 10 of Dickens' later, Victorian Gothic, I will make some suggestions about the source and meaning of the leverage on class and gender relations offered by these new presentations of homophobia in the late eighteenth century.

CHAPTER SIX

Murder Incorporated:
Confessions of a Justified Sinner

"Is it as potent as it used to be?"
"What do you speak of, deary?"
"What should I speak of, but what I have in my mouth?"
—Dickens, *Edwin Drood*[1]

J AMES Hogg's *Private Memoirs and Confessions of a Justified Sinner* is
a late (1824), and perhaps only arguably, Gothic novel: to classify it
as Gothic one has to admit the native (Scottish) scene and vernacular religion into what had been signalized, so far, chiefly as a genre about
Catholic Europe. *Caleb Williams* and *Wuthering Heights,* however, neither depending on the overseas picturesque, precede and follow it into
the current Gothic canon. Reasons for considering it Gothic are that it is
ambiguously supernatural, that it is lurid, that it is "psychological" (i.e.,
literalizes and externalizes, for instance as murder or demonic temptation, conflicts that are usually seen as internal), that its action seems to
be motivated by religious absolutes, and, most importantly, that it richly
thematizes male paranoia. Precisely because the novel has such a (not strictly
Gothic) grounding in the native and the vernacular, because the characters are racy and textural and the class conflicts exact and anxious, it is a
good place to look at some articulations of male paranoia, to test the
conjunctions of desire and persecution with gender and empowerment.

Like many Gothic novels, this one begins by seeming to offer neatly
demarcated pairs of doubles, whose relationships degenerate under the

power pressures of the novel into something less graphic and more insidious.[2] The novel famously offers two distinct narratives of almost the same events; there are two distinct paranoid-style persecutions of one man by another; one character is able to turn into a physical double of other characters; and so forth. But there is also a pairing of opposites, brothers—a less Gothic device—that provides the overtly moral and social engine of the book, and lays out a schema of values by which the Gothic code is, at least provisionally, supposed to be read. But just as in our reading of Sonnet 144, where the semantic, *ethical* presentation of gender *opposites* undermined and contaminated the supposedly symmetrical, syntactic presentation of *structural counterparts,* so it is in this novel.

The two brothers in the novel may or may not have the same father; their social and familial coordinates are widely different. According to the "Editor's Narrative" that constitutes almost the first half of the book, their mother is a Glasgow woman, "sole heiress and reputed daughter of a Baillie Orde"[3] ("Baillie" is roughly equivalent to "Alderman"), and "the most severe and gloomy of all bigots to the principles of the Reformation" (p. 4). "She had imbibed her ideas from the doctrines of one flaming predestinarian divine alone"—one Robert Wringhim, who goes with her to perform the ceremony when, as a young woman, she is sent off to the country to marry a rich, much older landowner, George Colwan, laird of Dalcastle. The marriage is unhappy—"The laird was what his country neighbours called 'a droll, careless chap,' with a very limited proportion of the fear of God in his heart, and very nearly as little of the fear of man" (p. 4)—and in the face of his wife's persistent sexual refusal, the laird establishes her and later her spiritual guide in a separate set of rooms in the top part of his mansion-house.

The pairing of contrasted values implicit in this marriage, of the landed gentry with the urban bourgeoisie, becomes even more acute and discordant in the next generation. The paternity of each son is mysterious on more than one narrative level: there is an open conjecture, meant to amount to an assumption, that the younger son is Robert Wringhim's, but everyone in the novel including the "editor" assumes that the elder son is the laird's, even though the "Editor's Narrative" offers no significant reasons for differentiating the circumstances in which the two were conceived. Nevertheless, each boy is more or less firmly assigned to one camp. The older one is named "George" after the laird, takes his surname unproblematically, and is brought up in the lower half of the house with the laird. But the second son is not acknowledged by his mother's husband, and finally "Mr. Wringhim, out of pity and kindness, took the lady herself as sponsor for the boy, and baptized him by the name of Robert Wringhim—that being the noted divine's own name" (p. 18).

Thus, without any very secure "genetic" basis, the boys are assigned to class milieux that the novel presents as starkly contrasting; and in a possible triumph of nurture over nature, each one seems ideally suited to his assignment. The narrator describes George in the terms that, in the Victorian novel, will come ever more overtly to denominate the British racial ideal. He is "a generous and kind-hearted youth; always ready to oblige, and hardly ever dissatisfied with anybody" (p. 18); much slower than his brother in "scholastic acquirements," George is "greatly his superior in personal prowess, form, feature, and all that constitutes gentility in the department and appearance" (p. 19).[4] Young Robert Wringhim, on the other hand, "was an acute boy . . . had ardent and unquenchable passions, and, withal, a sternness of demeanour from which other boys shrunk. He was the best grammarian, the best reader, writer, and accountant in the various classes that he attended, and was fond of writing essays on controverted points of theology" (p. 19). His mother's religiosity is redoubled in Robert. The editor's favorite word for him is "demure": "His lips were primmed so close that his mouth was hardly discernible. . . . His presence acted as a mildew on all social intercourse or enjoyment";[5] he is a physical coward and, according to his own account, a compulsive liar.

In many ways the terms in which class and religion intersect here are familiar from as far back as *Twelfth Night*, via *Hudibras*. Rather than begin with young Robert's sociological and characterological placing, however, I would like to start with an apparently less descriptive comparison: between this dour young Calvinist and Sparkish, the wealthy, puppyish young would-be man about town in *The Country Wife*. In our discussion of Sparkish in chapter 3, we emphasized his misunderstanding—at least, his fatally partial understanding—of the circuit of male transactions in women. Understanding correctly (in the terms of the play's world) that the ultimate function of women is to be conduits of homosocial desire between men, Sparkish makes the mistake of underestimating the investment that must be made in the fiction of desiring women; and his insufficiently mediated desire to enter into relation with the men he admires results in *his* being feminized, in turn, in relation to them.

Young Wringhim is like Sparkish—like an extreme of Sparkish—in his explicit devaluation of women. For Wringhim, this devaluation has a religious meaning: "In particular," he says in his own account of his life,

> I brought myself to despise, if not to abhor, the beauty of women, looking on it as the greatest snare to which mankind are subjected, and though young men and maidens, and even old women (my mother among the rest), taxed me with being an unnatural wretch, I gloried in my acquisition; and, to this day, am thankful for having escaped the most dangerous of all snares. (p. 103)

When we move—temporarily—from Wringhim's overt, "unnatural" devaluation of women to his unmediated bonding with men, we are moving into the most convoluted and conflicted realm in the novel. To begin with, the two distinct parts of the novel—the Editor's Narrative and Wringhim's "Confessions" proper—although covering the same events from two different perspectives, actually describe two quite different male-homosocial bonds. The centerpiece of the Editor's narrative is the intense, persecutory relationship between young Robert and his brother George—culminating in Robert's murder of George. The centerpiece of Robert's own narrative of these events, however, is his even more intense, persecut*ed* relationship with a male character whom the narrator has hardly even mentioned—one Gil-Martin, apparently the Devil himself. Each of the two narratives, that is, seems to give an account of a relationship that might fit fairly readily into the set of psychosocial categories we have been dealing with so far; but to fit them together as accounts of the *same* events is complicated.

To begin with Robert's relation to his brother George is to begin in the (ex post facto) familiar world of Dostoevsky.[6] When the two young men come together—apparently for the first time—in young adulthood, during a particularly inflammable political moment in Edinburgh, Robert's strategy toward his dashing, popular, athletic brother is a maddeningly literal version of the "feminine" one that we would today call passive-aggressive. When George and his entourage are at tennis, and "the prowess and agility of the young squire drew forth the loudest plaudits of approval from his associates," Robert "came and stood close beside him all the time that the game lasted, always now and then putting in a cutting remark by way of mockery." Throughout the game, Robert

stood so near [George] that he several times impeded him in his rapid evo-
lutions, and of course got himself shoved aside in no very ceremonious way.
Instead of making him keep his distance, these rude shocks and pushes, accompanied sometimes with hasty curses, only made him cling closer to this
king of the game. . . . [T]he next day, and every succeeding one, the same
devilish-looking youth attended him as constantly as his shadow. (p. 21)

Nothing can be done to shake Robert's attendance on the young gentlemen's game: asked to keep out of the range of the ball, " 'Is there any
law or enactment that can compel me to do so?' " he asks, "biting his lip
with scorn." "With a face as demure as death," he

seemed determined to keep his ground. He pretended to be following the
ball with his eyes; but every moment they were glancing aside at George.
One of the competitors chanced to say rashly, in the moment of exultation,
'that's a d——d fine blow, George!' On which the intruder took up the word,
as characteristic of the competitors, and repeated it every stroke that was given.
(p. 22)

Things get worse. Robert precipitates a tussle with George, in which
he is himself bloodied, and makes himself

an object to all of the uttermost disgust. The blood flowing from his mouth
and nose he took no pains to stem, neither did he so much as wipe it away;
so that it spread over all his cheeks, and breast, even off at his toes. In that
state did he take up his station in the middle of the competitors; and he did
not now keep his place, but ran about, impeding everyone who attempted
to make at the ball. They loaded him with execrations, but it availed nothing; he seemed courting persecution and buffetings, keeping steadfastly to
his old joke of damnation, and marring the game so completely that in spite
of every effort on the part of the players, he forced them to stop their game
and give it up. (pp. 23–24)

However one may read the affect in Robert's "malignant" (p. 21)
glances—and it does seem worlds removed from Sparkish's ingenuous
admiration for "the wits"—it is nevertheless clear that, like Sparkish, Robert
is submitting to feminization in order to get close to—really, get under
the skin of—a more powerful and prestigious man of higher class. The
bloody nose, especially, is an emblem of a specifically female powerlessness: as Janet Todd points out, it occurs in eighteenth-century novels at
moments of sexual threat against women.[7] In a later tussle Robert's nose

"again gushed out blood, a system of defence which seemed as natural to him as that resorted to by the race of stinkards" (p. 412), and he again refuses to wash the blood off. Clearly, the tools for advancement he perceives himself as possessing are those belonging to the castrated, to the visibly and even disgustingly powerless. His strength is that of having nothing to lose in the way of prestige: he can be a bad sport, kick his brother when he's down, make an obstructionist stand on the letter of the law—make a pure guerrilla nuisance of himself—through the empowerment of sheer abjection. His very physical presence is flaccid and unresistant: his brother can seize him "by the mouth and nose with his left hand so strenuously that he sank his fingers into his cheeks" (p. 41), and when his dead body is dug up in the Epilogue, "All the limbs, from the loins to the toes, seemed perfect and entire, but they could not bear handling. Before we got them returned again into the grave they were all shaken to pieces, except the thighs, which continued to retain a kind of flabby form" (p. 227). In his abjection, Robert cannot desire women enough to be able to desire men through them; instead, identifying hatingly with them he hatingly throws himself at the man who seems to be at the fountainhead of male prestige. The uncanny "pursuit" of George by Robert that is the subject of the Editor's Narrative offers a portrait of male homosocial desire as murderous ressentiment. It is closer—more shared, more familial, less mediated—than the pristinely stratified ascendancy of cuckoldry in *The Country Wife,* but also far more violent and repressive. The newly virulent, newly personalized element, as we have suggested, is homophobia.

For George, as for his brother Robert, bonds with men are the organizing fact of his social life: he is often seen, and always seen as successful, in groups of young, aristocratic men. Unlike Robert, however, George relates to his male acquaintance as a man, because he has the knack of triangulating his homosocial desire through women. This need be done only in the most perfunctory way. For instance, George on his way to church meets a friend "who was bound to the Greyfriars to see his sweetheart, as he said: 'and if you will go with me, Colwan,' said he, 'I will let you see her too, and then you will be just as far forward as I am'" (p. 35). Or carousing with his friends, he and they "adjourn to a bagnio for the remainder of the night" (p. 48).

In his happy and confident (however minimal) wielding of women as mediators of male transactions, George is merely reproducing as he habitually does the habits of his (at any rate, legal) father, the laird of Dalcastle. The first disagreement between the laird and his bride, at their wedding, had occurred when he "saluted every girl in the hall whose appearance was anything tolerable, and requested of their sweethearts to take the same freedom with his bride, by way of retaliation" (p. 5). Later, on the bride's running home to her father, her status as a worthless, transparent counter for male relationships becomes explicit in what Robert M. Adams calls "a fine scene of folk-humor" (p. xii). Her father, pretending to be outraged by the laird's treatment of her, in turn flogs *her* as her husband's representative:

> ". . . wi' regard to what is due to his own wife, of that he's a better judge nor me. However, since he has behaved in that manner to *my daughter,* I shall be revenged on him for aince. . . ."
>
> So saying, the baillie began to inflict corporal punishment on the runaway wife. . . . "Villain that he is!" exclaimed he, "I shall teach him to behave in such a manner to a child of mine . . . ; since I cannot get at himself, I shall lounder her that is nearest to him in life." (p. 10)

Of course, his purpose is to drive her back to her husband, and in this he succeeds.

The first half of the novel, then, has shown us, in the Editor's bluff masculist version, the persecution, the supernatural-seeming pursuit, and ultimately the murder of the attractively masculine George by his sinister, feminized, uncanny brother. The second half, Robert's own narrative, tells a slightly different, redistributed story: George is not a central character, and instead we hear about the courtship, persecution, and eventual entrapment of the rather pathetic, schizoid, feminized Robert by one "Gil-Martin," a glamorous, uncanny male stranger whom he persists in imagining to be the Czar Peter of Russia. In this relationship, we learn, somehow lies the explanation for the peculiar happenings retailed in the Editor's Narrative.

It is in the second half of the novel that a genuinely erotic language of romantic infatuation between men is introduced. The explicit affect is, at least at first, very different from the one that had prevailed between Robert and George in the first half. At the same time, the language that describes the two bonds is curiously echoic. For instance, when Robert first sees the stranger,

> he cast himself in my way, so that I could not well avoid him; and, more than that, I felt a sort of invisible power that drew me towards him, some-

thing like the force of enchantment, which I could not resist. As we approached each other, our eyes met and *I can never describe the strange sensations that thrilled through my whole frame at that impressive moment.* (p. 106; emphasis mine)

This eye contact is like the glance with which Robert has mysteriously followed George:

> To whatever place of amusement [George] betook himself, and however well he concealed his intentions of going there from all flesh living, there was his brother Wringhim also, and always within a few yards of him, generally about the same distance, and ever and anon darting looks at him that chilled his very soul. *They were looks that cannot be described; but they were felt piercing to the bosom's deepest core.* (p. 34; emphasis mine)

When Robert is struck, at the sight of the stranger, by the fact that "he was the same being as myself!" (p. 106), the stranger says, "You think I am your brother . . . ; or that I am your second self. I am indeed your brother" (p. 107). Again, George has felt in the first half of the novel that Robert was appearing to him "as regularly as the shadow is cast from the substance, or the ray of light from the opposing denser medium" (p. 35), while Robert in turn says of Gil-Martin, "He was constant to me as my shadow" (p. 120). When Robert begins—perhaps tardily, having been entangled into committing two murders—to find the stranger creepy and oppressive, he describes the stranger in terms of disgust and fascination that his brother might have used to describe the clinging, bloody, passive rag of a man who tripped him up on the tennis courts:

> I felt as one round whose body a deadly snake is twisted, which continues to hold him in its fangs, without injuring him, further than in moving its scaly infernal folds with exulting delight. (p. 175)

Robert's strategy of spooking his brother's circle by parroting their own words back at them is like the strategy Gil-Martin in turn uses toward Robert in theological discussion:

> in everything that I suggested he acquiesced, and, as I thought that day, often carried them to extremes, so that I had a secret dread he was advancing blasphemies. He had such a way with him, and paid such a deference to all my opinions, that I was quite captivated, and, at the same time, I stood in a sort of awe of him, which I could not account for, and several times was seized

with an involuntary inclination to escape from his presence by making a sudden retreat. (p. 108)

Many of the parallels between the two homosocial relationships are clearly meant to have a literal, rather than a merely echoic, correspondence. For instance, Robert's apparition has not merely dogged his brother, but made a habit of materializing always at a particular point on his right (p. 35). Robert, correspondingly, when he imagines himself haunted, "always beheld another person, and always in the same position from the place where I sat or stood, which was about three paces off me towards my left side" (p. 139). When we go back to Gil-Martin's assertion that he *is* Robert's "brother," we see that that is importantly true in two senses: first, in that scene of their initial meeting, he looks identical to Robert himself; second, later in the events narrated, he looks identical to Robert's actual brother George (p. 76). In fact, Gil-Martin is able at will to take on the exact appearance of anyone (at least, any man) he chooses. We also learn, in Robert's "Confessions," that during much of the time of Robert's supposed persecutions of his brother as described in the Editor's Narrative, Robert was, or imagined himself to be, home in bed in a peculiar trance; and in the latter reaches of the narrative, when "Robert" seems to be carrying on murderous depredations all over the countryside, Robert himself perceives himself as merely being asleep.

In short, the novel's strong suggestion is that Gil-Martin in the shape of Robert is the author of much of the carnage; or, psychologizing that, that Gil-Martin performs these acts as a projection of Robert's unconscious wishes. That much is a critical commonplace. (We should note that at the beginning of the events narrated, it is relatively easy for both us and Robert to keep track of the distinction between Robert and Gil-Martin, even when Gil-Martin is disguised as Robert; later, conforming to the common Gothic pattern, that clarity degenerates rapidly.) What is most striking for our purposes, however, is not the mere presence of Gil-Martin as an eroticized, paranoid double for Robert, but the importance in that context of his slipperiness of identity—and specifically, of the fact that he is Robert's "brother" in two senses: that he can move back and forth between impersonating Robert and impersonating George.

The significance of this is to dramatize precisely the inextricability of identification from desire that makes male homosexuality a necessary structuring term for male heterosexual empowerment (see chapter 1). Oedipal schematics to the contrary, there is no secure boundary between wanting what somebody else (e.g., Daddy) has, and wanting Daddy. The protean Gil-Martin represents the fluidity of that bond: Robert both loves and fears Gil-Martin *both* because Gil-Martin mirrors himself in his murderous abjection *and* because Gil-Martin mirrors the empowered male other. A scene that takes place in Robert's bed is the perfect expression of this uncrystallizable, infusory flux of identification and desire. It is during the apparent trance state that occupies him while Gil-Martin seems to be out haunting George in Robert's guise:

> I was seized with a strange distemper. . . . I generally conceived myself to be two people. When I lay in bed, I deemed there were two of us in it; when I sat up I always beheld another person. . . . It mattered not how many or how few were present: this my second self was sure to be present in his place, and this occasioned a confusion in all my words and ideas that utterly astounded my friends . . . over the singular delusion that I was two persons my reasoning faculties had no power. The most perverse part of it was that I rarely conceived *myself* to be any of the two persons. I thought for the most part that my companion was one of them, and my brother the other; and I found that, to be obliged to speak and answer in the character of another man, was a most awkward business at the long run. (p. 140)

We might mention that the confusion of identities in this bedroom scene is echoed in two other texts we will be considering later: the attack on John Harmon in *Our Mutual Friend,* and the rape of T. E. Lawrence in *The Seven Pillars of Wisdom* (see chapter 10). Steven Marcus, disapprovingly, describes this deliquescence of identity (or identification) in the direction of desire as a feature of sadomasochistic pornography; based on his own examples as well as these, however, I think it would be more accurate to associate it with the conjunction of sexual compulsion and male homosocial desire.[8]

To give a name—"the inextricability of desire from identification in male homosocial empowerment"—to the slipperiness of Gil-Martin's identity, is I think to denominate a crucial area of psychological concern in this novel. At the same time, the sheer confusion caused by this slipperiness— the proliferation of faces, identities, paranoias, families, overlapping but subtly different plots—also requires a move away from the focus on intrapsychic psychology, and back toward a view of the social fabric as a whole. One of the meanings of the cognitive mess seems to be that the chains of symbolic transactions in the novel do, after all, take place within a relatively discursive system, one that is constituted by and offers room for deferral and displacement.

One of the odd things about this novel is that although the Editor and the Dalcastles apparently take a cheerful, complaisant view of the oppression of women in the context of male transactive desire, the novel as a whole and particularly the Editor's Narrative are nevertheless unusually graphic and explanatory in exploring its mechanisms and effects. We have already seen, for instance, that the grievances of the laird's wife—in being treated by both her husband and her father as an exchangeable token of their own power—are detailed intelligibly, although without any sympathy, by the narrator. After his wife ceases to cohabit with him, the lusty old laird consoles himself with the company of a Miss Logan, a "fat bouncing dame" (p. 12), whom both the laird and the narrator treat with great affection. Nevertheless, the novel makes plain that she, too, is victimized by him, at least economically: after years of faithful service in the roles of surrogate wife and of housekeeper, child-rearer, and nurse, she cannot, in his declining days, get him to pay enough attention to mere worldly things to settle his affairs on her behalf (p. 51).

Again, as we have seen, one of the guarantees of young George's attractive masculinity had been his willingness to romp among his male friends at a "bagnio." Unexpectedly, however, the Editor's Narrative also offers at a different moment a much more critical view of the meaning of that casual use of prostitutes. Lurking—waiting for custom—outside the bagnio that night, and hence a witness to the murder of George, has been a prostitute, Arabella Calvert, who becomes an important character in the Editor's Narrative; telling her story in her own words, she supplies a point of view very different from the narrator's own. For instance, she "knew"— "and never for any good," she says (p. 56)—both the old and the young George, and thinks of them without infatuation. A well-born woman ruined by a lord, "she had been imprisoned; she had been scourged, and branded as an impostor; and all on account of her resolute and unmoving fidelity to *several* of the very worst of men, every one of whom had abandoned her to utter destitution and shame" (p. 64). In Edinburgh, on the fateful night, she solicits a young gentlemen, a friend of George's; during their assignation, however, he notices that she speaks like a lady, and sentimentally begs her to "take heart. Tell me what has befallen you; and if I can do anything for you . . . you shall command my interest." She continues:

> "I had great need of a friend then, and I thought now was the time to secure one. So I began. . . . But I soon perceived that I had kept by the naked

truth too unvarnishedly, and thereby quite overshot my mark. When he learned that he was sitting in a wretched corner of an irregular house, with a felon, who had so lately been scourged and banished as a swindler and impostor, his modest nature took the alarm, and he was shocked, instead of being moved with pity. His eye fixed on some of the casual stripes on my arm, and from that moment he became restless and impatient to be gone." (pp. 66–67)

The truth of her situation—passed literally from male hand to hand and repeatedly left to be punished "in the place of" the men who have owned her (p. 65)—is far too brutal for the man's intended, Yorick-style pathos and recuperation. Its most memorable emblem is her vision of her death by hanging as a thief: "I think of being hung up, a spectacle to a gazing, gaping multitude, with numbers of which I have had intimacies and con-nections" (p. 55).

It is not only in the "heterosexual" plot of the two Georges that female sexuality is shown as a corrosive, punishing, and punished commodity, however. In fact, although Robert Wringhim's story condenses into a schema of desire and struggle between masculine men and feminized men, it cannot be understood except through the proscribed sexuality of a woman—his mother. Specifically, it is the *social* forces of religious and class anxiety that are brought to bear on him most acutely through the question of his mother's sexuality.

As usual in this novel, the question of maternal sexuality is displaced every which way including backward: the legitimacy of Rabina, the mother, herself, is treated as dubious (pp. 3, 10, 44). This apparently random an-imadversion prepares the ground for the question of Robert's own legit-imacy (although, as mentioned earlier, the question of George's legiti-macy is never raised). The dubiousness of Robert's legitimacy, of his paternity, is, however, the mainspring of his character and homosocial situation. He is brought up in the menage of his mother and Robert Wringhim the elder, to whom he bears a remarkable physical similarity—though as the pastor himself points out,

"there are many natural reasons for such likeness, besides that of consan-guinity. They depend much on the thoughts and affections of the mother; and it is probable that the mother of this boy, being deserted by her worth-less husband, having turned her thoughts on me, as likely to be her protec-tor, may have caused this striking resemblance." (p. 97)

The pastor himself, however, does not seem to feel quite secure about this very plausible explanation. He fires his man for having the temerity to doubt it. Furthermore, it seems likely that a consciousness of his own transgression is the main energy behind his wracking struggles with God for an assurance of the boy's salvation.

> "I have struggled with the almighty long and hard. . . . but have been re-pulsed by him who hath seldom refused my request; although I cited his own words against him, and endeavoured to hold him at his promise, he hath so many turnings in the supremacy of his power, that I have been re-jected." (p. 91)

The day on which Wringhim the elder announces that he has finally wrested an assurance of the boy's salvation from God is the very day that young Robert first meets Gil-Martin, and the elements of the murderous plot are finally all in place.

It seems likely, then, that a beginning of young Robert's feminization has been in his father's use of him as a gambling chip in an inexplicit deal with God: forgive my transgression (without my ever having to confess to it), and (to prove that all is forgiven) save my son. This is the Calvinist version of the bargain made by Catholic parents in two other Gothic fic-tions, Diderot's "La Religieuse" and Maturin's *Melmoth the Wanderer,* who try to pay for the illicitness of their children's conception by donating the children themselves to religious orders. The Protestant, internal siting of the transaction in this case, however, and the tacitness and illogic of its terms even in the mind of the transactor, make its schizogenic effects on the child fully plausible even on the strictly psychological level.

Within the context of this transaction, young Robert's aversion to his mother becomes quite explicable. He himself, professing to find it puz-zling, actually explains it:

> though I knew her to be a Christian, I confess that I always despised her motley instructions, nor had I any great regard for her person. If this was a crime in me, I never could help it. I confess it freely, and believe it was a judgment from heaven inflicted on her for some sin of former days, and that I had no power to have acted otherwise towards her than I did. (p. 104)

There is no explicit indication in Robert's "Confessions" that he believes himself to be illegitimate, but this passage, exercising his characteristic and now compulsive pharisaism on the person who first occasioned it, suggests that his behavior is at any rate appropriate to that knowledge. Robert seems to grow up, religiously, in the consciousness that only men (Robert the elder, God—if not the old or the young laird) can legitimate him, and that women can only illegitimate him. To the minister he is indebted, he says, "under Heaven," for the "high conceptions" that saved him after the laird disavowed his paternity.

The very first vignette of Robert's home life shows him precociously reaching toward the minister for religious vindication at the expense of his mother: pouncing on her at catechism for responding by rote and with an insufficiently ingenious vengefulness toward sinners, he evokes this delicious version of the Yorickian primal scene:

> "What a wonderful boy he is!" said my mother.
> "I'm feared he turn out to be a conceited gowk," said old Barnet, the minister's man.
> "No," said my pastor, and *father* (as I shall henceforth denominate him). "No, Barnet, he *is* a wonderful boy; and no marvel, for I have prayed for these talents to be bestowed on him from his infancy; and do you think that Heaven would refuse a prayer so disinterested? No, it is impossible. But my dread is, madam," continued he, turning to my mother, "that he is yet in the bond of iniquity." (pp. 90–91)

In this little drama of family constitution, we see the zeal and misogynistic trustfulness with which little Robert takes up his father's ambition to reformulate the family—excluding the mother—in homosocial terms as a transactive bond among God, old Wringhim, and Robert. The lie of Wringhim's claim to "disinterestedness" about the boy's attainments is the foundation of this new male family. Robert's position in it is, however, chronically undermined by Wringhim's ability to turn back toward the mother, who is—however devalued and denied—nevertheless a party to the original transgression that the new family exists to deny. Old Robert understands and to some extent manipulates the lie that excludes the mother; young Robert believes and thus is victimized and himself excluded by it. Hence, old Robert reprobates the mother, while young Robert murders her. (For another funny version of theologicial controversy-as-primal-scene, see p. 17).

Although old Robert, though a true believer, is nevertheless (through his heterosexuality) in a relatively manipulative position with respect to the received truths of religion, it is interesting that in class and political terms, he in turn finds himself playing exactly young Robert's manipulated, Sparkish-like role: that of the zealot who univocally acts out the essentially cynical, divided ideologies of others. During the congregation of political parties in Edinburgh, the Duke of Argyle and his friends made such use of him as sportsmen often do of terriers, to start the game, and make a great yelping noise to let them know whither the chase is proceeding. They often did this out of sport, in order to tease their opponent; for of all pesterers that ever fastened on man he was the most insufferable: knowing that his coat protected him from manual chastisement, he spared no acrimony, and delighted in the chagrin and anger of those with whom he contended. But he was sometimes likwise *of real use* to the heads of the Presbyterian faction, and therefore was admitted to their tables, and of course conceived himself a very great man. (p. 20)

The elder Robert's strategies in the political arena are like the younger Robert's on the tennis court. And of course, the younger Robert inherits his class placement and class ressentiment from his putative father, and they are the building-blocks of his "personal" legalistic, self-righteous, class-marked style. Defending his stand on the tennis court,

he let [Gordon, one of the young gentlemen] know that "it was his pleasure to be there at that time; and, unless he could demonstrate to him what superior right he and his party had to that ground, in preference to him, and to the exclusion of all others, he was determined to assert his right, and the rights of his fellow-citizens, by keeping possession of whatsoever part of that common field he chose."
  "You are no gentleman, Sir," said Gordon.
  "Are you one, Sir?" said the other.
  "Yes, Sir. I will let you know that I am, by G—!"
  "Then, thanks be to Him whose name you have profaned, I am none. If *one* of the party be a gentleman, *I do hope in God I am not!*" (p. 33)

Thus, although the novel's paranoid dramas are acted out in "Oedipal" terms, the Oedipal family that frames them is clearly a site whose definition is an object of struggle, not a given. The three-person family of father, mother, child—and then that of God, father, child—is willfully, arbitrarily, in effect violently carved out of the large messy material of too many fathers, too few acknowledgments of paternity, too much female sexuality, two different classes.

An important thematic emblem for the links among the various male figures in the novel's convoluted and finally violent ring of homosocial desire is the two-edged sword. This emblem appears, in addition, braided together with some thematics of anality or of penetration from the rear. For instance, on the morning when Wringhim the elder finally dedicates young Robert to God's service, intending to bind up the loose ends of the male triangular transaction for good—" 'I give him unto Thee only, to Thee wholly, and to Thee for ever' "—he concludes,

> "May he be a two-edged weapon in Thy hand and a spear coming out of Thy mouth, to destroy, and overcome, and pass over; and may the enemies of Thy Church fall down before him, and be as dung to fat the land!" (p. 111)

When George is murdered by Robert, it is with a two-edged sword, and "both the wounds which the deceased had received had been given behind" (p. 51). The weapon, a gilded one, had been pressed on Robert, "much against my inclination," by Gil-Martin (p. 152). Golden weapons are themselves a related motif: Robert has had an (apparently heaven-sent) vision of "golden weapons of every description let down in [a cloudy veil], but all with their points towards me" (p. 125); and he becomes infatuated with "two pistols of pure beaten gold" that Gil-Martin produces:

> the little splendid and enchanting piece was so perfect, so complete, and so ready for executing the will of the donor, that I now longed to use it in his service. (p. 126)

The last golden weapon in the novel is brandished behind Robert during his final degeneration, by Gil-Martin who is using it both to protect him and to prod and subjugate him:

> I was momently surrounded by a number of hideous fiends, who gnashed on me with their teeth, and clenched their crimson paws in my face; and at the same instant I was seized by the collar of my coat behind, by my dreaded and devoted friend, who pushed me on and, with his gilded rapier waving and brandishing around me, defended me against all their united attacks. Horrible as my assailants were . . . I felt that I would rather have fallen into their hands than be thus led away captive by my defender at his will and pleasure. (p. 211)

A more figurative two-edged weapon, earlier in the book, is Psalm 109, which Wringhim sings in his evening prayers after a legal offensive by the Wringhims has been turned back against them by the laird's party.

Set thou the wicked over him,
And upon his right hand

> *Give thou his greatest enemy,*
>   *Even Satan, leave to stand.*
>
> And, when by thee he shall be judged,
>   Let him remembered be;
> And let his prayers be turned to sin
>   When he shall call on thee.
>
> .   .   .
>
> Let God his father's wickedness
>   Still to remembrance call;
> And never let his mother's sin
>   Be blotted out at all.
>
> .   .   .
>
> As cursing he like clothes put on,
>   Into his bowels so,
> Like water, and into his bones
>   Like oil, down let it go. (pp. 31–
> 32)

This scene is clearly the source of the one in *The Mayor of Casterbridge* in which Henchard, cursing the formerly beloved Farfrae musically in the words of the same psalm, initiates a circuit of blight that eventually settles on himself in terms taken literally from the curse.[9] In *Confessions*, some of the terms of the curse alight on both the younger men: *each* has Satan standing to hand; each dies young; each (though in different senses) is given to cursing, and is cursed; since they have the same mother, the ineradicability of her "sin" is exactly what makes their fates inextricable, and makes the different styles of paternal "wickedness" such an explosive combination. Prefiguring *The Mayor of Casterbridge*, however, and also as in the legal proceeding that precipitates the curse in *The Confessions,* the worst consequences fall on Robert himself; the final lodging place of the two-edged sword is in the liquefaction of his own bowels and bones.

It is important and prophetic that even at this relatively early moment in the construction of the modern terms of the homosocial spectrum, "homosexual" thematics appear only in a subordinated yoking with an apparently already-constituted homophobia. Specifically in this case, the bowels and backside as the place of vulnerability to violence, pain, and domination proleptically take the place of any location there of possible satisfactions. Bonds, between men, of fascination and of unmediated power-exchange already take the form of two-edged weapons (in the brother's back, in the Lord's mouth), not of two-edged pleasures. The pleasures may be inferrable, but only from the forms of violence that surround them. Even the charm, for Robert, of Gil-Martin's enthralling society, comes as a reaction against paternal and fraternal denial; and it seems, itself, threatening almost from the first: "he acquired such an ascendancy over me that I never was happy out of his company, nor greatly so in it" (p. 120). "The sexual" itself, in any form—in any genital form—is not a part of young Robert's experience; but the double bind of the structures of sexual repression nevertheless is.

From this apparent disruption of order between homophilic and homophobic thematics, we can learn two things. First, we should be reminded by it that however radically the terms of the homosocial spectrum, and the meanings of homosexual identity, were changing during the two centuries after the Restoration, the thematics and the ideological bases of homophobia were probably the most stable and temporally backward-looking elements of the entire complex: the punitive fate of Edward II, the drama of *Edward II,* and the punitive thematics surrounding Robert Wringhim certainly have more in common than do the actual social or erotic forms in which each was situated.

At the same time, we can, I think, take the priority in this novel—in this period—of homophobic over homophilic thematics as underwriting our speculation about a main function of homophobia in its modern, psychologized form. Consistent with what we suggested in the last chapter, the internal homophobic pressures on young Robert have the effect, not in the first place of repressing a pre-existent genital desire within him toward men, but of making him an excruciatingly *responsive* creature and instrument of class, economic, and gender struggles that long antedate his birth. As he pushes blindly, with the absurdly and pathetically few resources he has, toward the male homosocial mastery that alone and delusively seem to promise him a social standing, the psychologized homophobic struggle inside him seems to hollow out an internal space that too exactly matches the world around him. Between the conflicted blood- and property-bond to his brother outside, and the far more conflicted bond of narcissistic fascination with the murderous "inner" brother, Robert becomes only the barest membrane of a person: a mere, murderous potential, violent against women and men alike, and capable of being seized and used by and in the service of any social force.

As I have already suggested, I consider it likely that the main subject of the "paranoid" classic Gothic as a whole can best be described in the terms I have been using for Hogg's novel. Some criticism has discussed how close the preoccupation with doubles and with persecution in these novels is to something (today) recognizably like male homosexual thematics.[10] What I wish to emphasize, by contrast, is the focus on homophobia as a tool of control over the entire spectrum of male homosocial organization. This emphasis seems potentially more precise and revealing. Most broadly, it allows us to read these novels as explorations of social and gender constitution as a whole, rather than of the internal psychology of a few individual men with a "minority" sexual orientation. There are several concomitant advantages to this. First, it gives us more, and more interesting, terms for discussing the positions of women in these novels and the societies they portray. Second, the "evidential" questions associated with any literary-critical discussion—never mind a historical one—of individual male homosexuality have most often been couched in peculiarly unilluminating terms, as of accusation and defense.[11] Aside from the inappropriateness of these adversarial terms for the discussion of fictional characters and preoccupations, and apart even from the unacceptably homophobic, and evidentially distorting, assumptions that underlie the treatment of homosexuality as an accusation, the legalistic frame of discussion of ascribed homosexuality disguises or denies the importance of much more fundamental and entirely unanswered questions about the constitution and social meaning of male homosexuality itself.

If there is a loss or a danger in my shift of emphasis from the homosexual to the homophobic content of the Gothic, it would lie in the potential blurring, the premature "universalization," of what might prove to be a distinctly homosexual, minority literary heritage. Feminist critics have long understood that when the male-centered critical tradition has bestowed the tribute of "universality" on a woman's writing, it is often not an affirmation but rather a denial of the sources of her writing in her own, female specificity. The extra virulence of racism in our culture has minimized the danger of this particular spurious naturalization of the work of writers of color, but the ambiguous, prestigious spectre of "universality" has nevertheless exerted a structuring and sometimes divisive effect on the history of at any rate Black American culture. Similarly, a premature recuperation (as being about the entire range of social gender constitution) of a thematic array that might in the first place have a special meaning for homosexual men as a distinctively oppressed group—which, beyond the reach of any unanswered questions, they unmistakably do constitute in our society as it is—would risk cultural imperialism.

Still, it is apt to be a critic able to read and speak as a participant in gay male culture who can recognize and situate such thematic arrays most authoritatively.[12] Obviously, I am not that critic. But also, interestingly, such critics have not so far been much attracted—at least in their writings—to the Gothic paranoid tradition before Wilde, in spite of its obvious focus on hypercharged relationships between men. Their relative neglect endorses, I think, my own contention: that even motifs that might ex post facto look like homosexual thematics (the Unspeakable, the anal), even when presented in a context of intensities between men, nevertheless have as their *first* referent the psychology and sociology of prohibition and control. That is to say, the fact that it is about what we would today call "homosexual panic" means that the paranoid Gothic is specifically not about homosexuals or the homosexual; instead, heterosexuality is by definition its subject.

The writing on the paranoid Gothic that is most closely relevant to this discussion has come, accordingly, not from a gay male but from a feminist perspective. For instance, the history of feminist readings of *Frankenstein,* including particularly Mary Jacobus's sketch of a feminist Girardian reading,[13] makes amply clear several ways in which the kind of analysis I am proposing would find resonances in that text. A remarkable reading of *Caleb Williams* by Alex Gold, Jr., both plots Caleb's story precisely onto Freud's analysis of paranoia (in relation to the repression of male homosexual desire), and then shows how fully Godwin portrays the constitution of *all* desire under the aspect of "the brutal erotics of property,"[14] of class, gender, and generational oppression. Different as it is from mine, Gold's analysis, like mine, locates the node of late-eighteenth-century usefulness and misleadingness for twentieth-century readers precisely at the matter of "sexualization." Gold writes,

> The [psychoanalytic] theory of paranoia can account for the emotional patterning in *Caleb Williams* because Godwin is exploring a political theory of passion which contains all the dynamic elements described in purely internal terms in the psychoanalytic account.[15]

Besides (but, as we have discussed, in relation to) their thematization of homophobia, the paranoid Gothic novels, and especially these two, have in common a relation to the family like the one I have sketched in Hogg: in *Frankenstein* and in *Caleb Williams* as in the *Confessions,* the hero intrusively and in effect violently carves a *small, male, intimate* family for himself out of what had in each case originally been an untidy, nonnuclear group of cohabitants. The deforming dominance in the Gothic of an image (however distorted) of the nuclear family household, in novelistic contexts where a much more varied and naturalistic tableau of in-laws, adopted children, unmarried adult siblings, quasidomestic servants, and domestic servants, actually obtained, is a link between the world of the Gothic and the world of *Sentimental Journey*.[16] As in *Sentimental Journey*, too, it is the ideological imposition of the imaginary patriarchal Family on real, miscellaneous, shifting states of solitude, gregariousness, and various forms of material dependence, that rationalizes, reforms, and perpetuates, in the face of every kind of change, the unswerving exploitations of sex and of class.

CHAPTER SEVEN

Tennyson's *Princess:*
One Bride for Seven Brothers

THE last two chapters have focused on the importance of the Gothic in the exploration of men's bonds with men. The paranoid Gothic was the novelistic tradition in which the routing through women of male homosocial desire had the most perfunctory presence; paradoxically, as a result, it was also the tradition that demonstrated the absolute signifying power, at least from the late eighteenth century on, of that "heterosexual" minim. As we discussed in chapter 5, it was (and is) the very minimalness, the arbitrariness, of the differentiation between male heterosexuality and its "opposite" that has lent this distinction its power to organize complicated, historical transactions of power, including power of or over women.

In this chapter and the next, our argument will move forward in time but also toward the "mainstream" of English Victorian culture. From the Gothic preoccupation with the minim and the absolute, with compulsion and prohibition, we will move to broader, more comprehensive ideological fictions whose ostensible structure is different: it is the liberal structure of "dialectic." The three fictions discussed in these two chapters are all, consciously, historical and political arguments. The ostensible importance of women in them is not minimal, but indeed lavish. Plot elements of paranoia, of male possession by men, are relatively absent, as are the recognizable thematics of homophobia. (These "Gothic" elements will be reintroduced into our present account through Dickens, briefly in this chapter and more fully in chapters 9 and 10.) It has seemed easiest for critical consensus to interest itself in the Gothic on "private" terms and in mainstream Victorian fictions on "public" terms; but just as the psychological harrowings of the Gothic are meaningful only as moves in a public discourse of power allocation, so the overtly public, ideological work of writers like Tennyson, Thackeray, and Eliot needs to be explicated in the supposedly intrapsychic terms of desire and phobia to make even its political outlines clear. *The Princess* in particular claims to be a major public statement, in a new form, about the history and meaning of femininity; but male homosocial desire, homophobia, and even the Gothic psychology of the "uncanny" are ultimately the structuring terms of its politics— and of its generic standing as well.

To generalize: it was the peculiar genius of Tennyson to light on the tired, moderate, unconscious ideologies of his time and class, and by the force of his investment in them, and his gorgeous lyric gift, to make them sound frothing-at-the-mouth mad.

Tennyson applied this genius with a regal impartiality that makes him seem like a Christmas present to the twentieth-century student of ideology, but made him something less reassuring to many of his contemporaries. We have suggested that the whole point of ideology is to negotiate invisibly between contradictory elements in the status quo, concealing the very existence of contradictions in the present by, for instance, recasting them in diachronic terms as a historical narrative of origins. For a writer as fervent, as credulous, and as conflicted as Tennyson to get interested in one of these functional myths was potentially subversive to a degree that, and in a way that, Tennyson himself was the last to perceive. Where he did perceive it, it was most often as a formal struggle with structural or stylistic incoherence in his work. These formal struggles, however, also answered to the enabling incoherences in his society's account of itself.

If, as we shall discuss in the next chapter, *Henry Esmond* is an ahistorical diagram of bourgeois femininity disguised as an account of historical change, *The Princess* is in some respects the opposite. Its myth of the origin of modern female subordination is presented firmly *as* myth, in a deliberately a-chronic space of "Persian" fairy tale. On the other hand, the relation of the myth to its almost aggressively topical framing narrative is so strongly and variously emphasized that the poem seems to compel the reader to search for ways of reinserting the myth into the history. The mythic narrative is sparked by a young woman's speculation about the male homosocial discourse from which she is excluded:

—what kind of tales did men tell men,
She wonder'd, by themselves?[1]

Its substance, as well, is about the enforcement of women's relegation
within the framework of male homosocial exchange. Some effects of un-
canniness result from this magnetic superposition of related tales—along
with more explicable historic and generic torsions.

The "mythic" central narrative begins with the astonishing vision of a
feminist separatist community, and ends with one of the age's definitive
articulations of the cult of the angel in the house. The loving construction of a female world, centered on a female university, looking back on
a new female history and forward to a newly empowered future; and then
the zestful destruction of that world root and branch, the erasure of its
learning and ideals and the evisceration of its institutions—both are the
achievements of Tennyson's genius for ideological investment. In the
fairytale feudal setting, there are two kingdoms, a northern and a southern; and the crown prince of the northern kingdom has grown up bound
by a childhood proxy-engagement to the princess of the southern kingdom. When the time comes for the marriage, however, no princess is
forthcoming. The Prince learns from the southern king that Princess Ida
has become a feminist, and with two widows from her court, has talked
the king out of a summer palace at the northern frontier of the southern
kingdom, where the three women have founded "an University for maid-
ens." The Prince and his two friends head north again to the frontier.
Learning that only women are allowed in the neighborhood of the University—"Let no man enter in on pain of death," the gates say—they sneak
in pretending to be women from the north who want to be educated.
Once in, they are discovered to be men by various of the inhabitants, but
each time promising (falsely) to keep quiet and leave at once, they per-
suade the women not to betray them to the Princess to be killed. Meanwhile the Prince is smitten with the noble, impassioned Princess, and each
of his friends also finds a woman to pursue. Finally one of the friends
gets a little drunk and, finding that he cannot conceal his contempt for
the women any longer, bursts out with an insulting song in front of the
Princess—"Forbear, Sir," the Prince exclaims, and the gaff is blown. In
the chaotic aftermath the Princess almost drowns and the Prince saves
her life; whereupon she pardons his life but sends him back home.

Meanwhile, however, a military confrontation has been shaping up between the men of the two kingdoms over her father's failure to hand over

the young bride as originally bargained for. Our Prince, genuinely impressed by the Princess's pride and dedication, argues at first against the use of violence or compulsion, but soon enough he finds himself with his friends and soldiers entering battle against Princess Ida's brothers and their soldiers. Under threat of a military invasion from the north, and subverted by the dissent and demoralization that the men have caused in the women's community, the Princess herself has had to agree to abide by the outcome of the battle, and to give herself up to the Prince if her brother's side loses. As it happens his side wins, but there is general bloodshed on the frontier; our Prince is given up for dead; but he survives, and he and the other wounded from both sides are taken to be cared for in the University, now turned into a hospital, where the women forget their studies and their feminism and fall wholesale in love with the men to whom they are ministering. The Princess, nursing the Prince back to life from his grievous wounds, begs him to forgive her for her mad, destructive vision, and he does. "My bride," he says, "My wife, my life"—

> "this proud watchword rest
> Of equal; seeing either sex alone
> Is half itself, and in true marriage lies
> Nor equal nor unequal" (vii.282–85)

> "Yield thyself up: my hopes and thine are one:
> Accomplish thou my manhood and thyself;
> Lay thy sweet hands in mine and trust to me." (vii.343–45)

We will be saying more in the next chapter about the ideological meanings of alternative narratives of the history of the English family. However, one important feature of the myth propounded in *The Princess*'s inner narrative is that it traces the origin of nineteenth-century bourgeois gender arrangements directly back to the feudal aristocracy. Even there, however, the angel in the house does not seem to be new; for the Prince describes his ideal of womanhood as coming directly from his own mother, and describes it in terms that any middlebrow Victorian would have recognized:

>   one
> Not learned, save in gracious household ways,
> Not perfect, nay, but full of tender wants,
> No Angel, but a dearer being, all dipt

> In Angel instincts, breathing Paradise,
> Interpreter between the Gods and men,
> Who look'd all native to her place, and yet
> On tiptoe seem'd to touch upon a sphere
> Too gross to tread, and all male minds perforce
> Sway'd to her from their orbits as they moved,
> And girdled her with music. Happy he
> With such a mother! (vii.298–309)

Toward this destiny (presented as both idealized past and paradisal future) Ida, too, is being propelled. At the same time, it is significant that this nostalgic portrait of the Prince's mother is not arrived at until the last pages of the poem; for the poem until then at least gestures at a critique of the aristocratic feudal family that, if not thorough or consistent, is nevertheless part of its purpose. Although the mother who is its product is a good old angelic mother, the family that has created her is the bad old baronial family:

> My mother was as mild as any saint,
>
> .   .   .
>
> But my good father thought a king a king;
> He cared not for the affection of the house;
> He held his sceptre like a pedant's wand
> To lash offence, and with long arms and hands
> Reach'd out, and pick'd offenders from the mass
> For judgment. (i.22–29)

The old king thinks his son is lily-livered as a wooer:

> "Tut, you know them not, the girls.
>
> .   .   .
>
> Man is the hunter; woman is his game:
> The sleek and shining creatures of the chase,
> We hunt them for the beauty of their skins;
> They love us for it, and we ride them down.
> Wheedling and siding with them! Out! for shame!
> Boy, there's no rose that's half so dear to them
> As he that does the thing they dare not do,
> Breathing and sounding beauteous battle, comes
> With the air of the trumpet round him, and leaps in
> Among the women, snares them by the score

> Flatter'd and fluster'd, wins, tho' dashed with death
> He reddens what he kisses: thus I won
> Your mother, a good mother, a good wife,
> Worth winning" (v.144–60)

The Prince is an authentic liberal. His tactic in response to his father here is Horner's: he presents Princess Ida's feminism as a mirror-image extreme of his father's crudely patriarchal style, and himself as forging a new dialectic between them, arriving at the moderating terms of a compromise. To Ida,

> "Blame not thyself too much," I said, "nor blame
> Too much the sons of men and barbarous laws" (vii.239–40)

As we see when Ida is forced to turn into a version of the Prince's mother, however, far from forging a new order or a new dialectic he is merely finding for himself a more advantageous place within the old one. Finding one, or preserving it: since one way of describing the Prince's erotic strategy is that, Yorick-like, while maintaining the strict division of power and privilege between male and female, he favors (and permits to himself) a less exclusive assignment of "masculine" and "feminine" personal traits between men and women, in order that, as an "effeminized" man, he may be permitted to retain the privileged status of baby (*within* a rigidly divided family) along with the implicit empowerment of maleness. (The privileged avenue from a baby's need to a woman's sacrifice is one of the most repetitively enforced convictions in this inner narrative, and most especially in the lyrics.) In short, the Prince's strategy for achieving his sexual ends in battle differs from his father's only in a minor, stylistic detail: he gets what he wants by losing the battle, not by winning it.

The meaningfulness of the concept of fighting *against* a man *for* the hand of a woman can barely be made to seem problematical to him, however. And in general, the Prince's erotic perceptions are entirely shaped by the structure of the male traffic in women—the use of women by men as exchangeable objects, as counters of value, for the primary purpose of cementing relationships with other men. For instance, it never for one instant occurs to him to take seriously Ida's argument that an engagement contracted for reasons of state, by her father, without her consent, when she was eight years old, is not a reason why the entire course of her life should be oriented around the desires of a particular man. Simi-

larly, as in Tennyson's own life, the giving of a sister in marriage to cement the love of the brother for another man is central in this narrative.
Although romantic love is exalted in the Prince's view, as it is not in his
father's, nevertheless its tendency in the mythic narrative must always be
to ratify and enforce the male traffic in women, not to subvert it.

This emphasis on a chivalric code in which women are "privileged" as
the passive, exalted objects of men's intercourse with men, is part of the
point of drawing a genealogy straight from the Victorian bourgeois family to the medievalistic courtly tradition. To cast the narrative in terms of
a "Prince" and a "Princess" is both a conventional, transparent fairytale
device, and a tendentious reading of history. Like the aristocratic siting
of the genealogical narrative in *Henry Esmond,* it accomplishes several
simplifying purposes. First, it permits a view of the Victorian middle-class
family that denies any relation between its structure and its economic
functions. By making the persistence and decadence of a stylized aristocratic family look like a sufficient explanation for contemporary middle-
class arrangements, it renders economic need invisible and hides from the
middle-class audience both its historical ties to the working class and also
the degree to which, while nominally the new empowered class or new
aristocracy, most of the middle class itself functions on a wage system for
males and a system of domestic servitude for females. Even though the
fit between the structure of the ideologically normative family and the
needs of capital for certain forms of labor-power is anything but seamless, nevertheless the new middle-class family reflects these imperatives in
its structure at least as strongly as it reflects internal contradictions left
over from the aristocratic family of feudal times. Thus, the appeal to high
chivalry obscures the contemporary situation by glamorizing and in fact
dehistoricizing it.

As we will see, though, the mock-heraldry of tracing the bourgeois family
back to aristocratic origins in feudal society is not the only ideologically
useful way of legitimating it. The *Adam Bede* model (see chapter 8), the
genealogy through the yeoman and artisan classes, has its uses as well:
for instance, instead of excluding work and the facts of economic necessity, it incorporates them centrally, but in a form (individual artisanship
evolving into a guildlike system of workshop production) that both af-
firms some of the features of modern industrial discipline (such as the
exclusion of women) and conceals its discontinuity from more individualistic modes of work.

Why then is Tennyson's defense of contemporary social arrangements in *The Princess* cast in the archaizing, aristocratic mold? It is through this question, I think, that we can move to a consideration of the fascinating frame narrative of the poem. For the poem takes place in a very particular England of the present (i.e., 1847), an England that, with Tennysonian daring, seems almost to represent a simple projection into the present of the inner narrative's fantasy of a feudal past. Like *Wives and Daughters, The Princess* begins on a great estate, on the day of the year on which it is opened up to the tenantry and neighborhood:

> Thither flock'd at noon
> His tenants, wife and child, and thither half
> The neighbouring borough with their Institute
> Of which he was the patron. I was there
> From college, visiting the son, . . .
> . . . with others of our set,
> Five others: we were seven at Vivian-place. (Prologue 3-9)

As these lines suggest, *The Princess* is unlike *Wives and Daughters* in locating its point of view among those who might be at Vivian-place even on a normal, non-open-house day; it is also different from any Gaskell novel in viewing all the activities of the neighborhood, *including* the industry-oriented sciences of the Institute, as firmly and intelligibly set within a context of aristocratic patronage. In fact, with a characteristic earnest bravado, Tennyson goes out of his way to underline the apparent incongruity of the juxtaposition of on the one hand ancient privilege and connoisseurship, and on the other hand modern science; like a small-scale exposition of arts and industry, the open grounds of Vivian-place are dotted for the day with "a little clock-work steamer," "a dozen angry model [engines] jett[ing] steam," "a petty railway," a miniature telegraph system where "flash'd a saucy message to and fro/ Between the mimic stations," and so forth, displayed along with the permanent family museum of geological specimens, Greek marbles, family armor from Agincourt and Ascalon, and trophies of empire from China, Malaya, and Ireland (Prologue 73–80, 13–24). The assertion that science, or technology, is the legitimate offspring of patronage and connoisseurship, that all these pursuits are harmonious, disinterested, and nationally unifying, that the raison d'être of the great landowners is to execute most impartially a national consensus in favor of these obvious desiderata—the frame narrative assumes these propositions with a confidence that is almost assaultive.

Along with the breathtaking ellipsis with which *class* conflict is omitted
from Tennyson's England, the aristocratic-oriented view of progress-as-
patronage affects the *gender* politics of the poem, as well. The feminism
presented in Princess Ida's part of the poem is a recognizable, searching,
and, in its own terms, radical feminism. Some of the elements of it that
are taught or practiced at the University include separatism, Lesbian love,
a re-vision in female-centered terms of Western history, mythology, and
art, a critique of Romantic love and the male traffic in women, and a
critique of the specular rationalism of Western medical science. How is
it possible for this elaborately imagined and riveting edifice to crumble at
a mere male touch? What conceptual flaw has been built into it that allows it to hold the imagination so fully on its own terms, and yet to melt
so readily into the poem's annihilatingly reactionary conclusion?

I am suggesting, of course, that its weakness is precisely the poem's
vision of social change as something that occurs from the top down. For
Princess Ida's relation to the University and in fact to the whole progress
of feminism in the mythical southern kingdom is only an intensification
of Sir Walter's relation to "progress" among his tenants: she is the foun-
der, the benefactor, the theorist, the historian, and the beau ideal of a
movement whose disinterested purpose is to liberate *them,* to educate *them,*

> Disyoke their necks from custom, and assert
> None lordlier than themselves. . . . (ii.127–28)

Ida's main feeling about actual living women is impatience, a sense of
anger and incredulity that she cannot liberate them and their perceptions
in a single heroic gesture:

> for women, up till this,
> Cramped under worse than South-sea-isle taboo,
> Dwarfs of the gynaeceum, fail so far
> In high desire, they know not, cannot guess
> How much their welfare is a passion to us.
> If we could give them surer, quicker proof—
> Oh if our end were less achievable
> By slow approaches, than by single act
> Of immolation, any phase of death,
> We were as prompt to spring against the pikes,
> Or down the fiery gulf as talk of it,
> To compass our dear sisters' liberties. (iii.260–71)

In an imaginative world where even a genuinely shared interest can be embodied and institutionalized only in the form of *noblesse oblige,* it is not surprising that a merely personal snag, encountered by the crucial person, succeeds effortlessly in unraveling the entire fabric. A top-down politics of the privileged, sacrificial, enlightened few making decisions for the brutalized, unconscious many will necessarily be an object of manipulation (from inside or outside), of late-blooming self-interest on the part of the leaders, of anomie and sabotage on the part of the led. A feminism based on this particular nostalgia will be without faith or fortitude, a sisterhood waiting to be subverted.

Part of the oddity of Tennyson's poem, however, is that the ideological structure that permits him in the inner narrative to tumble the feminist community down like a house of cards, is the same one whose value and durability for class relations he is blandly asserting, in the frame narrative. It may be this that caused his contemporaries to view the poem as a whole with such unease, an unease which however both he and they persisted in describing as formal or generic.

Tennyson describes the male narrator as being caught between the different *formal* and *tonal* demands of his male and female listeners:

> And I, betwixt them both, to please them both,
> And yet to give the story as it rose,
> I moved as in a strange diagonal,
> And maybe neither pleased myself nor them. (Conclusion 25–29)

Indeed, like the slippages of political argument, the formal and generic slippages between frame and inner narratives are very striking, and do catch up and dramatize the issues of class and gender, as well. For instance, the status of the inner narrative as collective myth, as a necessary ideological invention, is underlined by the indeterminacy about its authorship. During the Vivian-place party, the telling of the story, like a woman, is passed from hand to hand among the young men. The identification is directly made between the collectiveness of the male involvement in women and in storytelling: the idea of storytelling had started with an earlier Christmas reading-party of the seven young men from the University, where, Walter tells his sister Lilia,

> Here is proof that you [women] were miss'd: . . .

> We [men] did but talk you over, pledge you all
> In wassail . . .
>
>   —play'd
> Charades and riddles as at Christmas here, . . .
> And often told a tale from mouth to mouth (Prologue 175–79)

It is to initiate and place the Vivian-place women in the context of this proceeding that the inner story in *The Princess* is begun. Walter jokes of it as an occasion for making a gift of his sister to his friend—

> "Take Lilia, then, for heroine" clamour'd he,
> . . . "and be you
> The Prince to win her!" (Prologue, 217–19)

The story is to be a "Seven-headed monster," of which each male narrator will

> be hero in his turn!
> Seven and yet one, like shadows in a dream. (Prologue, 221–22)

As we have seen, the interior of the "Seven-headed monster" story, the belly of the beast, is no less structured by the male exchange of women than the circumstances of its conception had been. But there is a more unexpected and off-centered, thematic echo between inside and out, as well. The odd comparison of the male narrative communion to that of "shadows in a dream," almost unintelligible in its immediate context, leaps to salience in relation to one of the most notoriously puzzling features of the internal narrative. The Prince inherits from his family, perhaps through a sorcerer's curse, a kind of intermittent catalepsy,

> weird seizures, Heaven knows what:
> On a sudden in the midst of men and day,
> And while I walk'd and talk'd as heretofore,
> I seem'd to move among a world of ghosts,
> And feel myself the shadow of a dream. (i.14–18)

This fugue state is described throughout the poem with the words "shadow" and "dream," and most often simply "shadow of a dream."

> While I listen'd, came
> On a sudden the weird seizure and the doubt:
> I seem'd to move among a world of ghosts;
> The Princess with her monstrous woman-guard,
> The jest and earnest working side by side,
> The cataract and the tumult and the kings
> Were shadows; and the long fantastic night
> With all its doings had and had not been,
> And all things were and were not. (iv.537–45)

The link between the seizures and the "seven and yet one" narrative frame does not disappear from the poem: one of the fugue states, for instance, corresponds to one of the moments when the narrative voice is being passed from one male storyteller to another. Its link to the use of sisters to cement emotional and property relations between men also recurs. Psyche, one of the Princess's companions, is the sister of Florian, a companion of the Prince's whom he considers

> my other heart,
> And almost my half-self, for still we moved
> Together, twinn'd as horse's ear and eye. (i.54–56)

Cyril, the Prince's other companion, falls in love with Psyche—and he asks,

> What think you of it, Florian? do I chase
> The substance or the shadow? will it hold?
> I have no sorcerer's malison on me,
> No ghostly hauntings like his Highness. I
> Flatter myself that always everywhere
> I know the substance when I see it. Well,
> Are castles shadows? Three of them? Is she
> The sweet proprietress a shadow? If not,
> Shall those three castles patch my tatter'd coat?
> For dear are those three castles to my wants,
> And dear is sister Psyche to my heart. . . . (ii.386–96)

Real estate can give body and substance to the shadowy bonds—of women, of words, of collective though hierarchical identification with a Prince—that link the interests of men.

I have no programmatic reading to offer of the meaning and place-ment of the Prince's cataleptic seizures. Surely, however, they are best described as a wearing-thin of the enabling veil of opacity that separates the seven male narrators from the one male speaker. The collective and contradictory eros and need of their investment in him—and through him, in each other—seem to fray away at his own illusion of discrete existence. Is the Prince a single person, or merely an arbitrarily chosen chord from the overarcing, transhistorical, transindividual circuit of male entitlement and exchange? He himself is incapable of knowing.

In chapters 9 and 10, we will be looking toward Dickens' last writings for fantasy versions of worldly male exchange. A slightly earlier Dickens novel is directly relevant here, however. In *Great Expectations,* Pip is sub-ject to fuguelike states rather like the Prince's. The most notable is the one that occurs during Orlick's murderous attack on him at the lime-kiln:

> He drank again, and became more ferocious. I saw by his tilting of the bottle that there was no great quantity left in it. I distinctly understood that he was working himself up with its contents, to make an end of me. I knew that every drop it held, was a drop of my life. I knew that when I was changed into a part of the vapour that had crept towards me but a little while before, like my own warning ghost, he would . . . make all haste to the town, and be seen slouching about there, drinking at the ale-houses. My rapid mind pursued him to the town, made a picture of the street with him in it, and contrasted its lights and life with the lonely marsh and the white vapour creeping over it, into which I should have dissolved.
>
> It was not only that I could have summed up years and years and years while he said a dozen words, but that what he did say presented pictures to me, and not mere words. In the excited and exalted state of my brain, I could not think of a place without seeing it, or of persons without seeing them. It is impossible to over-state the vividness of these images, and yet I was so intent, all the time, upon him himself . . . that I knew of the slightest action of his fingers.[2]

For Pip, as (I am suggesting) for the Prince in Tennyson's poem, the psychologically presented fugue state involves, not an author's overiden-tification with his character, but a character's momentary inability to ex-tricate himself from his author. Pip's sudden, uncharacteristic power of imagination and psychic investiture—as in his later delirium in which "I was a brick in the house wall, and yet entreating to be released from the giddy place where the builders had set me; . . . I was a steel beam of a vast engine, clashing and whirling over a gulf, and yet . . . I implored

in my own person to have the engine stopped, and my part in it ham-
mered off" (ch. 57)—is disturbing *to him,* and resembles nothing so much
as Dickens' own most characteristic powers, as a personality, as a hypnotist, and of course as a novelist. This abrupt, short-lived, deeply disruptive fusion of authorial consciousness with a character's consciousness
occurs in both works under three combined pressures. These are:

First, a difficult *generic* schema of male identifications, narrators, per-
sonae;

Second, a stressed *thematic* foregrounding of the male homosocial bond;

Third, undecidable confusions between singular and plural identity.

We have discussed all three of these elements in *The Princess* and how
they are tied up in the passage "from mouth to mouth" of the "Seven-
headed monster," which links the generic and the thematic problems of
the poem. In *Great Expectations* the elements are on the whole kept more
separate; only the lime-kiln scene brings them together so combustibly.
Throughout the novel, of course, the delicately calibrated and varying
distance between old Pip and young Pip has been generically constitutive, but in a way that left the exuberant voice of "Dickens," or perhaps
of Dickens himself, unusually occluded. Thematically, this scene is one of
several very powerful ones in this paranoid novel to bring men together
under a wildly exacerbated homosocial bond of rivalry. "How dared you,"
asks Orlick, "come between me and a young woman I liked?" Of course,
the degree to which Pip is psychically implicated throughout the novel
in Orlick's violence against women—signally, Mrs. Joe—has attracted a
great deal of critical attention already. But what we have seen most of is
Orlick skulking after *Pip,* Pip hounding *Orlick.*

The confusion of one man and many men, and the problem of the author's status in that confusion—so central in *The Princess*—are oddly displaced and doubled in this scene from *Great Expectations.* On the one hand,
the problem is Pip's, when his consciousness suddenly multiplies as Orlick's bottle empties. On the other hand, it is attached to Orlick himself,
or his new associates. He brags:

> "I've took up with new companions, and new masters. Some of 'em writes
> my letters when I wants 'em wrote— do you mind?—writes my letters, wolf!
> They writes fifty hands; they're not like sneaking you, as writes but one."

Orlick especially relishes this last phrase ("them as writes fifty hands," he
repeats, "that's not like sneaking you as writes but one"). It is not the

first thing in the novel that has thematically linked Orlick with the other wicked male characters, such as Compeyson and Drummle: all three are characterized as lurking, skulking, following in the rear of other men, "coming up behind of a night in that slow amphibious way" (ch. 26).[3] All three also commit violence on women, in complicity with other men.[4] In fact, in piecing together the plot of the novel, it is hard to keep this group of violent, heterosexually possessive men distinct from one another. It is startling, however, to have this many-headed monster of male exchange and violence suddenly lending a wild expressiveness to the previously mute and brutish Orlick. And it is more startling that he expresses his boast in terms (rather like "doing the police in different voices") that suddenly vault *him* to a place in the novelist-surrogate sweepstakes alongside Pip. The cataclysmic pressure of male homosocial complicity is uncannily supra-individual. At its most stressed moments, it can bridge class at the same time as generic/ontological difference—it can melt into one the forge and the forger, or the man who works with his hands and the man who writes fifty of them.

I have mentioned that the collectiveness of male entitlement is not incompatible with, but in fact inextricable from, its hierarchical structure. This fact, too, has formal as well as political importance in *The Princess.* Even though, among the seven young men, young Walter Vivian is surely the one who is closest to the Prince in power and privilege, it is instead the nameless narrator of the frame narrative—the visiting friend, a young poet—who takes responsibility for having put the Prince's narrative into its final form. Thus some of the political shape of this poem might be attributed to its being an argument on behalf of an aristocratic ideology, aimed at an aristocratic as well as a bourgeois audience, but embodied through a speaker whose relation to patronage is not that of the patron but of the patronized. In addition, the confusion—or division—of genre in *The Princess* has an even more direct and explicit link to the division of gender; for the narrative, feminist content and all, is attributed entirely to the young men, while the ravishing lyrics that intersperse the narrative, often at an odd or even subversive angle to what is manifestly supposed to be going on, are supposed to be entirely the work of women in the group:

> the women sang
> Between the rougher voices of the men,
> Like linnets in the pauses of the wind. (Prologue 236–38)

Certainly it is among the ironies of this passionate and confused myth of the sexes, that it has come to be valued and anthologized almost exclusively on the basis of its lyrics, its self-proclaimed "women's work." Perhaps in the eyes of those who actually enjoyed hegemonic privilege, a mere poet could in that age *not* be trusted with the job of articulating a justification for them, however ready he felt himself for the task. Perhaps in their view, if not in Tennyson's, poet's work and women's work fell in the same ornamental, angelic, and negligible class.

Tennyson's project, his poet-narrator's project, and the Prince's project, then, are all like Wycherley's and Horner's projects: through an apparent self-renunciation to embody, to hold together, the contradictions of male homosocial and heterosexual desire within a given society, in order to parlay a sublimated *knowledge* into a measure of social *control*. *The Country Wife* is, from the viewpoint of cognitive as well as formal control, an almost perfect play; *The Princess* is, from the viewpoint of any form of control, a disastrous poem. And as we shall continue to see, no text does or can wield, over the modern, homophobically cloven terrain of male homosocial desire, the extraordinarily concentrated cognitive command of Wycherley's earlier fiction. If nowhere else—if not in thematics, if not in subject matter—then the electrified barrier of homophobia will do its crazing work on genre itself, on the bond between the man who writes the book and the man who officiates in it. "The lyric leak,"[5] Henry James' phrase for the the spreading, corruptive stain on novels of authorial desire indulged or denied, is itself an aspect of modern homosexual panic.

CHAPTER EIGHT

Adam Bede and Henry Esmond: Homosocial Desire and the Historicity of the Female

THE discussions of novels from the paranoid Gothic tradition, in chapters 5 and 6, were based on two important assumptions about historical periodization. The first, discussed explicitly in chapter 5 and based largely on scholarship about sexuality per se—signally male sexuality—and often specifically about attitudes toward male homosexuality, locates a crucial but temporally elusive historical fulcrum somewhere in or since the late seventeenth century. This fulcrum is the transfer of sexual regulation from religious institutions and ideologies to a complex of secular institutions and ideologies such as the state and the sciences of medicine and individual psychology. As we have seen, this transfer of assignment entailed an increasingly stressed and invasive homophobic division of the male homosocial spectrum. Our discussion so far has focused on the resultant changes in men's experience of living within the shifting terms of compulsory heterosexuality. It has been clear that women had a kind of ultimate importance in the schema of men's gender constitution—representing an absolute of exchange value, of representation itself, and also being the ultimate victims of the painful contradictions in the gender system that regulates men. This conception of women's role may be an unwarrantably flat and ahistorical one, however, even within the limits of a study of *male* homosocial desire.

The second assumption about periodization, which has more tacitly undergirt our readings so far in the novel, and became more active with

The Princess in the last chapter, has to do with the changing constitution of the family under emerging industrial capitalism. In various ways, a hypothesis about the increasing importance and the changing ideological significance of the so-called nuclear family will be a referent for our reading of masculinity in nineteenth-century England. Because of the strong identification of women's roles with the family during this period, it is to this hypothesis that we can look in shifting our focus temporarily from the historicity of men's bonds themselves to the historicity of women's relations to men's bonds.

The feminist periodization that hypothesizes an important change in European femininity, and in the European family, under industrialism, goes back at least as far as Engels' *Origin of the Family, Private Property, and the State.* Some version of it is by now a staple in virtually all historically oriented feminist scholarship. It is closely tied to the importance that feminist social scientists (most influentially anthropologists) place on the different shapes and intensities, in different cultures, of the distinction between the "domestic" and the "public."[1] As Joan Kelly-Gadol describes cultures that are "at the end of the scale where the domestic and public orders are clearly distinguished from each other,"

> Women . . . steadily lose control over private property, products, and themselves as surplus increases, private property develops, and the communal household becomes a private economic unit, a family (extended or nuclear) represented by a man. The family itself, the sphere of women's activities, is in turn subordinated to a broader social or public order—governed by a state—which tends to be the domain of men. This is the general pattern presented by historical or civilized societies.[2]

Feminist historical scholarship, following Engels, has tended to see eighteenth-century England, leading toward industrial capitalism and toward a newly narrow focus on the nuclear family, as an especially symptomatic point in the consequential, growing split between "public" and "domestic" spheres.

Although historically oriented feminism (which I will here condense as "Marxist feminism," overriding for the purposes of this argument many very serious differences of approach among many scholars and thinkers) finds this change real and important, the forms of feminism that I have been grouping together under the rubric "radical" (see Introduction iii) deemphasize its importance. In the recent give-and-take between Marxist and radical feminism, an important crux has been the issue of priority—

chronological priority, explanatory priority, *or* functional/teleological priority—between industrial capitalism and the male-dependent family household. The following questions, coarsely formulated as they are, are among the immediate, practical feminist issues at stake in this discussion of priority: Is it men as a group, or capitalists as a class, that chiefly benefit from the modern sexual division of labor? How close is the fit between the functions of the gendered family and the needs of capitalism? Is the gendered family necessary for capitalism? Will changes in one necessarily effect changes in the other, and if so, how?

Alternative reconstructions of the *pre*capitalist family naturally accompany each move in this debate. In another coarse formulation, one could say that radical feminism tends to see within history a relatively unchanging family, in which not only the fact but the basic structures of patriarchal domination have remained stable by resisting or assimilating economic difference or change; while Marxist feminism, again caricaturally, tends to historicize the gendered family catastrophically, to see it as taking its present oppressive form or forms relatively late, chiefly under the pressure of capitalism, and in a fairly direct response to the needs of capital.

In the more sophisticated middle ground that is emerging between these positions, it is appearing that European capitalism was, as it were, born into, or bred in, a pre-existent language of the family. (By "language" here I do *not* mean only ideology, but a complex structure for combining actual persons and functions along the axes of kinship and cohabitation.)[3] Like most languages, this one was multiple, contradictory, and redundant; also like most European languages, it was already intensively and complexly gendered. On the other hand, to the actual speakers of a language, if not the forms themselves then at least the salience, rationale, and meaningfulness of its inherited gender forms are always to some extent up for grabs. And just so did the coming of industrialism reopen negotiations on the salience, rationale, and meaning of pre-existent gender divisions in what was to become the class-marked family of industrial capitalism.

I am using a linguistic metaphor for this process, but, again, not because I mean to suggest that the ideological realm was the theater in which it mainly was enacted. The pattern by which wage work came to take place at a distance from the home, by which men were paid a "family" wage and women a "supplementary" wage for what might be the same work, by which women became a reserve labor force and at the same time had almost sole responsibility at home for the reproduction of male and female labor power; the differentials of salary, occupation, and often even of food consumption; the institution of childrearing by a single person of a single sex—these facts are obviously not ideological constructions in any very hermetic sense of "ideology." At the same time, complicated processes of meaning and reinterpretation must clearly have been close to the very center of mutual class and gender foundation during this period. To that extent it is certainly appropriate for us, as students of the relations of meaning, to work at tracing out the stitchery of ideology in its "invisible reweaving" of future to past and of class to gender.

My project in this chapter is, of course, more modest and much more specific than to adjudicate the issues between a "radical-feminist" and a "Marxist-feminist" reading of the transition to the nineteenth century in England. It is more modest because of the many limitations involved in working on historical questions through the reading of literature; it is much more specific because it is ultimately aimed at the question of male homosocial desire. I am going to be looking here at Thackeray's *Henry Esmond* and Eliot's *Adam Bede,* still against the background of *The Princess:* three nineteenth-century narrative fictions that consciously offer historical or mock-historical accounts of women's changing family roles in relation both to women's own sexuality and to male homosocial desire. *Bede* and *Esmond,* like *The Princess,* end with a ratification of the female role usually identified with the bourgeois Victorian "angel in the house." On the way to that ratification, however, each offers a very different genealogy in preindustrial, feudal relations for what by the end of each has turned into the normative, male-headed nuclear family. Each presents family structure and the meaning of femininity and of masculinity as needing to be redefined in newly "modern" terms. In *Bede* and *Esmond,* a magnetic and preemptive drama of heterosexual transgression occasions even as it obscures a transfer of power between classes. And in all three, the tableau of legitimation of "modern" class and gender arrangements is something that takes place on firmly male-homosocial terms: it is a transaction of honor between men over the dead, discredited, or disempowered body of a woman.

I am going in this chapter to be using the two novels, *Henry Esmond* and *Adam Bede,* to embody a dialectic between Marxist-feminist and radical-feminist views of the historicity of women's status in relation to male homosocial desire. In *Adam Bede,* as in any serious historical novel, a trajectory of myth organizes landscapes of sociology. In *Adam Bede,* both the exquisite sociology and the overarching myth have the same catastrophic structure that we have already seen in the Marxist-feminist account of the economic foundations of the gendered middle-class family. Of course, it is more than arguable whether Eliot would have accepted the *disastrous* connotations of the word "catastrophic" to describe this shift. Nevertheless, a (relatively speaking) big bang theory of class and gender foundation is so finely articulated here, that the feminist scholar/professor *moyen marxisante* can comfortably base half of her women's studies survey on this text alone.

The explanatory power of this novel for our current theoretical crux comes from the authority and fullness with which it places its characters in relation to apparently timeless gender roles; but then from the specificity with which it anchors those roles in the productive and conservative economy of particular families at particular nodes of the social fabric; and finally from the resolute directionality with which the mythic plot pushes those families into new relations that, for some of the familial roles, mean extinction, and for others radical and alienating reorganization.

In the survey of preindustrial society at the beginning of the novel, it is of course the Poysers' farm that most strikingly represents the integrated agricultural workplace described by Marxist feminists, in which the spheres of men's work and women's work overlap substantially.[4] Partly because commodities and services rather than cash are the main medium of exchange, the dairy and textile products over whose production Mrs. Poyser reigns are never clearly differentiated as being for domestic use as against market trade. Neither is Mr. Poyser's farming. Not only are the home and the workplace not physically distinct, that is, but the modes of production and consumption that characterize them are very similarly structured and, hence, similarly valued.

Demographically, as well, the Poyser family is very elastic. A muse of cliometry alighting on the hearth would have her evening's work cut out for her in cataloging and categorizing the group. There are three direct generations of the Poyser family; then there are Dinah and Hetty, two nieces, one living there as a guest, but the other as a servant; then there are the real servants and farm-laborers. But again, in this omni-industrious household everyone not only works hard, but works relatively similarly. Surely it matters, economically, whether one is or is not in line to inherit the tenancy of the farm or ownership of the splendid linens; but in a household economy where manual and managerial labor are only barely distinguished, and more importantly where commodities, services, room and board, companionship, and training in skills are exchangeable on a complex market that does not claim to translate them all into one common rationalized measure, the different capacities in which groups of people live or work in the same household do not easily fit into the gross alternatives, "family" and "servant," or again "men's sphere" and "women's sphere." The family in this sense stretches along the axes of both kinship and cohabitation, apparently not reducing either to the terms of the other.[5]

Of course, Mrs. Poyser's personal authority and incisiveness make the warmest of sense in the context of this economically integrated family. She is not sparing of her words, but pointedness rather than diffuseness is their trait: they are pointed because her pointing hand is a visibly consequential one; her say in the production of family goods and power requires no dilation or mystique. In this we could compare her with Lisbeth Bede, Adam's mother, whose speech, by contrast, shows so many of the traits associated by Robin Lakoff[6] with "female language": repetitiousness, querulousness, self-deprecation, insistence on irrelevant details, "anxious humours and irrational persistence," and, in addition, "a sort of wail, the most irritating of all sounds where real sorrows are to be borne, and real work to be done."[7] Her speech is always vexingly beside the point of the "real"—apologetic and defiant at the same time, "at once patient and complaining, self-renouncing and exacting, brooding the livelong day over what happened yesterday, and what is likely to happen tomorrow, and crying very readily both at the good and the evil" (I,4). "But," Eliot adds to this description, as if to contradict herself, "a certain awe mingled itself with her idolatrous love of Adam, and when he said, 'leave me alone,' she was always silenced."

When we first see Lisbeth, she is standing at the door of her house, where she lives with only her husband and sons. She is watching with practiced eyes "the gradually enlarging speck which for the last few minutes she has been quite sure is her darling son Adam" (I,4), on his way home from the shop where he works as a carpenter. Lisbeth, we are told, is a hard worker herself—she knits "unconsciously," she cleans compulsively, she carries pails of water on her head in from the spring. But it is hard not to associate the fearful hemorrhage of authority and consequentiality from her language, with the physical alienation from her household of the male workers and, by the same economic process, of the emerging monetary nexus. The work she performs in the household is descriptively circumscribed as "domestic" and conservative, *as opposed to* economically productive. Her voice, correspondingly, which presents itself as that of maternity, is really that of perceived dependence, of the talking dog: "We are apt to be kinder to the brutes that love us than to the women that love us," here remarks George Eliot (not then known to be a woman). "Is it because the brutes are dumb?" (I,4) Mrs. Poyser, too, is an energetic lover of her children, but the fretful category of "the women that love us" could never be applied to her; her language is incapable of irrelevance, because she in *her* home is in a position to create relevance.

Fertile and continuous as the Poysers' arrangement originally looks, and fragile and ill-assorted as the Bedes' does, the basic historical trajectory of *Adam Bede* is to move the novel's normative vision of family from the Poysers' relatively integrated farm to the Bedes' highly specified nuclear household. *As part of this transition,* the normative female role must change from Mrs. Poyser's to one like Mrs. Bede's. By the Epilogue of the novel, no one is left in the Poyser household who seems likely to grow up into Mrs. Poyser; Arthur Donnithorne's only child is, of course, dead; but Dinah and Adam have their baby Adam and their baby Lisbeth, whose function is to refract their parents' and namesakes' values on into the future. Of course, the degree to which the novel is not a feminist one in its *valuations* is clear from the lengths to which it goes to make this change seem palatable; but the full measure of the lengths which, as it also clearly shows, there are to go for that purpose, demonstrates the thoroughness of its feminist *analysis.*

The main vehicle for this change in the normative female role is Dinah Morris. Dinah's career in the novel has been extraordinarily full, not only in its intensity, but in its aptitude for catching up the important strands of women's fate as a gender during this period. Although she is Mrs. Poyser's niece, and one of the inhabitants of the Hall Farm as the novel begins, she is also the only character in the novel who has a direct experience of the concentration of industry: she supports herself by working at a cotton mill in Snowfield. At the same time, she is visiting her aunt at the Hall Farm as part of a round of itinerant Methodist preaching. Dinah's mode of life, then, when the novel begins, seems to exemplify certain promises of individualism and autonomy held out to young working women around the time of the beginning of the industrial revolution. Her pay for the work at the mill is, as she puts it, "enough and to spare" (I,8) for her individual needs; orphaned early, she lives alone by choice; and no institutional constraints, and no very potent ideological ones, seem to offer to interfere with the mobility and resoluteness with which she can publicly dedicate her talents to the cause she has chosen.

Dinah's Methodism, predictably, is a two-edged sword in the service of her autonomy. At the beginning of the novel, though, the terms that Methodism offers the young female preacher seem to be fairly clear and fairly advantageous, even by the standards of a worldly individualism: by offering a heightened submission to a single, divine male authority, omniscient and omnipotent, she is to be able to function on at least equal terms with *all* the creatures, men as well as women, on the reduced plane of the human. The seriousness of her vocation justifies her independence from her aunt's family and her geographical mobility, and it also permits her to decline a very eligible offer of marriage without being subject to undue social pressure to accept. Her eloquence as a preacher is a source of attention, prestige, and great influence for her. The terms in which she describes her eloquence to others, however, always de-emphasize her own control over it:

> "[I]t seemed as if speech came to me without any will of my own, and words were given to me that came out as the tears come, because our hearts are full and we can't help it. . . . But, sir, we are led on, like the little children, by a way that we know not." (I,8)

Or Dinah's exercise of her art and influence may be recuperated through the image of maternal compulsion: she tells Mrs. Poyser,

> "I can no more help spending my life in trying to do what I can for the souls of others, than you could help running if you heard little Totty crying at the other end of the house." (I,7)

Plainly, the price to be paid for the extraordinary authority carried by Dinah's voice, which is public in a way that even Mrs. Poyser's is not, is just the insistence that that voice is the instrument of a higher patriarchal utterance not her own. The source of this authority is so very high, nevertheless, that it gives her for the moment a concrete and potent leverage over mere human men. At this *particular* juncture, that is to say, as so often in history, "patriarchy" is not a monolithic mechanism for subordinating "the female" to "the male"; it is a web of valences and significations that, while deeply tendentious, can historically through its articulations and divisions offer both material and ideological affordances to women as well as to men. "She for God only, he for God in her" seems for a long time to be the structure of Dinah's relationship with at any rate the Methodist men in the novel, and to a large extent with the other men as well. And the power that goes with that position is not a merely circumscribed and transcendent one, but a secular one as well.

But given that the story must end, as Milton's does, with the modern male-dominated nuclear family, what is to be done, ideologically, with a paradise in which Eve was created first and stronger, she for God only, he for God in her? Of course, in novels, that is what love is for. The change in Dinah as she "falls in love" with the impervious Adam begins with the emergence of a new, silent, doglike eros whose only expressive faculty is through the eyes, and whose main erogenous zone is the feather-duster:

> . . . how the duster behaved in Dinah's hand—how it went into every small corner, and on every ledge in and out of sight—how it went again and again round every bar of the chairs, and every leg, and under and over everything that lay on the table, till it came to Adam's papers and rulers, and the open desk near them. Dinah dusted up to the very edge of these, and then hesitated, looking at them with a longing but timid eye. (II,26)

Interestingly, it is only around this part of the novel that the Biblical/Miltonic associations of Adam's given name, as opposed to the stolid Saxon associations of his surname, begin to become salient in relation to Dinah. This occurs as Dinah begins to ask herself with a new urgency and uncertainty who is, after all, really for God in whom.

> "Nay, Adam; it seems to me that my love for you is not weak; for my heart waits on your words and looks, almost as a little child waits on the help and tenderness of the strong on whom it depends. If the thought of you took slight hold of me, I should not fear that it would be an idol in the temple. But you will strengthen me." (II,28)

The scene in which Dinah finally accepts Adam carries this tendency to its extreme, for she seems to hear his voice, not as that of the Biblical Adam, but as God's. He comes upon her climbing a hill:

> It happened that just as he walked forward, Dinah had paused and turned round. . . . Adam was glad; for, with the fine instinct of a lover, he felt that it would be best for her to hear his voice before she saw him. He came within three paces of her and then said, "Dinah!" She started without looking round, as if she connected the sound with no place. "Dinah!" Adam said again. He knew quite well what was in her mind. She was so accustomed to think of impressions as purely spiritual monitions, that she looked for no material visible accompaniment of the voice.

> But this second time she looked round. What a look of yearning love it
> was that the mild grey eyes turned on the strong dark-eyed man! She did
> not start again at the sight of him; she said nothing, but moved towards him
> so that his arm could clasp her round. (II,30)

Although earlier in the novel, splits of signification and institutional
structure between the heavenly father and the earthly male had offered
Dinah the space and leverage for some real power of her own, those enabling gaps are closing up here. In fact, the regime of meaning that had
empowered her forms precisely the ground for her present surrender. Dinah finds here that her heavenly Master's voice *is*, simply, Her Master's
Voice; now voiceless herself, she can only quiver, whimper, or gaze hu-
midly in response to it.

Importantly, too, the circumscription of Dinah's power and sphere at
the end of the novel is far from taking place only in the realm of individual psychology, even though that is where the novel has most scope for
making it appear voluntary and exciting. Changes in the composition of
the industrial workforce, apparently enforced as much by working men
as by capitalists, severely curtailed women's access to well-paid or steady
industrial work as the factory system developed during this period, although the novel masks this fact by the assumption that marriage would
in any case mean, for Dinah, settling down for good in her husband's
village and a cessation of wage work. The novel does make explicit, however, that even had Dinah never married, she would have had to give up
the preaching that had been the source of her independence and power,
since in 1803 the right to preach was taken away from Methodist women.
Chillingly, it is only in Adam's voice, in the Epilogue, that we hear what
he claims is Dinah's defense of this rule:

> "Most o' the women do more harm nor good with their preaching—they've
> not got Dinah's gift nor her sperrit; and she's seen that, and she thought it
> right to set th'example o'submitting. . . . And I agree with her, and approve
> o' what she did." (II, p. 374)

Also chillingly, the Epilogue begins with Dinah in just the same canine
posture in which we first saw Lisbeth Bede: poised on the threshold of a
house, straining her eyes out to catch the first possible glimpse of a returning Adam. In fact, Seth points out the continuity:

"Trust thee for catching sight of him if he's anywhere to be seen. . . . Thee't like poor mother used to be. She was always on the look-out for Adam, and could see him sooner than other folks, for all her eyes got dim." (II, p. 372)

If one listens to Top-40 radio, one thinks here irresistibly of Sheena Easton's hit from a year or two ago, "My baby takes the morning train/ He works from nine to five and then/ He takes another home again/ To find me wa-a-a-a-aiting," with its insinuating whisper between the choruses—"Only when he's with me—I come to life!/ Everything he gives me—makes me feel all right!"[8] That nine-to-five regularization of productive work, as much as its alienation from the household, is an underpinning of the statutory tableau of sphere ideology, in which the woman who cannot venture out of "her" sphere stands poised waiting for the man who, owning it, enters it freely but at regularly foreseeable hours specified by the needs of his own masters.

In fact, an especially incisive although tendentiously handled locus of Eliot's sociology in *Adam Bede* is the growing rationalization, the placing on a basis of measurable and interchangeable units, of male work, as it is increasingly differentiated from the increasingly feminized sphere of the household. The hours are not yet "nine to five," but the very first scene of the novel shows a conflict between a pre-industrial task orientation and a factorylike time discipline: as the church clock strikes six, all the carpenters in the Burge workshop throw down their tools from their unfinished tasks—all but Adam, who chides, "I hate to see a man's arms drop down as if he was shot, before the clock's fairly struck, just as if he'd never a bit o' pride and delight in 's work" (I,1). Adam's ideological appeal here, as often in the novel, is to the values of an individualized, pre-industrial artisanry, in which the maker is unproblematically identified with the artifact, and extracts from it the full value of his labor in it. It is important, though, that Adam is speaking from the position of heir-apparent to Jonathan Burge who owns the workshop, and therefore as a prospective beneficiary of the alienated profits of this more collectivized labor. It makes economic sense *for him* to want to reimpose the now emptied-out values of "pride and delight" in work; but the sharp differentiation made by Wiry Ben, his colleague and soon-to-be-employee, between the time for "work" and the time for "play," corresponds more closely to the immediate, less mystified situation of the salaried workers. Outside the sphere of labor relations, the "stiff and masterful" (I,11) Adam is actually a hero of abstraction and rationalization: he "wrote a beautiful hand that you could read off, and could do the figures in his head—a degree of accomplishment totally unknown among the richest farmers of that countryside" (I,9). And what is perhaps clearest about Adam's personality is how fully it is shaped by the leverage on the world given him by rationalized work.

> "There's nothing but what's bearable as long as a man can work. . . . the natur o' things doesn't change, though it seems as if one's own life was nothing but change. The square o' four is sixteen, and you must lengthen your lever in proportion to your weight, is as true when a man's miserable as when he's happy; and the best o' working is, it gives you a grip hold o' things outside your own lot." (I,11)

In contrast to that, the work of the (diminished) household, now become "women's work," remains stubbornly task-oriented and unrationalized: care of children, the sick, or the elderly cannot stop when the clock strikes, nor does the square root of a potroast give one a grip hold o' things outside her own lot. The result of these historical dislocations of work, as Eliot shows, is that the space and time of women's work are ideologized as not only separate but anachronistic in relation to the realm of "real" work. In other words, the ideological soil for Dinah's relegation to the narrow sphere of "angel in the house" had been amply prepared by her early ministry, but that ministry could have borne very different fruit, as well; it is only on the material ground of catastrophic change in the economic structure and functions—and context—of the family, that her particular worldly relation to the transcendent becomes the engine of so narrow and specialized a fate.

Eliot's choice of the rural artisan class rather than representatives of urban industrialism as the vehicle for her genealogy of the English middle-class family was a shrewd one for her gentle defense of the status quo: as we mentioned in the last chapter, it permits her to suggest that the values of modern industrial society are genetically—and appropriately—individualistic, couched in the mode of private property. Furthermore, the terminological slippage "bourgeois family"–"middle-class family"–"working-class family," a slippage that is both a crucial tool of capitalist ideology *and* a yet-unmet challenge to Marxist analysis,[9] is handsomely accommodated by Adam's quiet slippage upward from worker to owner, which is much less emphatically presented than the more clearly "historical" shift of his economic base away from personal aristocratic patronage.

So far we have been using *Adam Bede* to exemplify a proto Marxist-feminist view of the inextricability of gender arrangements from economic division. A corollary of that view is that the one-directional development of economic forms toward industrial capitalism in the eighteenth and nineteenth centuries had correspondingly deep and irreversible effects on the construction of femininity, and of gender relations, as we now experience them. In *Adam Bede,* the most revealing locus of this change will be the fate of Dinah Morris, as she moves from a position of relative power and independence in a loose relation to an agriculture-based extended family, to a much more circumscribed position as mother of an intensively gendered bourgeois nuclear family that is in a marginal relation to the site of economic production.

Henry Esmond, like *The Princess,* while it seems to dramatize a related shift at the level of the transfer of power from the aristocracy to the bourgeoisie, actually, as we shall see, grounds this apparent shift in a pre-existent division of power and roles between men and women, the structure and content of which are already those of the bourgeois nuclear family. Because it shows a relatively constant form of gender division and subordination as *presiding* over historical change in other areas, *Henry Esmond* is perhaps most appropriately considered a proto radical-feminist novel. The main locus in the novel for the reproduction and conservation of gender roles and of male ascendancy is the question of female sexuality. Female sexuality itself, however, is meaningful in the novel chiefly within the context of the exchange of power and of symbolic goods between men; and the scene of female sexuality, whether it be that of the virgin or of the whore, seems regularly and fittingly to end, with the banishment of the woman, in an "affair of honor" between men.

Eliot chooses the rural artisan class for her mythic genealogy of the family; Thackeray has a very different idea. The characters in *Henry Esmond* come from a different class and play for much higher stakes—Earldoms and Marquisates. In some important respects, however, the basic trajectory is the same. In each novel, at any rate, the perceived norm moves from a demographically elastic, untidy family led by an incisive woman, to a small, well-defined family led by a man, and in which the woman's role is both economically undercut and intensively and circumscriptively moralized.

In *Henry Esmond,* a family that begins as rakish, reactionary, Catholic, Jacobite aristocracy, in the picturesque and (in this rendering) chivalric England of Queen Anne, turns within a few years to a piously Protestant, Whiggish, obsessionally domestic home circle of, essentially, solid mid-Victorian citizens.[10] Isabel, the dominant woman of the first, Jacobite family, had been one of those old women in whom Thackeray specialized: a childless selfish Catholic pagan matriarch, powerful, wealthy, semiliterate, with the ruins of beauty and coquetry, a checkered and fairly explicit sexual history, and absolutely no natural ingredients. Rachel, the normative mother of the final family, on the other hand, joys in nursing her loved ones back to health, uses no makeup, studies foreign literatures in her spare time (although "she was a critic, not by reason but by feeling"),[11] is sexually both repressive and possessive to an almost murderous or suicidal degree, has no money of her own . . . in short, the beloved, avenging Angel in the House.

The actual historical legitimation of this new family and new female role in *Henry Esmond* is more graphic and explicit than in *Adam Bede,* because the aristocratic siting of the tale makes familial legitimacy a more available image.[12] Henry Esmond, the new paterfamilias, legitimates the new form of family in two ways: first, he turns out, unexpectedly, to *be,* not a bastard as had been thought, but the legitimate heir to the family's title, the 5th Viscount Castlewood; but second, from that position of power he renounces the title and withdraws from the aristocratic world, symbolically casting his lot instead with the future, with the more modest and private values of the respectable bourgeoisie.

It is characteristic of Thackeray's bravado to underline the historicism of his myth of familial history by intertwining it with genuine world-historical events and persons—world-historical at least at the summer-stock or touring-company level. Most notably, the Jacobitism that is the badge of the old aristocratic values and gender roles is called into question in the very concrete form of the Pretender James Edward. The climactic night when the Pretender squanders, for a sexual adventure, his chance to succeed Queen Anne on the English throne marks the very moment that Henry Esmond becomes a Whig, and the very moment that his plans and desires fall conclusively on Rachel. Surely here, if anywhere, is a portrayal of the bourgeois family as the result of the catastrophic, one-way devolution of the forces of class conflict.

But so much that is most Thackeray in the novel goes in another direction. The problem here is not that he is not a feminist. Of course Thackeray was no more a feminist than David Ricardo was a communist; but Thackeray, like George Eliot, was an inspired specialist in the analysis of gender roles as forms of power, and for that reason it behooves feminists to situate our theoretical formulations in some intelligible relation to their findings. The contradiction in *Henry Esmond* is something more oblique: that for all the novel's finely wrought thematization of historical change in gender relations, the feminism that its analysis truly prefigures is instead the radical and *a*historical critique of patriarchy. If anything, the structure of other kinds of political change is itself subordinated to what is seen as the stable and self-reproducing structure of the gendered family.

For instance, in *The Virginians,* the sequel to *Henry Esmond,* one character says, "Every woman is a Tory at heart. Pope says a rake, but I think t'other is the more charitable word."[13] The remark is symptomatic of Thackeray's insistent yoking-together of the sexual and the political, so that "rake" and "Tory" become exchangeable quantities. No less symptomatic, though, is his fondness for the "*every* woman is—" formulation to begin with; and its effect in turn is to dehistoricize, and hence *de*politicize, the term "Tory," so that political parties themselves come to represent not a struggle of interests but an assignment of static personality types. Besides, one might ask, if *Henry Esmond* showed the once-and-for-all weaning-away of the modern bourgeois family from forms of sexuality and gender relations shaped by a "reactionary" feudalism, then why, in this novel that is its sequel, are we hearing once again about the "naturally" reactionary sexuality of women? And the embarrassments posed by the later novel to the earlier one are only beginning with this question; for from start to finish, *The Virginians* is only an explicit reprise, in the terms of cynical farce, of the grave drama that had first been played, in the terms of catastrophe, in the novel set two generations before.[14]

In fact, what makes *Esmond* plausible as a great *historical* novel, as a novel in which something changes, is only the cleverness with which it is framed, with which it seems to show us that its events happen and could happen only once. But as *The Virginians* makes clear, a slip of the frame, by which *Esmond* might have ended a few years later, or even only a few weeks later, would have shown the dead alive again, lost reputations found or done without, the shattered pitcher back at the well for more. *Henry Esmond* shows us the pastoral cat let out of the bag; *The Virginians* offers us, so to speak, the Cats Repastured. Yet oddly, the great strength of *Esmond,* not as a historical novel perhaps but as a novel of gender constitution, is exactly here, in its presentation of gender roles as things that cannot help but reproduce themselves. If *Adam Bede* offers a sociology of sexual change, *Henry Esmond* is almost in spite of itself an analysis of the mechanisms of sexual continuity.

The great question of *Henry Esmond* seems, as we have said, to be whether the modern family will keep the raffish "reactionary" shape of the Jacobite feudal aristocracy, with its loose ends of both male and female power, filiation, and desire, or take on the tighter and chaster form that is seen as appropriate to bourgeois work and values. The most dramatic form in which this apparent question is enacted is the choice that Henry himself has to make between two women: Rachel, who, as we have seen, already embodies the new-style angel in the house; and her daughter Beatrix, who takes after her aunt Isabel and is growing up to be hell on wheels in the promiscuous old style. (By the time of *The Virginians,* it is patent that Beatrix, with age, has quite simply turned into Isabel.) Now, so far as *Esmond* merely dramatizes the terms of a single moment of choice, it does pose and enact this historical crux of the family. But as a novel that moves through time, even aside from its relation to *The Virginians,* it does something quite different: it shows, with extraordinary continuity and force, old-style Beatrix *as* the daughter of new-style Rachel. The kind of woman Beatrix turns into is both so brilliantly the result of her mother's style of nurturance, and at the same time so clearly the mirror of the ancien regime of femininity whose overthrow *by* her mother it is the novel's apparent purpose to record, that one is left with the image, not of determinate historical change, but of a self-reproducing and incessant narrative of schism within femininity itself, unraveling backwards into the past.

Thackeray's great, inexhaustible subject is the poetry of the unhappy family, but the accent must be on *the* unhappy family. They are not exactly all alike, but the lines of conflict and the personality conformations seem most often to reflect the Victorian bourgeois family, even when the setting of time, rank, place, or even demographic composition might suggest something very different. So that even the household of Rachel's first marriage, when she is Viscountess of Castlewood, with an extended entourage that includes, among others, the chaplain's entire family and the apparently illegitimate son of her husband's cousin, is pure Biedermeier: the inner enforcing mechanism of sphere ideology is firmly in place in her. Her unhappiness is in the first place about her husband's absences from home; her consolations come through cultivation of mind and soul, and these inevitably divide her ever more completely from her husband's sphere of physical action and physical pleasure; her most piercing emotions are attached to jealousy and to the suppression or concealment of sexual desire (I,7; I,11). It is made explicit that her jealousy is caused by the accurate perception of a simple scarcity of love or power available to women (I,11; I,13); and responding to this scarcity, Rachel in turn, although as an idealized mother she is supposed to be an *embodiment* of familial love, turns out to be a cripplingly narrow channel for it (Preface, p.7). Rachel not only monopolizes the love of the men around her, but reserves all *her* love for *them*—first for her husband and son, but soon for Henry Esmond, the saturnine little changeling in the domestic nest. Beatrix, in adulthood, says in one of her revelatory outbursts to Henry,

> "she cares more for Frank's little finger than she does for me—I know she does: and she loves you, sir, a great deal too much; and I hate you for it. I would have had her all to myself; but she wouldn't. In my childhood, it was my father she loved—(oh, how could she? I remember him kind and handsome, but so stupid, and not being able to speak after drinking wine). And then it was Frank; and now, it is heaven and the clergyman. How I would have loved her! From a child I used to be in a rage that she loved anybody but me; but she loved you all better—all, I know she did." (III,3)

In a family whose first principle is a radical cleavage of concerns between father and mother, bridged only by the mother's jealousy, Beatrix is taught early to feel jealousy—which, "if spoken in the presence of Lord Castlewood, tickled and amused his humour; he would pretend to love Frank best, and dandle and kiss him, and roar with laughter at Beatrix's jealousy" (I,8). Unlike her mother, however, and under the tutelage of her seductive father, Beatrix learns not only to feel jealousy, but to manipulate it in others.

> She had long learned the value of her bright eyes, and tried experiments in coquetry. . . . not a little to . . . the joy of her father, who laughed his great laugh, and encouraged her in her thousand antics. Lady Castlewood watched the child gravely and sadly. . . . From her mother's sad looks she fled to her father's chair and boozy laughter. She already set the one against the other: and the little rogue delighted in the mischief which she knew how to make so early. (I,11)

Beatrix's sexual manipulativeness will prove, however, not only a necessary strategy for survival in the gendered family, but at the same time the grounds for the denial to her of love and authority within the same family.

In short, the first brilliance of *Henry Esmond* is to show with apparently timeless authority, in a past tense that keeps turning to present tense, and through a third-person that keeps turning to the first person, the process by which the virgin and the whore beget each other. Thackeray's description is remarkable for not depending on any crudely hydraulic channeling of a reified substance called Sexual Desire, be it male or female: that is, men do not turn some women into whores because they have turned others into virgins but still require their natural quota of sexual discharge; nor do women split between a virginal superego that says no and a whorish id that is raring to go. Instead, in an analysis that strikingly dramatizes some recent feminist readings of Freud (see Introduction ii and iii, and chapter 1), Thackeray depicts sexuality as a highly charged and volatile signifier for differentials of power that take their shape from the social/political concommitants of gender difference. Specifically, both woman-as-virgin and woman-as-whore take on sexual significance within the context of circulation, exchange, and the gift; and what women make of women, as moral or social creatures but most signally as sexual creatures, occurs primarily (though not exclusively) under the pressure of a signifying relation in which both the sender and the intended recipient of the message are male.

Beatrix's erotic situation is an exquisitely detailed double bind. We can begin (but *only* begin) by examining the female homosocial bond in which it seems most immediately to reside. The most sustained and consistent and (at least after the first reading) dramatically visible pressure of desire in *Henry Esmond* is that of Rachel, her mother, for Henry himself. But Rachel's desire occurs entirely within, and in the terms of, the enforcing familial dichotomies of prohibition/transgression, fidelity/infidelity, repression/revelation; if it is potentially subversive of those, it subverts them only from within, and therefore silently, apolitically, and in a mode that permits no solidarity with other women. Thus, although—extraordinarily—her mother's desire for Henry is fully visible to Beatrix, it offers no legitimation to any desires of her own. Instead, the moralistic discourse which the mother silently though agonistically circumvents in her own life is imposed all the more monolithically on the daughter. Beatrix's situation is like Satan's or the Frankenstein monster's: Satan wants only what God wants (and has), but because God writes the lexicon of good and evil, Satan in laying claim to his desires is reduced to two unsatisfactory alternatives: first, a belated, servile, second-hand acquiescence in "the good," which can not get him what he wants, or second, a posing of himself in opposition to God ("Evil be thou my good"[15]), in terms that because they are already taken from God's lexicon put him in an unstable semiotic situation that is bound to degenerate in terms ripe for moralization. In each case, Beatrix's and Satan's, the disabling, unadmitted split between the parental practice and the prescriptive parental definitions is the same, and the two adult children share a similar range of tones among the plangent, the hollow/defiant, and the abject (e.g., III,3; III,7). What is different is that Rachel, as a woman, is not the author of her lexicon nor even an important beneficiary of it. Instead, although this excruciating woman-to-woman relationship is the novel's great distinction, it functions as only half of a scissors mechanism, holding poor Beatrix and her would-be sexuality against the far sharper blade of male homosocial desire.

What is the situation of the men in the novel? In contrast to the mixed messages that Beatrix gets, and the room for (need for) manipulation between the male and female parental spheres, "The young heir of Castlewood," at any rate, "was spoiled by father and mother both. He took their caresses as men do, as if they were his right" (I,11). After his father's death, Frank takes over his father's role of describing Beatrix to herself "indulgently" in the most damagingly sexualized terms; he both promotes her, and reserves the right always to condemn her, as someone who manipulates her sexual allure to advantage. "Look who comes here!—ho, ho! . . . 'Tis Mistress Trix, with a new riband; I knew she would put one on as soon as she heard a captain was coming to supper" (II,7). Rachel, as we have seen, displays the same rapidity in crystallizing her damning judgment of the traits in which she has educated her daughter; but it is perhaps less damaging because less genial, obtuse, and impersonal, the vessel of jealousy in her throbbing so close to the translucent surface of ethical judgment (e.g., II,8; II,15; III,3).

In fact, Henry himself plays the same game with Beatrix: what he defines as *lovable* in her is exactly the same catalog of traits that he defines as morally damning, and to which he holds out a contrast in her mother (e.g., II,15); so that his erotic servitude to her, compulsive as it feels, exists only on the ground of a more or less willed suspension of judgment, a judgment with which he is always free to threaten her and which he finally allows to descend on her with extraordinary punitive force.

As I have suggested, the whipsaw noose of condemning women and desiring them for exactly the same traits is drawn tightest in certain triangular transactions for women between men. The prototype of this transaction in *Esmond* has occurred early in the novel: in Rachel's position in the middle of her first husband's passionate friendship for the dissolute Lord Mohun. Castlewood's infatuation is sudden and imperious, "my Lord Castlewood kissing the other lord before he mounted on horseback, and pronouncing him the best companion he had met for many a long day";

> and when my Lady said there was something free in the Lord Mohun's looks and manner of speech which caused her to mistrust him, her lord burst out with one of his laughs and oaths; said . . . that Mohun was the prettiest fellow in England; . . . and that he would let Mohun know what my Lady Prude said of him. (I,12)

Determining that "Mohun is the best fellow in England; and I'll invite him here, just to plague that . . . frigid insolence" (I,12), Castlewood asserts his mastery over his wife by thrusting her at his friend, who, once arrived,

> was no sooner in his nightcap and dressing-gown than he had another visitor whom his host insisted on sending to him: and this was no other than the Lady Castlewood herself with the toast and gruel, which her husband bade her make and carry with her own hands in to her guest. (I,13)

Needless to say, although there seems to be no serious threat to Rachel's physical fidelity as far as her own feelings are concerned, this triangular relationship becomes a dangerously freighted conduit of all kinds of apparently exchangeable symbolic goods: of money in the form of Castlewood's gambling debts to Mohun, of religion in the form of Rachel's desire to reform Mohun, of sexual one-upmanship in the form of Mohun's desire to cuckold Castlewood. The result is a duel in which Rachel becomes a widow, even though her husband has had no serious doubts about her fidelity.

> "Did I ever doubt that she was pure? It would have been the last day of her life when I did. Do you fancy I think that *she* would go astray? No, she hasn't passion enough for that. She neither sins nor forgives. I know her temper— and now I've lost her, by Heaven I love her ten thousand times more than ever I did—yes, when she was young and beautiful as an angel— . . . when she used to look with her child more beautiful, by George, than the Madonna in the Queen's Chapel. I am not good like her, I know it. . . . And I felt she didn't belong to me: and the children don't. And I besotted myself, and gambled, and drank, and took to all sorts of devilries out of despair and fury." (I,14)

With these words, Castlewood at the end of his life makes clear that it is exactly her purity, the commodity that made the whole point of his thrusting her at Mohun in the first place, that is at the same time the ground of her value for him and the ground of his continuing, and now conclusive, abandonment of her.

Just as Rachel's sexual *goodness* both takes on exchange value, and becomes a strangling double bind for her, in the context of an intense, transactive homosocial desire between men, so Beatrix's sexual *badness* is activated in the same ways by the same male homosocial structure. We have seen how her brother Frank both promotes and criticizes her carefully nurtured aptitude for judicious flirtations; but he does more than that. When Beatrix seems in a position to make an advantageous match with his friend, the young Lord Blandford, Frank acts as an aggressive go-between, giving Blandford a lock of her hair, extorting a signed avowal of love from him, and threatening Blandford with a duel if he does not acknowledge the Castlewood family to be worthy of his hand; though at the same time, Frank feels free to condemn "Trix" for her worldliness in affairs of the heart (II,8).

The political climax of the novel, the crisis of the Jacobite plot, is also the climax of this plot that founds Beatrix's sexuality in a detour of male homosocial desire. The Castlewood family's involvement with the dynastic claims of the Stuarts is long-standing, and has historically been expressed through the gift of women, for instance in the form of Isabel's sexual services to Charles II and his brother (I,2). The strands that tie Beatrix's menfolk to the young Pretender are complicated; but among them is Henry's determination that his suit for Beatrix will "stand or fall" (III,8) by the success of his scheme to smuggle James Edward into England and onto the throne; while the scheme itself depends on James Edward's sharing a birthday with Frank Castlewood, resembling him physically, having his portrait painted as Frank, and finally impersonating him. The prospective rewards for this exploit would include James's retroactive ability to make good the marquisate secretly granted by his father to the Castlewood family; as well as, Henry thinks, Beatrix's ultimate acceptance of himself.

Impelled by this intoxicating blend of upwardly mobile personal identification, romantic patriotism, family tradition, political ambition, and sexual desire, Henry and Frank smuggle the young prince into the Castlewood household. Henry watches the women's preparations for him with approval:

> The chamber was ornamented with flowers; the bed covered with the very finest of linen; the two ladies insisting on making it themselves, and kneeling down at the bedside and kissing the sheets out of respect for the web that was to hold the sacred person of a King. (III,9)

What is more, it is arranged that the ladies themselves will wait on the young visitor; and when he arrives, Beatrix is wearing the family diamonds given to her by Esmond, for "it had been agreed between them, that she should wear these brilliants on the day when the King should enter the house, and a queen she looked, radiant in charms, and magnificent and imperial in beauty" (III,9).

Of course, no sooner have the Castlewood men succeeded, through their exertions both practical and imaginative, in bringing this "King" and "Queen" together in the service of Castlewood family ambitions, than the terrified scapegoating of female sexuality begins.

> She appeared . . . radiant, and with eyes bright with a wonderful lustre. A pang, as of rage and jealousy, shot through Esmond's heart, . . . and he clenched his hand involuntarily, and looked across to Castlewood, whose eyes answered his alarm-signal, and were also on the alert. (III,9)

And that night,

> "I have done the deed," thought [Esmond], sleepless, and looking out into the night; "he is here, and I have brought him; he and Beatrix are sleeping under the same roof now. Whom did I mean to serve in bringing him? Was it the Prince? was it Henry Esmond? . . ." The eager gaze of the young Prince, watching every movement of Beatrix, haunted Esmond and pursued him. The Prince's figure appeared before him in his feverish dreams many times that night. (III,9)

Spurred by his jealousy, Henry finally leads Frank and Rachel in a horrifying, irreparable scene of not-quite-accusation of Beatrix, aimed at getting her out of London and "harm's way." Her denunciations of them are wrenching and undeniable: to Henry she says "you are the chief of the conspiracy against me"; "I give back these family diamonds, which belonged to one king's mistress, to the gentleman that suspected I would be another"; to Frank, "Keep your oaths, my lord, for your wife"; to her mother,

> "Farewell, mother; I think I never can forgive you; something hath broke between us that no tears nor years can repair. I always said I was alone: you never loved me, never—and were jealous of me from the time I sat on my father's knee." (III,10)

No wonder the victors in this scene are left "scared, and almost ashamed of our victory. It did indeed seem hard and cruel that we should have conspired the banishment and humiliation of that fair creature. We looked at each other in silence."

In the upshot, Beatrix is proved to be indeed the whore she has been made into. With a note hidden in *Eikon Basilike,* she tempts the Prince out to the place of her imprisonment, on what by coincidence turns out to be the very night that he most needs to be in London; and the damnation pronounced on her character by each member of the remaining family is entirely beyond appeal. None of them ever sees her again. Interestingly, however, the generations-long male homosocial transaction, in which this destructive heterosexual relationship had been a brief detail, proves at this juncture more durable—even, within certain terms, *successful*. Henry, as head of the family, angry at the Pretender, formally renounces the Castlewood family's fealty to the Stuart succession, and there is a brief, formal gesture that represents a duel; after which Esmond

> falling back a step dropped his point with another very low bow, and declared himself perfectly satisfied.
>
> "Eh bien, Vicomte," says the young Prince, who was a boy, and a French boy, "il ne nous reste qu'une chose a faire": he placed his sword upon the table, and the fingers of his two hands upon his breast:—"We have one more thing to do," says he; "you do not divine it?" He stretched out his arms:— *"Embrassons nous!"* (III,13)

If this male embrace does not represent the triumph of the Castlewood ambitions in the anticipated, Jacobite form, it does however ratify a more authoritative social foundation. It represents the ultimate moral legitimation, the passing on of the torch of history from the discredited old order to Henry Esmond and the small, male-headed, prescriptively gendered bourgeois nuclear family that he seems about to found. This tableau of bonding, in which an aristocratic male hands over his moral authority to a newly bourgeois male, over the sexually discredited body of a woman, offers an arresting image of what appears to be a distinct historical moment of class foundation. Its apparent historical distinctness is, however, in the context of this novel, apparently illusory; since, as we have seen, the transhistorical structure by which female sexuality itself is defined and reproduced, and used and discredited, is condensed in exactly the same triangular and male-homosocial terms, which the novel also shows as repetitious and incessant.

Explicit in our discussion of the not-quite historical genealogies of femininity in *Henry Esmond* and *The Princess* has been a focus on what we have treated as a transhistorical, or perhaps more problematically ahistorical, triangular structure of male exchange of women. Even when we look in our proto "Marxist-feminist" historical novel for "radical-feminist" sexual structure, however, we have not far to go. In *Adam Bede,* the signally sexual plot is the one around Hetty. Like the Jacobite plot of *Henry Esmond,* too, this one culminates in what I have been describing as a tableau of male homosocial bonding—"in which an aristocratic male [Arthur in this case] hands over his moral authority to a newly bourgeois male [Adam], over the sexually discredited body of a woman [Hetty]." This scene in *Adam Bede,* which is the last in the novel and in fact occurs offstage, has the same claims as the *Henry Esmond* scene to being historically constitutive: its ideological purpose is clearly to ratify the authority of the bourgeois male both in economic/political terms, and as head of the emerging nuclear family. In each novel, however, the supposedly foundational nature of this tableau is undermined because it occurs, for one reason or another, ex post facto. In *Henry Esmond* it is ex post facto because the entire, generations-long chain of events that has led up to it has apparently all along been shaped by almost exactly the same forms of almost exactly the same divisions that are supposedly just now being constituted. In *Adam Bede,* it is ex post facto because the novel in its other plot, the Dinah plot, has already done such a careful job of siting these changes—*as* changes—historically in economic and demographic terms.

Thus the specifically sexual power plot of each novel, though it may seem substantively to echo or mirror the more overtly political plot of historical gender and class relations, does so in a form that is temporally both displaced and condensed. In other words, as we have already discussed in section ii of the Introduction, sex as such not only resembles and conveys but represents power, including—but not only—the power relations of gender. This signifying relation of sex to the various forms of power is very intimate and often direct, but it is neither simple nor innocent.

Even the condensation alone of a sexual plot, in the context of a directly historical fiction, can be wildly tendentious. Let me exemplify this briefly in terms of the marriage plots, the plots of family foundation, that we have already treated in *Adam Bede, The Princess,* and *Henry Esmond.* In each of these fictions the condensed evolution of the family proceeds at such a clip, and the "accidents" of the story are arranged in such a way, that each hero "happens" to marry a woman who appears at a crucial moment to be more powerful than he is: Rachel because she is, to all intents and purposes, Henry Esmond's mother; Dinah because Adam is shattered over Hetty's fate, and because her own religious mandate has temporarily let her seem to represent an authority more forceful and patriarchal even than his own; Princess Ida because she is more single-minded, more passionate, more educated, more eloquent, more emotionally forceful, and of course, at the end, much healthier than the Prince. Like Princess Ida, Rachel in *Esmond* has fallen in love with, while nursing, a delirious, utterly dependent invalid who appeared to be dying. Dinah, in *Bede,* imagining her religious power to be inalienable, has fallen in love with a man who bitterly needs her consolations. In each case, it has been the woman who has appeared to be *more* closely tied to the sources of political, intellectual, material, and/or rhetorical authority. The watchword of Ida's feminism is "Better not be at all/ Than not be noble"[16]—and when she first propounds this doctrine, its ethical meaning is firmly tied to its grounding in political power.

Of course, each of these forms of apparent power is destined to undergo a direct translation into a form of bourgeois female powerlessness. The physical vigor of the healthy survivor becomes the humility of the nurse. The vocal authority of the preacher becomes the marginality of the religious quietist. The political clout of the nobility becomes the paralysis of the ethically "noble" (i.e., silent) Victorian heroine. However, for the brief moment of the genealogical fiction, the transaction by which the woman binds herself over to the man, which is presented in each of these fictions as coinciding with the transaction by which the feudal order gives over to the bourgeois—for that brief moment, the transaction appears to be between a woman so powerful, and a man so powerless, that no subsequent use of the power that has been ceded to the man could ever endanger the woman's interests.

And indeed the language of transcendence that continued to disguise the relative powerlessness of bourgeois women kept the same ideological shape: the power of women was assigned the same metaphysical, superstitious, ungrounded status that was supposed also, in the nineteenth century, to inhere in the power of the hereditary aristocracy. In each case, the *displacement* of power relations onto a historical fiction of class relations, and their temporal *condensation* in an erotic narrative, was a way of rationalizing gender inequality, and other inequalities, in the face of an egalitarian public rhetoric.

One important result of this mutual mapping onto each other of class and gender was that bourgeois women became publicly allegorized, in mystifying and for the most part disempowering ways, as representing the traits of a class higher than their husbands'. Women's sexuality, in these marriage plots, has been the space of a chiasmic switching between gender and class power. As in our ideological archetype "A man's home is his castle" (Introduction iii), an archaizing image of control—in these cases condensed as the women's disposal of their own bodies—has been used as a cover under which the material grounds of that control can be prospectively withdrawn.

The more signally, because transgressively, *sexual* plots of the two historical novels—the Beatrix and Hetty plots—display this figure even more insistently. As we have noted, each sexual plot can seem to represent a transhistorical, graphic absolute of Structure: the triangular traffic in women, that busy, transactive stasis that is the setpiece of every form of structuralism. At the same time, however, it is important that these transactions in the two novels occur within a fictive, tendentious, but none the less historically meaningful and purposeful, European class discourse about the vicissitudes of aristocratic *droit de seigneur.* The class discourse of "seduction," here, is distinct from for instance the discourse of rape that has insistently characterized American racism (see Introduction ii).

The frame called sexuality in these historical myths offers a privileged space for the emptying and filling of "eternal" forms with profoundly and specifically manipulative meanings. The mechanism of this, in the transgressively sexual plots, is easy to see. It is the crossing by which women like Hetty and Beatrix enter into sexuality, not as an avenue to pleasure but as the only avenue to power; and emerge from it, far more abject and denuded of power, retroactively identified as embodiments of sexuality itself. This plot is familiar from *Paradise Lost.* For each woman, the sexual narrative occurs with the overtaking of an active search for power of which she is the *subject,* by an already-constituted symbolic power exchange between men of which her very misconstruction, her sense of purposefulness, proves her to have been the designated *object.*

This crossing of subjects within "female" sexuality is congruent with

Freud's account of the retroactive constitution of individual sexuality it-self.[17] Historically, as well, however, the very inclusions and definitions of the sexual are variable and themselves political. In a sense, none of the plots we have discussed is a sexual one: the marriage plots are about marriage, an institution, hence clearly economic and political, while the heroines of the "sexual" plots are both clearly described as being sexually numb, but ambitious. Conversely, look at the relationships that embody what we have been calling here "male homosocial desire"—between Adam and Arthur, say, or between the Prince and Florian, or between the Prince and the tight band of men who "speak" him, or between Castlewood and Mohun, or between all the Castlewood men and their Stuart hero. Political as these relationships clearly are, fraught with the exchange of every kind of symbolic, economic, and cultural meaning and power, each relationship also could be—not only theoretically, but under different historical configurations might have been—classified as sexual, and for reasons themselves tendentious. In such a case, not only the prestige but the "heterosexual" force, the power of these men and these bonds to organize the lives of women, could have been compromised and qualitatively changed, even had the relationships themselves been exactly the same.

From a twentieth-century American perspective, however, these three mainstream early- and mid-Victorian texts, unlike the paranoid Gothic texts discussed in chapters 5 and 6, seem not to engage the homosexual/homophobic division of the male homosocial spectrum in especially marked ways. Each treats the compulsory routing of homosocial desire through heterosexual love more or less as a matter of course. Nevertheless, in each text that routing is both stressful and heavily freighted with political meaning. Perhaps the most generalizable and important for our ongoing narrative is this: that in the presence of a woman who can be seen as pitiable or contemptible, men are able to exchange power and to confirm each other's value even in the context of the remaining inequalities in their power. The sexually pitiable or contemptible female figure is a solvent that not only facilitates the relative democratization that grows up with capitalism and cash exchange, but goes a long way—for the men whom she leaves bonded together—toward palliating its gaps and failures.

CHAPTER NINE

Homophobia, Misogyny, and Capital: The Example of *Our Mutual Friend*

EIGHT years ago, writing a narrative poem about a musicologist with a writing block, I included a little literary joke: a fictional psychoanalyst in the poem was writing a fictional essay for *Thalassa: A* (fictional) *Journal of Genitality,* on the then-fictional topic,

"Sustained Homosexual
Panic and Literary Productiveness" (which includes
close readings from *Our Mutual Friend*). . . .[1]

It didn't amount to much as a joke, but at any rate it does record the slightly incredulous beginnings of my thinking about this present project, and their inextricability from a reading of late Dickens. At that time I probably imagined a reading couched in more biographical terms than it now seems to me feasible to do well, or interesting to do speculatively. In a more historical and political framework, though, it still seems important to delineate the force of Dickens' contribution to the "Gothic" project: the psychologization and political naturalization of homophobia about men.

In chapter 5, on the Romantic Gothic, we sketched a fragmentary, mythical phylogeny of the English novel, which Dickens' career seems to recapitulate at the level of ontogeny. *The Pickwick Papers* at any rate, although written after almost all the Gothic novels mentioned in chapter 5, has much in common with the pre-Gothic *Sentimental Journey:* constitutive elements of its picaresque include the hypercharged and hyperarticulated paternalism of the bond between male servant and male employer; the apparent affective sunniness and unproblematicality of its (far more open, less psychological) gynephobia; and most importantly, the structuring, "explanatory," and coercive authority, for gender as well as class relations, of an image of the family that is in fact appropriate to none of the affectional or cohabitant groupings in the novel.

Also as in *A Sentimental Journey,* the profound and insistent bonds of love between men do not seem to engage with any intimate prohibition. (They also do not seem to engage with any form of genitality; but, as we have already seen, the at any rate literary portrayal of homophobic prohibition seems far more readily triggered than the portrayal of homosexual genitality in any event.) "Homosexual panic"—the modern, intrapsychic, potentially almost universal extension of the secularization of homosexual anathema—seems not to have touched these men or these bonds. They might still be in the England of the sixteenth century, when sodomy was a capital crime, but men found it almost impossible to recognize it in their own or their neighbors' behavior, even in bed.[2]

By the time of *Great Expectations, Our Mutual Friend,* and *Edwin Drood,* however, Dickens' writing had incorporated the concerns and thematics of the paranoid Gothic as a central preoccupation. Specifically, each of these novels sites an important plot in triangular, heterosexual romance—in the Romance tradition—and then changes its focus as if by compulsion from the heterosexual bonds of the triangle to the male-homosocial one, here called "erotic rivalry." In these male homosocial bonds are concentrated the fantasy energies of compulsion, prohibition, and explosive violence; all are fully structured by the logic of paranoia. At the same time, however, these fantasy energies are mapped along the axes of social and political power; so that the revelation of intrapsychic structures is inextricable from the revelation of the mechanisms of class domination.

In the half-century or so between the classic Gothic and Dickens, the terms of engagement between homophobia and class structure had become ever more differentiated. The normative status of the rural gentry in Hogg had to a large extent devolved onto (some version of) the English middle class—mediated by genealogical narratives like *Henry Esmond* and

The Princess. And an anxious self-definition of that class, in male-homo-social terms, as against those both above and below on the social ladder, was effected, as well as critiqued, by neo-Gothic writers such as Dickens. In this chapter and the next, I am going to be focusing on these political strains in Dickens' use of the paranoid Gothic. This chapter will make primary use of *Our Mutual Friend,* with some additional reference to other nineteenth-century English fiction, to explore the uses of homophobia in the domestic political terms of mid-Victorian England. In the next chapter, I will use *The Mystery of Edwin Drood* as the focus of a discussion of homophobia and the literature of British imperialism.

Our Mutual Friend has had an emboldening effect on at any rate the thematic project of *Between Men,* because it is so thick with themes associated with male homophobia and homosexuality. After all, *Our Mutual Friend* is *the* English novel that everyone knows is about anality. The inheritance at the center of the plot is immensely valuable real estate that contains a cluster of what Dickens calls "dust heaps." Layers of scholarly controversy have been devoted to the contents of Victorian dust heaps; and, led by Humphry House's *The Dickens World,* many critics have agreed that human excrement was an important (and financially valuable) component of the mounds. Such critics as Earle Davis, Monroe Engel, J. Hillis Miller, and Sylvia Bank Manning have given this thematic element a good deal of play, often, as F. S. Schwarzbach says, "with the intention of establishing whether Dickens did or did not understand Freud's later formulation of the psychic relation between human waste and money."[3] But although many of those who write about Dickens' conjunction of excrement and money refer to Freud, sometimes by way of Norman O. Brown, most of the substance of Freud's (and Brown's) argument is missing from their accounts. Their point is most often far simpler and essentially moralistic: that money and excrement are alike because (more or less) they are worthless, *bad.* Thus Earle Davis writes,

> Economically speaking, [Dickens'] world could see no difference between unearned increment and diffused excrement. . . . [I]n every part of London he saw mankind straining and struggling over a dung heap. . . . His pen became an excretory organ spouting out a sizzling cover for all the organic corruption which lay festering in the values that money set, the awful offal of Victorian standards.

Davis concludes his "post-Freudian" reading with the ancient favorite text of Chaucer's Pardoner:

> At the bottom of all is money, the love of money at the cost of everything
> else. It is the overweening desire for money which lands most people in the
> filth of Hell.[4]

Perhaps it would be more precise, then, to say that *Our Mutual Friend*
is the only English novel that everyone *says* is about excrement in order
that they may *forget* that it is about anality. For the Freudian insights,
elided in the critics' moralistic yoking of filth and lucre, are erotic ones.
They are insights into the pleasures, desires, bonds, and forms of eros
that have to do with the anus. And it is precisely the repression of these
pleasures and desires that, in Freud, turns feces into filth and filth into
gold. A novel about the whole issue of anal eroticism, and not merely a
sanitized invective against money or "filthy lucre" or what critics have come
to call "the dust-money equation," would have to concern itself with other
elements in the chain Freud describes: love between man and man, for
instance; the sphincter, its control, and the relation of these to sadism;
the relations among bodily images, material accumulation, and economic
status. It would also offer some intimations, at least, of adult genital desire, and repression, in relation to the anus. Furthermore a novel that
treated these issues would necessarily cast them in the mold of a particular, historical vision of society, class, power, money, and gender.

One curious thematic marker in *Our Mutual Friend* that has gone crit-
ically unnoticed, and that the novel itself tends to muffle, is a name. An
important character in the novel chooses to call herself Jenny Wren, but
we are told—just once—that that is not the name she was born with.
Her real name is Fanny Cleaver. Unlike the later, funny, almost childishly
deflationary name, Fanny Assingham, in *The Golden Bowl,* Fanny Cleaver
is a name that hints at aggression—specifically, at rape, and perhaps at
homosexual rape.[5] The pun would seem a trivial accident, were it not a
small pointer to something much more striking: that there are two scenes
in *Our Mutual Friend* whose language does indeed strongly suggest male
rape.[6] These are Bradley Headstone's attack on Rogue Riderhood (discussed below), and the attack on John Harmon in chapter 13 (discussed
in the next chapter). Another thematic "clue" functions at a different level
to solicit the twentieth-century reader's attention to the male homosocial
components in the book. One of the male protagonists lives in domestic
happiness with another man, and at moments of particular intensity he
says things like, "I love you, Mortimer."[7]

In some simple sense, therefore, this must be a novel that delineates something close to the whole extent of the male homosocial spectrum, including elements of homosexual genitality. Just what version of male homosociality most concerns it, however? The sweet avowal, "I love you, Mortimer," almost promises the sunny, Pickwickian innocence of encompassing homosocial love rendered in the absence of homophobia. At the same time, to give a *woman* a name like Fanny Cleaver may suggest something almost opposite: homophobia, in the absence of homosexuality. And those golden dust heaps are the emblem of a wholly abstracted anality: they do not refer us to any individual or sentient anus. To understand the very excess, the supervisibility of the homosocial/homophobic/homosexual thematics in this novel requires us to see that for Dickens the erotic fate of every female or male is also cast in the terms and propelled by the forces of class and economic accumulation.

Let me begin by tracing a chain of Girardian triangles within one of the novel's plots, a chain reaching from the lowest class up to the professional class. It begins with the three members of the Hexam family: Gaffer Hexam, the father, an illiterate scavenger who makes his living by fishing corpses from the Thames and robbing them; Lizzie Hexam, his beautiful, good, and loyal daughter; and Charley Hexam, his son, whom Lizzie protects from their father's violent resentment until Charley is old enough to run away and go to school. These three comprise the first triangle.

Charley is determined and industrious enough to go from a Ragged School to a National School, where he becomes a pupil-teacher under the sponsorship of a young schoolmaster, Bradley Headstone. Bradley, like Charley, began as a pauper, and Dickens says, "regarding that origin of his, he was proud, moody, and sullen, desiring it to be forgotten." Yet an intense bond soon develops between the schoolmaster and young Charley. After the father's death, Bradley advises Charley to have no more to do with his impoverished, illiterate sister. Charley begs Bradley to come meet Lizzie first, however, and Bradley finds himself, as if by compulsion, violently in love with her.

The triangles of the Hexam family and of Charley, Lizzie, and Bradley are complicated by another triangle. Eugene Wrayburn, a young barrister and one of the heroes of the novel, also falls in love with Lizzie. He, like Bradley, has an intense encounter with Charley before meeting Lizzie, although in this case the intensity takes the form of instant, almost allergic dislike on both sides. And Eugene has another, apparently nontriangular, love relationship—it is he who says, "I love you, Mortimer." Mortimer Lightwood is an old friend and protégé of Eugene's from public school, and the two, while making languid efforts to succeed in the law, make a household together.

Already contrasts of class are appearing under the guise of contrasts of personality and sexuality. One great evidence of class and control divides this little world in two as absolutely as gender does, though less permanently: the division of the literate from the illiterate. And after Gaffer's early death, only one of these people—Lizzie, the desired woman—remains illiterate. The quarrel between the schoolmaster and Eugene is over who will teach her to read. But even within the masculine world of literacy, the gradations of class are unforgiving. Charley's and Bradley's relation to knowledge is always marked by the anxious, compulsive circumstances of its acquisition. Dickens says of the schoolmaster,

> From his early childhood up, his mind had been a place of mechanical stow-age. . . . There was a kind of settled trouble in the face. It was the face belonging to a normally slow or inattentive intellect that had toiled hard to get what it had won, and that had to hold it now that it was gotten. (II,1)

Bradley seems always to be in pain, "like . . . one who was being physically hurt, and was unwilling to cry out" (II,11); his infliction of pain on others seems to come from even greater spasms of it within himself; talking to Lizzie about his desire to teach her to read, for example, he seems to be hemorrhaging internally:

> He looked at Lizzie again, and held the look. And his face turned from burning red to white, and from white back to burning red, and so for the time to lasting deadly white. (II,11)

In fact, to borrow an image from a patient of Freud's, the schoolmaster behaves socially like a man with a hungry rat in his bowels. And for him, the rat represents not money but more specifically his small private capital of knowledge. Or rather it represents the alienation from himself of the profit of his knowledge. For the knowledge never makes *him* wiser; it is quite worthless outside the schoolroom; it merely places him, more decisively even than illiteracy would, in a particular, low position in the line of production of labor for a capitalism whose needs now included a literate, rather than merely a massive, workforce. Bradley's one effort to invest his nest egg for his own profit—to teach Lizzie to read, as part of that triangular transaction with Charley—is imperiously overruled by Eugene, who wants to pay for his own person to do the teaching. "Are you her schoolmaster as well as her brother's?" asks Eugene scornfully, and instead of using his name, will only call him, "Schoolmaster." Bradley, as usual, loses control of his composure and complexion—for he is merely "used to the little audience of a school, and unused to the larger ways of men" (II,6).

Eugene, on the other hand, though not wealthy, is a gentleman and a public-school boy. His relation to his own store of knowledge is the confident one of inconspicuous consumption: he can afford to be funny and silly. He likes to say things like "But then I mean so much that I—that I don't mean" (II,6). Or

> "You know that when I became enough of a man to find myself an embodied conundrum, I bored myself to the last degree by trying to find out what I meant. You know that at length I gave it up, and declined to guess any more." (II,6)

Mortimer sees him affectionately as "this utterly careless Eugene." He has no consciousness of knowledge, or even of power, as something to be struggled for, although his unconscious wielding of them makes him not only more loveable and relaxed than Bradley but also much more destructive. The moral ugliness of Eugene's taunts against the schoolmaster is always less striking, in the novel's presentation, then the unloveliness of the schoolmaster's anxiety and frustration. Bradley the pauper, thinking to make himself independent by his learning, finds that he has struggled himself into a powerless, alienating position in an impervious hierarchical economy. Eugene Wrayburn, like Yorick imagining himself as marginal, passive, and unempowered in his relation to the economy, nevertheless speaks with the full-throated authority of a man near its very center.

Bradley's relation with Charley and Eugene's with Mortimer differ on the basis of class, and the position of Lizzie in each relationship is accordingly different. Charley's offer of Lizzie to his schoolmaster represents the purest form of the male traffic in women. Charley explains it to Lizzie this way:

> "Then *I* come in. Mr. Headstone has always got me on, and he has a good deal in his power, and of course if he was my brother-in-law he wouldn't get me on less, but would get me on more. Mr. Headstone comes and confides in me, in a very delicate way, and says, 'I hope my marrying your sister would be agreeable to you, Hexam, and useful to you?' I say, 'There's nothing in

the world, Mr. Headstone, that I could be better pleased with.' Mr. Head-stone says, 'Then I may rely upon your intimate knowledge of me for your good word with your sister, Hexam?' And I say, 'Certainly, Mr. Headstone, and naturally I have a good deal of influence with her.' So I have; haven't I, Liz?"

"Yes, Charley."

"Well said! Now you see, we begin to get on, the moment we begin to be really talking it over, like brother and sister." (II,15)

To Bradley, his triangle with Charley and Lizzie represents not access to power within the society but a dire sliding away from it; and this is true whether one takes his desire for Lizzie or for Charley to represent the main erotic bond. No wonder he says to Lizzie, in an example of his resentful style of courtship:

"You are the ruin—the ruin—the ruin—of me. . . . I have never been quit of you since I first saw you. Oh, that was a wretched day for me! That was a wretched, miserable day!" (II, 15)

No; the closest relation to patriarchal power for Bradley in this tangle comes in the link of rivalry between himself and Eugene Wrayburn. And it soon emerges that this is, indeed, for him, the focus of the whole affair. In the painful scene with Lizzie I have been quoting, Bradley makes a threat against Eugene, and when she responds, indignantly, "He is noth-ing to you, I think," he insists, "Oh yes he is. There you mistake. He is much to me." What? she asks.

"He can be a rival to me *among other things*. . . . I knew all this about Mr. Eugene Wrayburn, all the while you were drawing me to you. . . . With Mr. Eugene Wrayburn in my mind, I went on. With Mr. Eugene Wrayburn in my mind, I spoke to you just now. With Mr. Eugene Wrayburn in my mind, I have been set aside and I have been cast out." (II, 15; emphasis added)

After Lizzie has refused Bradley and left London, the desiring relation between Bradley and Eugene, far from dissipating, becomes hotter and more reciprocal. The schoolmaster decides—wrongly—that he can find Lizzie by following Eugene everywhere he goes, and, Eugene says,

"I goad the schoolmaster to madness. . . . I tempt him on, all over London. . . . Sometimes, I walk; sometimes, I proceed in cabs, draining the pocket of the schoolmaster, who then follows in cabs. I study and get up abstruse No Thoroughfares in the course of the day [while Bradley is teaching]. With

Venetian mystery I seek those No Thoroughfares at night, glide into them by means of dark courts, tempt the schoolmaster to follow, turn suddenly, and catch him before he can retreat. Then we face one another, and I pass him as unaware of his existence, and he undergoes grinding torments. . . . Thus I enjoy the pleasures of the chase. . . . just now I am a little excited by the glorious fact that a southerly wind and a cloudy sky proclaim a hunting evening." (III,10)

In Surtees's *Handley Cross*, Mr. Jorrocks declaims that " 'Unting" is "the image of war without its guilt, and only five-and-twenty per cent. of its danger," but it is less lucky than that for the men who are caught up in this chase. One day on a towpath Bradley attacks Eugene from behind; the two men struggle in an embrace, and Eugene, both arms broken, nearly drowns. Soon after that, another man, a lockkeeper with the sinister and important name Rogue Riderhood, who has been dogging and blackmailing Bradley Headstone, finds himself, too, attacked from behind. This is one of the scenes whose language is that of male rape:

Bradley had caught him round the body. He seemed to be girdled with an iron ring. . . . Bradley got him round, with his back to the Lock, and still worked him backward. . . . "I'll hold you living, and I'll hold you dead! Come down!"

Riderhood went over into the smooth pit, backward, and Bradley Headstone upon him. When the two were found, lying under the ooze and scum behind one of the rotting gates, Riderhood's hold had relaxed, probably in falling, and his eyes were staring upward. But, he was girdled still with Bradley's iron ring, and the rivets of the iron ring held tight. (IV,15)

Sphincter domination is Bradley Headstone's only mode of grappling for the power that is continually flowing away from him. Unfortunately for him, sphincter control can't give him any leverage at all with women—with Lizzie, who simply never engages with him, who eludes him from the start. It only succeeds in grappling more closely to him men who have already been drawn into a fascinated mirroring relation to him—Eugene, with whom he has been engaged in that reversible hunt, and Rogue Riderhood, in whose clothing he had disguised himself for the assault on Eugene. His initial, hating terror of Lizzie was a terror of, as he kept putting it, being "drawn" from himself, having his accumulated value sucked from him down the great void of her illiteracy and powerlessness. But, classically, he is the Pinchwife-like man who, fearing to entrust his relations with patriarchy to a powerless counter, a woman, can himself only be used as a woman, and valued as a woman, by the men with whom he comes into narcissistic relation.

In the novel's social mapping of the body, Bradley, like some other figures at the lower end of the respectable classes, powerfully represents the repressive divorce of the private thematics of the anus from the social forces of desire and pleasure. Dickens does precede Freud, Ferenczi, Norman O. Brown, and Deleuze/Guattari, among others, in seeing digestion and the control of the anus as the crucial images for the illusion of economic individualism: cross-culturally, Brown remarks, "the category of 'possession,' and power based on possession, is apparently indigenous to the magic-dirt complex."[8] One thematic portrayal of this exclusion is a splitting of the body between twin images of a distended gut and a distended disembodied head. Bradley Headstone (and note his name), the most wrackingly anal of the characters, also appears repeatedly as a floating "haggard head in the air" (III,10; III,11); Mr. Venus, a taxidermist and articulator of skeletons, with his shop full of hydrocephalic babies in jars, is himself given to "floating his powerful mind in tea" (III,7); illiterate "Noddy" Boffin dandles the head of his walking stick at his ear like the head of a floating "familiar spirit" or baby, and himself seems to turn into a great heavyheaded puppet at the end of the novel (IV,3; IV,13); and so on. The unanxious version of *homo digestivus* is the "hideous solidity" that the firmly bourgeois Podsnaps and their circle share with their "corpulent straddling" tableware:

> Everything said boastfully, "Here you have as much of me in my ugliness as if I were only lead; but I am so many ounces of precious metal worth so much an ounce; wouldn't you like to melt me down?" . . . All the big silver spoons and forks widened the mouths of the company expressly for the purpose of thrusting the sentiment down their throats with every morsel they ate. The majority of the guests were like the plate. . . . (I,11)

This strain of imagery, of course, culminates in the monstrous dust-heaps themselves. In short, one thing that goes on when the human body is taken as a capitalist emblem is that the relation of parts to wholes becomes problematic; there is no intelligible form of circulation; the parts swell up with accumulated value, they take on an autonomous life of their own, and eventually power comes to be expressed as power over reified doubles fashioned in one's own image from the waste of one's own body. Power is over dolls, puppets, and articulated skeletons, over the narcissistic, singular, nondesiring phantoms of individuality.

For Bradley Headstone, dissociation, anxiety, toil, and a crippling somatic self-consciousness mark the transition into respectability, and make heavy and humiliating work of his heterosexual involvement. How differently they manage these things in the upper classes. While Bradley's intentions toward Lizzie, however uneasy, had been strictly honorable, Eugene Wrayburn has no intentions toward her at all. Mortimer asks him,

> "Eugene, do you design to capture and desert this girl?"
> "My dear fellow, no."
> "Do you design to marry her?"
> "My dear fellow, no."
> "Do you design to pursue her?"
> "My dear fellow, I don't design anything. I have no design whatsoever. I am incapable of designs. If I conceived a design, I should speedily abandon it, exhausted by the operation." (II,6)

This is the opposite of Bradley's compulsive, grasping relation to power. Eugene sees himself as a little leaf borne upon a stream; and an image that is often associated with him is the pretty river that supplies power to the papermill where Lizzie finally gets work. But Eugene's lack of will is enormously more potent than Bradley's clenched, entrapping will, simply because the powerful, "natural" trajectory of this stream is eternally toward swelling the exploitive power of ruling-class men over working-class women. Resolute and independent as Lizzie is, weak and passive as *he* is, Eugene barely has to make a decision, much less form a design, in order to ruin her.

> The rippling of the river seemed to cause a correspondent stir in his uneasy reflections. He would have laid them asleep if he could, but they were in movement, like the stream, and all tending one way with a strong current. . . . "Out of the question to marry her," said Eugene, "and out of the question to leave her." (IV, 6)

It is traditional, in criticism of *Our Mutual Friend*, to distinguish two groups of thematic imagery, that surrounding the river and that surrounding the dust-heaps. If, as I have suggested, the dust-heaps can be said to represent an anthropomorphization of capital that is most closely responsive to the anxieties of the petit-bourgeoisie, then the river, in a sense, offers a critique of that in terms of a more collectively scaled capitalism, organized around alienation and the flow of currency. Its gender implications are pointed and odd: all the men in this waterside novel are strikingly incompetent about the water; there are seven drownings or near-drownings, all of males; men are always dragging each other into the river; and only one person, Lizzie, has the skill to navigate a rescue. At the same time, women are in control only in correctly understanding the current of power as always flowing away from themselves. Gazing into the river, both Lizzie and Eugene read in it the image of Lizzie's inability to resist ruin.

Just as Eugene's higher status enables his heterosexual relationship to be at once more exploitive and less guilty than Bradley's, so his desiring relationship with a man can be at once much more open and much less embroiled in repressive conflict than any of Bradley's. Interestingly, though it is more open, it also seems much less tinged with the sexual. Imagery of the sphincter, the girdle, the embrace, the "iron ring" of the male grasp, was salient in those murderous attacks on men by Bradley Headstone. By contrast it is utterly absent from the tenderer love between Eugene and Mortimer. They live together like Bert and Ernie on Sesame Street—and who ever wonders what Muppets do in bed? This thematic reticence, if it is reticence, in contrast to the hypersaturation with anal thematics of Bradley's part of the story, can perhaps best be accounted for not by some vague invocation of "Victorian prudery," but by thinking about how the libidinal careers of Victorian gentlemen were distinguished, in fiction and in ideology at any rate, from those of males of higher and lower class.

The obstacles to mapping this territory have been suggested before. The historical research on primary sources that would add texture and specificity to generalizations is only beginning to be done, or at any rate published; at the same time, the paradigms available for understanding the history of sexuality are in rapid and productive flux. The best that I can attempt here is perhaps to lay out in a useful codified form what the "common sense" or "common knowledge" of the (essentially middle-class) Victorian reader of novels might be likely to have been, buttressed by some evidence from biographies. I wish to make clear how tentative and how thoroughly filtered through the ideological lens of middle-class literature these generalizations are, but still to make them available *for* revision by other scholars.

With respect to homosocial/homosexual style, it seems to be possible to divide Victorian men among three rough categories according to class. The first includes aristocratic men and small groups of their friends and dependents, including bohemians and prostitutes; for these people, by 1865, a distinct homosexual role and culture seem already to have been in existence in England for several centuries. This seems to have been a milieu, at once courtly and in touch with the criminal, related to those in which the usages of the term "gay" recorded by John Boswell occurred.[9] It seems to have constituted a genuine subculture, facilitated in the face of an ideologically hostile dominant culture by money, privilege, internationalism, and, for the most part, the ability to command secrecy. Pope's lines on Sporus in "Epistle to Dr. Arbuthnot" do, however, presuppose his audience's knowledge that such a role and culture exist. This role is closely related to—is in fact, through Oscar Wilde, the antecedent of—the particular stereotype that at least until recently has characterized American middle-class gay homosexuality; its strongest associations, as we have noted, are with effeminacy, transvestitism, promiscuity, prostitution, continental European culture, and the arts.

For classes below the nobility, however, there seems in the nineteenth century not to have been an association of a particular personal style with the genital activities now thought of as "homosexual." The class of men about which we know most—the educated middle class, the men who produced the novels and journalism and are the subjects of the biographies—operated sexually in what seems to have been startlingly close to a cognitive vacuum. A gentleman (I will use the word "gentleman" to distinguish the educated bourgeois from the aristocrat as well as from the working-class man—a usage that accords, not with Victorian ideology, but with Victorian practice) had a good deal of objective sexual freedom, especially if he were single, having managed to evade the great cult of the family and, with it, much of the enforcing machinery of his class and time. At the same time, he seems not to have had easy access to the alternative subculture, the stylized discourse, or the sense of immunity of the aristocratic/bohemian sexual minority. So perhaps it is not surprising that the sexual histories of English gentlemen, unlike those of men above and below them socially, are so marked by a resourceful, makeshift, *sui generis* quality, in their denials, their rationalizations, their fears and guilts, their sublimations, and their quite various genital outlets alike. Biographies of English gentlemen of the nineteenth and early twentieth centuries are full of oddities, surprises, and apparent false starts; they seem to have no predetermined sexual trajectory. Good examples include Lewis Carroll, Charles Kingsley, John Ruskin, and a little later, T. E. Lawrence, James M. Barrie, T. H. White, Havelock Ellis, and J. R. Ackerley, who describes in an autobiography how he moved from a furtive promiscuous homosexuality to a fifteen-year-long affair of the heart with a female dog.[10] The sexuality of a single gentleman was silent, tentative, protean, and relatively divorced from expectations of genre, though not of gender.

In fiction, a thematically tamer but structurally interesting and emotionally—very often—turbid and preoccupying relationship was common between single gentlemen: Pendennis and Warrington, Clive Newcome and J. J. Ridley, the two Armadales of Collins' *Armadale,* the gentlemen of the Pickwick Club, resemble Eugene and Mortimer in the lack of remark surrounding their union and in the shadowy presence of a mysterious imperative (physical debility, hereditary curse, secret unhappy prior marriage, or simply extreme disinclination) that bars at least one of the partners in each union forever from marriage.

Of the sexuality of English people below the middle class, reliable accounts are difficult to assemble. Both aristocratic and (early twentieth-century) middle-class English male homosexuality seem to have been organized to a striking degree around the objectification of proletarian men, as we read in accounts by or of Forster, Isherwood, Ackerley, Edward Carpenter, Tom Driberg, and others; at the same time, there is no evidence (from these middle-class-oriented accounts) of a homosexual role or subculture indigenous to men of the working class, apart from their sexual value to more privileged men. It is possible that for the great balance of the non-public-school-educated classes, overt homosexual acts may have been recognized mainly as instances of violence: English law before the Labouchère amendment of 1885 did not codify or criminalize most of the spectrum of male bodily contacts, so that homosexual acts would more often have become *legally* visible for the violence that may have accompanied them than for their distinctively sexual content. In middle-class accounts of the working class, at any rate, and possibly within the working class itself, there seems to have been an association between male homosexual genitality and violence, as in Dickens' treatment of Bradley Headstone's anal eroticism in terms exclusively of murder and mutilation.

Since most Victorians neither named nor recognized a syndrome of male homosexuality as our society thinks of it, the various classes probably grouped this range of sexual activities under various moral and psychological headings. I have suggested that the working class may have grouped it with violence. In aristocrats—or, again, in aristocrats as perceived by the middle class—it came under the heading of dissolution, at the very time when dissolution was itself becoming the (wishful?) bourgeois-ideological name for aristocracy itself. Profligate young lords in Victorian novels almost *all* share the traits of the Sporus-like aristocratic homosexual "type," and it is impossible to predict from their feckless, "effeminate" behavior whether their final ruin will be the work of male favorites, female favorites, the racecourse, or the bottle; waste and wastage is the presiding category of scandal. (See chapter 8 for more on the femininine ascription of the aristocracy.) Fictional examples of this ambiguous style include Lord Frederick Verisopht (with his more "masculine," less aristocratic sidekick, Sir Mulberry Hawk), in *Nicholas Nickleby;* Count Fosco, (with his more "masculine," less aristocratic sidekick, Sir Percival Glyde) in *The Woman in White;* Lord Porlock, in *The Small House at Allington* and *Doctor Thorne;* in a more admiring version, Patrick, Earl of Desmond (with his more "masculine," less aristocratic sidekick, Owen Fitzgerald) in Trollope's *Castle Richmond;* and Lord Nidderdale (with Dolly Longstaffe) in *The Way We Live Now.* In each case there is explicit mention of only female erotic objects, if any; but in each case the allegedly vicious or dissolute drive seems more visibly to be directed at a man in more immediate proximity. Perhaps the most overtly sympathetic—at any rate the least grotesque, the closest to "normal"-seeming—of the men in this category is also one who is without a title, although within the context of the novel he represents the vitiated line of a rural aristocracy. That is Harold Transome, in *Felix Holt.* To his sexual history we receive three clues, each tantalizing in its own way: we hear—mentioned once, without elaboration—that the woman he had married in his Eastern travels was one whom he had bought as a slave;[11] we hear—mentioned once, without elaboration—that he has brought a (different) woman back with him from the East;[12] but the person of whom we hear incessantly in connection with Harold is his plangent, ubiquitous manservant-companion:

> "I don't know whether he's most of a Jew, a Greek, an Italian, or a Spaniard. He speaks five or six languages, one as well as another. He's cook, valet, major-domo, and secretary all in one; and what's more, he's an affectionate fellow. . . . That's a sort of human specimen that doesn't grow here in England, I fancy. I should have been badly off if I could not have brought Dominic."[13]

Throughout a plot elaboration that depends heavily on the tergiversations of a slippery group of servants-who-are-not-quite-servants, who have unexplained bonds from the past with Dominic, one waits for the omniscient, serviceable, ingratiating character of Dominic to emerge into its full sinisterness or glamor or sexual insistence—in vain, since the exploitive "oriental" luxuries of his master can be perceived only in a sexually irresolute blur of "decadence." (See chapter 10 for more on "orientalism" and sexual ascription.) Perhaps similarly, the lurid dissipations of the characters in *The Picture of Dorian Gray* are presented in heterosexual terms when detailed at all, even though (biographical hindsight aside) the triangular relationship of Basil, Dorian, and Lord Henry makes sense only in homosexual terms.

Between the extremes of upper-class male homosocial desire, grouped with dissipation, and working-class male homosocial desire, grouped perhaps with violence, the view of the gentleman, the public-school product, was different again. School itself was, of course, a crucial link in ruling-class male homosocial formation. Disraeli (who was not himself an Etonian) offers the flattering ideological version of Eton friendships in *Coningsby*:

> At school, friendship is a passion. It entrances the being; it tears the soul. All loves of after life can never bring its rapture, or its wretchedness; no bliss so absorbing, no pangs of jealousy or despair so crushing and so keen! What tenderness and what devotion; what illimitable confidence; what infinite revelations of inmost thoughts; what ecstatic present and romantic future; what bitter estrangements and what melting reconciliations; what scenes of wild recrimination, agitating explanations, passionate correspondence; what insane sensitiveness, and what frantic sensibility; what earthquakes of the heart, and whirlwinds of the soul, are confined in that simple phrase—a schoolboy's friendship![14]

Candid accounts agree that in most of the public schools, the whirlwinds of the soul were often acted out in the flesh. Like the young aristocrat, the young gentleman at those same public schools would have seen or engaged in a variety of sexual activities among males; but unlike the aristocrat, most gentlemen found neither a community nor a shared, distinctive sexual identity ready for adults who wanted more of the same. A twentieth-century writer, Michael Nelson, reports asking a school friend, "Have you ever had any homosexual inclinations since leaving Eton?" "I say, steady on," his friend replied. "It's all right for fellows to mess one another about a bit at school. But when we grow up we put aside childish things, don't we?"[15]

David Copperfield, among other books, makes the same point. David's infatuation with his friend Steerforth, who calls him "Daisy" and treats him like a girl, is simply part of David's education—though another, later part is the painful learning of how to triangulate from Steerforth onto women, and finally, although incompletely, to hate Steerforth and grow at the expense of his death. In short, a gentleman will associate the erotic end of the homosocial spectrum, not with dissipation, not with viciousness or violence, but with childishness, as an infantile need, a mark of powerlessness, which, while it may be viewed with shame or scorn or denial, is unlikely to provoke the virulent, accusatory projection that characterizes twentieth-century homophobia.

This slow, distinctive two-stage progression from schoolboy desire to adult homophobia seems to take its structure from the distinctive anxieties that came with being educated for the relatively new class of middle-class "gentlemen." Unlike title, wealth, or land, the terms that defined the gentleman were not clearly and simply hereditary but had somehow to be earned by being a particular kind of person who spent time and money in particular ways. But the early prerequisites for membership in this powerful but nebulous class—to speak with a certain accent, to spend years translating Latin and Greek, to leave family and the society of women— all made one unfit for any other form of work, long before they entitled one to chance one's fortune actively in the ruling class.

The action of *Our Mutual Friend* brings to a close that long abeyance in Eugene's life between, so to speak, being *called* and being *chosen* for the professional work of empire. (For instance, he has been called to the Bar, but no one has yet chosen to employ him.) His position is awash with patriarchal authority, the authority of the law itself, but none of it belongs to him yet. In just the same way, having been removed from his family as a child, he will soon be required to return—and in the enforcing position of *paterfamilias,* a position that will lend a retroactive meaning and heterosexual trajectory to his improvised, provisional relationship with Mortimer and his apparently aimless courtship of Lizzie. In the violence at the end of the novel, we see the implacability with which this heterosexual, homophobic meaning is impressed on Eugene's narrative: Bradley, his rival, nearly kills him by drowning; Lizzie saves him; while he seems to be dying, Mortimer interprets his last wishes as being that he might marry Lizzie; and when he comes back to life, he is already a married man. "But would you believe," Lizzie asks afterwards, "that on our wedding day he told me he almost thought the best thing he could do, was to die?" (IV,16)

There is one character to whom this homophobic reinscription of the bourgeois family is even more crippling than it is to Eugene, who already, by the end of the novel, looks almost "as though he had never been mutilated" (IV, 16). That person is, of course, Lizzie. The formal, ideological requirements for a fairytale "happy ending" for her are satis-fied by the fact that she is not "ruined" by Eugene, not cast into the ur-ban underclass of prostitution, but raised up into whatever class the wife of a Victorian barrister belongs to. Eugene is determined to fight for his right to have her regarded as a lady. But with all that good news, Dick-ens makes no attempt to disguise the terrible diminution in her personal stature as she moves from being the resentful, veiled, muscular, illiterate figure rowing a scavenger boat on the Thames, to being a factory worker in love, to being Mrs. Eugene Wrayburn *tout court*. Admittedly, Lizzie has been a reactionary all along. But she has been a blazing, courageous reactionary: she has defended and defied her violent father; she has sac-rificed everything for her beastly brother; she gave up a chance to form an alliance with an older woman, a tavern-keeper, just because the woman would not accept her father; she took off for the countryside to save her honor from the man she loved; and she unhesitatingly risked her life to save his life. But all her reactionary courage meets with a stiflingly reac-tionary reward. Lizzie stops being Lizzie, once she is Mrs. Eugene Wray-burn.

As we see how unrelentingly Lizzie is diminished by her increasingly distinct gender assignment, it becomes clearer why "childishness," rather than femininity, should at that moment have been the ideological way the ruling class categorized its own male homosexuality. As Jean Baker Miller points out in *Toward a New Psychology of Women*, an attribution of gender difference marks a structure of *permanent* inequality, while the re-lation between adult and child is the prototype of the *temporary* inequal-ity that in principle—or in ideology—exists only in order to be over-come: children are supposed to grow up into parents, but wives are not supposed to grow up into husbands.[16] Now, the newly significant class of "gentlemen," the flagship class of English high capitalism, was to in-clude a very wide range of status and economic position, from plutocrats down to impoverished functionaries. In order to maintain the illusion of equality, or at any rate of meritocratic pseudoequality, *within* the class of gentlemen, and at the same time justify the magnification of distinctions within the class, it clearly made sense to envision a long, complicated pe-riod of individual psychic testing and preparation, full of fallings-away, redefinitions, and crossings and recrossings of lines of identification. This protracted, baffling narrative of the self, a direct forerunner of the twen-tieth-century Oedipal narrative, enabled the process of social and vocational sorting to occur under the less invidious shape of different rates of individual maturation.

Not until this psychologistic, "developmental" way of thinking had been firmly established was the *aristocratic* link between male homosexuality and *femininity* allowed to become an article of wide public consumption—a change that was crystallized in the Wilde affair (see chapter 5 and Coda) and that coincided (in the 1890s) with the beginnings of a dissemination across classes of language about male homosexuality (e.g., the word "homosexual"), and with the medicalization of homosexuality through an array of scientific "third sex" and "intersex" theories.

But during all this time, for women, the immutability of gender inequality was being inscribed more and more firmly, moralistically, and descriptively in the structure of bourgeois institutions. As the contrasting bodily images in *Our Mutual Friend* suggest, woman's deepening understanding, as she saw the current flowing away under her own image, came for the most part at the cost of renouncing individual ownership and accumulation. The division of cognitive labor that emerged with the bourgeois family was not a means of power for women, but another part of the edifice of master-slave subordination to men. Sentient middle-class women of this time perceive the triangular path of circulation that enforces patriarchal power as being routed through them, but never ending in them—while capitalist man, with his prehensile, precapitalist image of the body, is always deluded about what it is that he pursues, and in whose service. His delusion is, however, often indistinguishable from real empowerment; and indeed it is blindest, and closest to real empowerment, in his triangular transactions through women with other men.

CHAPTER TEN

Up the Postern Stair:
Edwin Drood and
the Homophobia of Empire

"Well, then," said [Orlick], "I'm jiggered if I don't see you home!"
This penalty of being jiggered was a favourite suppositious case of his. He
attached no definite meaning to the word that I am aware of, but used it . . .
to affront mankind, and convey an idea of something savagely damaging. When
I was younger, I had had a general belief that if he had jiggered me personally, he would have done it with a sharp and twisted hook.
—Dickens, *Great Expectations*[1]

I N the last chapter, we had occasion to quote a homicidal schoolmaster
who addressed his lady-love in the following terms:

"I knew all this about Mr. Eugene Wrayburn, all the while you were drawing me to you. . . . With Mr. Eugene Wrayburn in my mind, I went on.
With Mr. Eugene Wrayburn in my mind, I spoke to you just now. With Mr.
Eugene Wrayburn in my mind, I have been set aside and I have been cast
out."[2]

In *The Mystery of Edwin Drood,* John Jasper, a homicidal music-master,
addresses the woman *he* loves in a similar rhythm.

"Rosa, even when my dear boy was affianced to you, I loved you madly;
even when I thought his happiness in having you for his wife was certain, I
loved you madly; . . . even when he gave me the picture of your lovely face

so carelessly traduced by him, which I feigned to hang always in my sight for his sake, but worshipped in torment for yours, I loved you madly."[3]

The erotic triangle of John Jasper, Edwin Drood, and Rosa Bud in Dickens' unfinished last novel is a recasting of the triangle of Bradley Headstone, Eugene Wrayburn, and Lizzie Hexam in the work that preceded it. In each triangle, the first-mentioned of the male rivals murderously attacks the second; probably each is himself killed before the end of the novel; and each of the women perceives instinctively that, far from loving her as *he* imagines he does, the violent rival is really intent on using her as a counter in an intimate struggle of male will that is irrelevant and inimical to her.[4]

In *Edwin Drood*, however, the recasting of Lizzie's erotic plot from *Our Mutual Friend*, close as it is, engages a different group of preoccupations. To begin with, the magnetism between the rivals in *Our Mutual Friend*, although intense, has to be inferred from the very violence of their hating intercourse; while in *Edwin Drood*, the love between them is the first and most overtly and insistently presented aspect of their relationship. Jasper is famous throughout Cloisterham for nothing so much as his "womanish" (ch. 13) devotion to his nephew, who unambivalently loves and admires him. There are passages between the two men that sound like outtakes from Shakespeare's Sonnets: in which young Drood's pink confident charm, his callow impercipience and selfishness, his innocent all-of-a-piece-ness, seem to stimulate his saturnine uncle to secret, creative extravagances of self-division and double meaning (e.g., ch. 2). The apparent intensity of Jasper's love means that, of course, his deep-laid plot to murder his beloved nephew suggests a serious problem of motivation. A facile solution—that Jasper has consciously and controlledly simulated, for years, all this love for his nephew—is available but entirely unsatisfactory. Instead, Dickens seems to have meant to use the opium addiction mentioned in the story, and/or the hypnosis that seems to be a lurking but unarticulated presence there, to give access to a psychological account of Jasper's personality as a psychotically divided one: one in which love for his nephew and a plan to murder him could coexist. Clearly, then, this is a novel in which the denied erotics of male rivalry are discussed more sentiently than in *Our Mutual Friend*—which means, a novel in which the mechanisms *of* the denial and division of male homosocial eros are more openly a subject.

Another change from the triangle in *Our Mutual Friend:* the difference

of class between the rivals in the earlier novel, to which Headstone's repressive rage, and Wrayburn's insouciance, had seemed to give an exact
psychological correlative, has disappeared in *Edwin Drood*. The rivals, being
uncle and nephew, are of the same class. And in general, gradations of
the professional bourgeoisie almost too subtle and plural to call class differences occupy most of the domestic landscape. Instead of class, the socially crucial signifying function is performed in *Edwin Drood* by race and
exoticism. The rivals are different because one is blond and one is dark;
and one is going off "to wake up Egypt a little" (ch. 8), while the other
endures the "cramped monotony" of Cloisterham (ch. 2). The implicit
frame of *Edwin Drood* has widened from England to the whole world of
Empire; and distinctions that the earlier novel had dramatized in terms
of English grammar and accent are more often dramatized here in terms
of geographical mobility, internationalism, and—especially—skin color.
As in Podsnap's discourse, though possibly not with exactly his set of
valuations, "the English" and "the un-English"—which means here the
Oriental, in various senses—are the dominant categories.

I am going to be arguing in this chapter, through *Edwin Drood* and
some related texts, that the literary availability of a thematics of Empire,
in a relation neither distant nor immediate to English imperalism itself,
changed the terms of the Gothic discourse of homophobia in several mutually reinforcing ways. To begin with, it replaced the consciousness of
class difference that had been endemic in the Gothic with a less discriminate, more dichotomous and fantasy-prone distinction between the domestic and the exotic. (This distinction, of course, had itself had a history
in the Gothic.) Second, the wider and more protected international can-
vas of opportunities for—and fantasies of—exploitive sexual acting-out
meant that the mechanisms of psychological dividedness, always important in the Gothic, were able to be, and needed to be, newly rationalized
and literalized in exotic terms: in opium addiction, and in hypnosis through
"oriental" techniques.[5] In addition to this, a partly Gothic-derived paranoid racist thematics of male penetration and undermining by subject
peoples became a prominent feature of national ideology in western Europe. Its culmination is an image of male rape.

In the famous "Terminal Essay" of his (1885–88) *Thousand Nights and
a Night*, Sir Richard Burton was to bring together the conclusions of his
decades of travel and of reading in nineteenth-century and earlier anthropology. His conclusions on male homosexuality were as follows:

1. There exists what I shall call a "Sotadic Zone," bounded westwards by the northern shores of the Mediterranean (N. Lat. 43°) and by the southern (N. Lat. 30°). . . . including meridional France, the Iberian Peninsula, Italy and Greece, with the coast-regions of Africa from Marocco to Egypt.

2. Running eastward the Sotadic Zone narrows, embracing Asia Minor, Mesopotamia and Chaldaea, Afghanistan, Sind, the Punjab and Kashmir.

3. In Indo-China the belt begins to broaden, enfolding China, Japan and Turkistan.

4. It then embraces the South Sea Islands and the New World where, at the time of its discovery, Sotadic love was, with some exceptions, an established racial institution.

5. Within the Sotadic Zone the Vice [pederasty] is popular and endemic, held at the worst to be a mere peccadillo, whilst the races to the North and South of the limits here defined practise it only sporadically amid the opprobrium of their fellows who, as a rule, are physically incapable of performing the operation and look upon it with the liveliest disgust.[6]

In short, the most exploratory of Victorians drew the borders of male homosexual culture to include exclusively, and almost exhaustively, the Mediterranean and the economically exploitable Third World.

Burton insists that the influence of the Sotadic Zone on "the Vice" is "geographical and climatic, not racial."[7] His insistence is characteristic of an important element of the racism that accompanied European imperialism, as distinct, for instance, from American racism: its genetic basis, where asserted at all, was much less crisply conceived. Americans, in the dichotomized fantasy of our racism, are Black or white, and from birth. Colonials, on the other hand, can "go" native: there is a taint of climate, morale, or ethos that, while most readily described in racial terms, is actually seen as contagious. The first chapter of *Edwin Drood* suggests yet another route to becoming racially declassed: through the ingestion of foreign substances. John Jasper, waking up in a London opium-den, on a bed that also contains "a Chinaman, a Lascar, and a haggard woman," notes that the (English) woman "has opium-smoked herself into a strange likeness of the Chinaman. His form of cheek, eye, and temple, and his colour, are repeated in her." Nor does the *influenza* seem to stop at her; in fact,

As he watches the spasmodic shoots and darts that break out of her face and limbs, like fitful lightning out of a dark sky, *some contagion in them seizes upon him;* insomuch that he has to withdraw himself to a lean arm-chair by the hearth . . . and to sit in it, holding tight, until he has got the better of *this unclean spirit of imitation.* (ch. 1; emphasis mine)

By the end of the chapter, on his return from London to his home in Cloisterham, Jasper is referred to as "a jaded traveller." From Jasper to jade: the Englishman has become orientalized by his contact with the Princess Puffer—and, by the same toke, insidiously feminized. We are not surprised to learn in the next chapter, when we are as it were officially introduced to Jasper, that his "manner is a little sombre. His room is a little sombre"; nor that his regard for his beloved nephew is constantly "hungry, exacting, watchful"; and least of all that "Mr. Jasper is a dark man" (ch. 2).

The orphans, Helena and Neville Landless, are the other orientalized Europeans in the novel.

An unusually handsome lithe young fellow, and an unusually handsome lithe girl; much alike; both very dark, and very rich in colour; she of almost the gypsy type; something untamed about them both; a certain air upon them of hunter and huntress; yet withal a certain air of being the objects of the chase rather than the followers. Slender, supple, quick of eye and limb; half shy, half defiant; fierce of look; an indefinable kind of pause coming and going on their whole expression, both of face and form, which might be equally likened to the pause before a crouch, or a bound. (ch. 6)

The Landlesses come by their savagery more cleanly and honestly than Jasper—they grew up in Ceylon, and were subjected to privation and do-mestic violence as children—and the effect of the exotic contagion on Helena, at any rate, is relatively virilizing and morally invigorating. It does, however, undermine Neville's health, probably fatally; and he worries aloud about his quick temper:

"I have been brought up among abject and servile dependents, of an inferior race, and I may easily have contracted some affinity with them. Sometimes, I don't know but that it may be a drop of what is tigerish in their blood." (ch. 7)

It is clear from even these two examples that the novel's moral reading of the imperialist view of race is rather complicated. The Landlesses are heroic; and the Englishman who is most their foil is Sapsea the incomparably English Mayor and auctioneer, complacently certain that he "knows the world" through his command of Chinese, Japanese, Egyptian, even Esquimaux inventory. Considering the arrest of Neville on suspicion of Drood's murder, "Mr. Sapsea expressed his opinion that the case had a dark look; in short (and here his eyes rested full on Neville's countenance), an Un-English complexion" (ch. 15). The novel presents Sapsea's insularity as a hideous joke; at the same time, it is Jasper, sinister in proportion as he is orientalized, who is most able to manipulate Sapsea's very chauvinism. And in a largely uncriticized version of English genetic and cultural *virtu*, it is Jasper's foil Crisparkle, the more than faintly silly Minor Canon, who seems to occupy the moral center of the novel: Crisparkle "fair and rosy, perpetually pitching himself head-foremost into all the deep running water in the surrounding country" (ch. 2), a fitness addict who every morning, "having broken the thin morning ice near Cloisterham Weir with his amiable head, much to the invigoration of his frame," then moves on to boxing, "hitting out from the shoulder with the utmost straightness, while his radiant features teemed with innocence, and soft-hearted benevolence beamed from his boxing-gloves" (ch. 6). Crisparkle's bounding—indeed, coercive—innocence is traceable to the proverbial playing-fields:

> Good fellow! Manly fellow!. . . . There was no more self-assertion in the Minor Canon than in the schoolboy who had stood in the breezy playing-fields keeping a wicket. He was simply and staunchly true to his duty alike in the large case and in the small. So all true souls ever are. So every true soul ever was, ever is, and ever will be. (ch. 17)

In fact, the English racial ideal that Crisparkle represents is redoubled when, from the depths of his public-school past, his "old fag," who had once saved his life, reappears, and "the two shook hands with the greatest heartiness, and then went to the wonderful length—for Englishmen—of laying their hands each on the other's shoulders, and looking joyfully each into the other's face" (ch. 21). The man who inspires this *tendresse* is a fitness nut like his old master, and even outdoes him in the matter of hygiene: "his bath-room was like a dairy" (ch. 22).

The novel, especially toward the beginning, takes a certain pleasure in exploring the fatuity of the Crisparkle type.

> "We shall miss you, Jasper, at the 'Alternate Musical Wednesdays' tonight;

but no doubt you are best at home. Good-night. God bless you! 'Tell me, shepherds te-e-ell me; tell me-e-e, have you seen (have you seen, have you seen, have you seen) my-y-y Flo-o-ora-a pass this way!' " Melodiously good Minor Canon the Reverend Septimus Crisparkle thus delivers himself. (ch. 2)

Nevertheless, Crisparkle's disastrous stupidity ("Like takes to like, and youth takes to youth," he says cheerily, setting up the meeting that will lead to the murder of Drood [ch. 6]), the physical coercion which his fitness mania allows him to practice under the guise of unruffled friendliness (ch. 8), and his bland and ignorant confidence in the universal applicability of his own sweet, muscular values, seem to be emphatically underwritten by the narrative voice of the novel. The version of male homosociality foregrounded and valued here (between Crisparkle and Tartar, between Crisparkle and Neville Landless) is hierarchical, on a basis that is conceived as one of merit—Crisparkle's "manliness," his Englishness; it is affectively intense but profoundly inexpressive; and it is clean, clean, clean.

In fact, Crisparkle's relation with Neville deviates from the ideal in two respects. The first is that Neville, probably because of his early exposure to "abject and servile dependents, of an inferior race," is more expressive of his feelings of gratitude to his mentor than is perhaps quite expected: there are tears (ch. 10), there are kissings of the Crisparkle hand (ch. 17). These are accepted by Crisparkle, but augur ill for, not Neville's morality, which seems fine, but some inner soundness or integrity in him. By the time the novel breaks off, it is looking as though Neville is not destined to survive his "Englishing"; morally refined to the point of inanition, he will die in the English climate of racism and cold, leaving English Rosa (with whom he is in love) to Crisparkle's other, more vital, more virile, simply more national protégé, Tartar.

The dark John Jasper's overfraught relation with *his* protégé, Drood, is meant to be counterposed against the wholesomeness of the rosy Crisparkle's mentorship. Nevertheless, as so often in these compartmentalizations of male homosocial bonds, the reprobated version is surprisingly congruent with the prescribed version. Crisparkle, all English, has charge of two "dark" young orphans, one male and one female, who are profoundly bonded; he loves one; the other will die. Jasper, himself "dark," has charge of two fair young orphans, one male and one female, who are profoundly bonded; he loves one; the other will die. So that specifically in Edwin's case, as in Neville's, the nurturing process is such that the beloved object apparently does not survive it. But also as in Crisparkle's bond with Neville, there is an overexpressiveness of love that is portrayed as a deep problem—and in this case, a moral problem.

Not surprisingly, it is under the influence of opium that Jasper's feelings about his protégé are allowed the greatest abandon. Even there, however, the erotic and the murderous seem to be inextricable in him. In one of the last scenes of the fragment as it stands, Princess Puffer interrogates Jasper about his opium dreams, which we are meant to infer have been preparatory, and now retroactive, fantasies of his murder of Drood. Both their affect and their compulsively repetitious, convulsive rhythm, however, are sexual. "When I could not bear my life, I came to get the relief [of having the fantasy], and I got it. It *was* one! It *was* one!" he insists. And,

> "I always made the journey [the murderous fantasy] first, before the changes of colors and the great landscapes and glittering processions [of the opium dream proper] began. They couldn't begin till it was off my mind. I had no room till then for anything else." (ch. 23)

The relation between the repeated, delicious violent reverie and the actual violence is as condensed and anticlimactic as the relation between erotic reverie and genital sex: "I did it so often, and through such vast expanses of time, that when it was really done it seemed not worth the doing, it was done so soon." Even in solitary fantasy, there is always the danger of a too-early climax, as well:

> "Hush! the journey's made. It's over. . . . Wait a little. This is a vision. I shall sleep it off. It has been too short and easy. I must have a better vision than this; this is the poorest of all. No struggle, no consciousness of peril, no entreaty—and yet I never saw *that* before. . . . Look at it! Look what a poor, mean, miserable thing it is! *That* must be real. It's over!"

The plot as we have it does not make clear what *"that,"* the "real," is, what Jasper has seen. The rhythm of the sentence, and of the dream itself, however, push our reading of it in the direction of the "poor, bare, forked animal," the poignant disappointment (in this context) of the sensation that, in Sterne, "terminated *in a general way,* in little better than a convulsion" (p. 297). And it has already been made amply clear in the novel that Jasper takes his imaginary "journeys" with an imagined "fellow-traveller"; and that the fellow-traveller is Edwin Drood. As for a thematic location for all this reverie, arousal, climax, revulsion, there is none offered in this scene; unless it is parodically pantomimed by the Princess while Jasper undergoes his silent, solitary ordeal:

> Twitching in an ugly way from time to time, both as to his face and limbs, he lies heavy and silent. The wretched candle burns down; the woman takes its expiring end between her fingers, lights another at it, crams the guttering frying morsel deep into the candlestick, and rams it home with the new candle, as if she were loading some ill-savoured and unseemly weapon. . . .

Not even the release of opium, then, allows Jasper to disentangle three crucial things: his love for his nephew, his need to do violence, and the rhythm of sexual desire. The erotic and the repressive, both tied to Edwin, are inextricable in Jasper. Furthermore, the De Quinceyan splendors of the opium theater are much less his object in seeking out the Princess Puffer, than an opportunity to re-rehearse a scene that may well be already consciously available to him. Why then does he resort to opium at all? What is the function for him and for the novel of his ingestion of the exotic substance?

The importance of opium becomes clearer, in this (Gothic) novel of doubles, if we view it as the double or foil of hypnosis: an alternative technology of consciousness and will. The two motifs are not automatically juxtaposed in the novel, because while opium is associated with the homosocial plot—the murderous journey with Edwin—Jasper's hypnotic powers are exercised over Rosa, in the heterosexual plot. In fact, Jasper's hypnotic power *is* his heterosexual plot: it is the ground of Rosa's hatred and fear of him, but also the only reason she notices him erotically at all.

As Fred Kaplan points out in *Dickens and Mesmerism*, the main meaning that hypnosis had for Dickens was as a channel of will. Its eros was the eros of domination. A brilliant hypnotist, Dickens never permitted himself to be hypnotized. What most engaged him about the technique was not the eeriness of the "sleep-waking" hypnotic subject, but the channelization and intensification of the mesmerist's will as it passes through the unresisting (or, more excitingly, the resisting) being of another. Most exciting of all was the figure of a proud woman forced to embody the meaning, to enact the will—even as she knows it is not hers—of a sufficiently focused man.[8] Of course, this is exactly the shape of the "love" that Jasper wishes to impose, and at times seems almost able to impose, on Rosa. As a music teacher and choirmaster, he is above all in a position to force another or others to utter "him," whatever they may wish to utter: "When he corrects me, and strikes a note, or plays a passage," Rosa says, "he himself is in the sounds, whispering that he pursues me as a lover, and commanding me to keep his secret" (ch. 7).[9]

The split between opium-consciousness and hypnosis-consciousness, then, seems to correspond not only to a divorce in Jasper's mind of homosocial from heterosexual desire, but also to a compartmentalization of passivity from active mobilization of the will. The man who channels his will-power as furiously as Jasper does toward Rosa, in these lessons, has need of a form of voluntary abdication as sudden, convulsive, and reliable as the one provided by his delicious recourse to the opium den. In addition, however, the very distinctness of these two sites, of these two technologies, is important and even necessary in enabling Jasper to maintain an illusion of psychic equilibrium. Feelings about women and feelings about men are, he needs to feel, *different*. The active and the passive are *entirely distinct*. What I feel toward the woman whose self I wish to erase is not hatred; it is love. What I feel toward the man I love to dream about is not love; it is hatred. My active, dominant will, which is heterosexual desire, is something intrinsic, within me, that I radiate outward, by which I master the world. It is hypnosis. This dangerous passivity, which is sometimes necessary to me as a release, and which is the site of my reveries about Edwin, is concretely localized. It is opium: an external substance, outside myself, which I can ingest *at will*.[10] And not only (the novel adds, in one of its voices) is it outside my body; it is outside my country: it is the Un-English. Rosa may munch serenely on her sticky Turkish Lumps-of-Delight candy; but for the English male, there is more at stake in Turkish pleasures. At stake, for instance, in the opium dream of the novel's first paragraph, is a Sultanly habit of impaling men on spikes (ch. 1).

Burton describes some related Oriental habits. Noting that "The Sotadic Zone covers the whole of Asia Minor and Mesopotamia now occupied by the 'unspeakable Turk,' a race of born pederasts,"[11] he dilates on the dangers of the area to travelers:

a favourite Persian punishment for strangers caught in the harem or Gynaeceum is to strip and throw them and expose them to the embraces of the grooms and negro-slaves. I once asked a Shirazi how penetration was possible if the patient resisted with all the force of the sphincter muscle: he smiled and said, "Ah, we Persians know a trick to get over that; we apply a sharpened tent-peg to the crupper-bone (os coccygis) and knock till he opens." A well-known missionary to the East during the last generation was subjected to this gross insult by one of the Persian Prince-governors, whom he had infuriated by his conversion-mania: in his memoirs he alludes to it by mentioning his "dishonoured person;" but English readers cannot comprehend the full significance of the confession. About the same time Shaykh Nasr, Governor of Bushire, a man famed for facetious blackguardism, used to invite European youngsters serving in the Bombay Marine and ply them with liquor till they were insensible. Next morning the middies mostly complained that the champagne had caused a curious irritation and soreness in la parte-poste.[12]

For Jasper, such images of violence are tolerable—they even fulfill a function—as long as they are geographically and psychically compartmentalized. Jasper conceives his integrity, his psychic equilibrium, safe as long as he can keep his opium life and his hypnotic life apart. Especially, active assertion (which is sexual desire) and passive enjoyment (which is—something else) must not be permitted to taint one another. As we have seen in our discussion of Hogg and the classic paranoid Gothic, however, it is of the essence of these doubled states, which begin as intelligibly or even controllably distinct, to invade and undermine one another. As the plot of *Justified Sinner* was to show Robert Wringhim unraveled and undone by that contamination, so the plot of *Edwin Drood* is to show the ruin of Jasper through the same "unclean spirit" of "contagion."

To judge from the way things stand when the novel breaks off, there are meant to be three main avenues of detection that lead to Jasper's conviction. The first of these is situated in the "scene of opium" itself. It is the Princess Puffer, who for reasons of her own, which might be blackmail and might be something yet to be revealed in her own history, is piecing together Jasper's story on the basis of utterances that he makes unconsciously during his opium trances. This represents a multiple undermining of what Jasper imagines is his relation to opium. First, it means simply that his opium-life is not hermetic and discrete. Perhaps because he has localized this form of consciousness in a discrete, external substance (contained in an ink-bottle!), he has imagined that his life under opium could be equally sealed-off; but it cannot. Second, it means that his behavior under opium is not, as he had schematically conceived it, purely passive. It is active, expressive of himself, and thus to some degree intrinsic in himself, as well: as in hypnosis, something of himself is broadcast. And third, although Jasper had conceived of the opium scene as purely the site of his homosocial intercourse with Edwin, he has forgotten or ignored the fact that even there, there is a woman—not a woman who fits into what he imagines to be his sexual life, but nevertheless a woman with motives, desires, and needs of her own. If the active and the passive are not different in essence, if women and the scene of male homosocial desire can be deeply implicated in one another, if passivity and abdication cannot be reliably located in a material, edible substance, outside the self, outside the national life of men—then what safety can there be?

The second path to Jasper's conviction is through Cloisterham, the scene of hypnosis and of Jasper's heterosexual life; here he is threatened by the incursions of opium-consciousness, of fits of narcolepsy or catalepsy, into the English scene of his active will. These fits are frequent, upsetting, and destructive; like the opium state itself, they may have a passively orgasmic rhythm and occur disconcertingly in relation to Edwin. In one scene Edwin is frightened by Jasper's lapsing into such a state; Jasper, attributing it to opium aftereffects, asks him to look away.

> With a scared face the younger man complies, by casting his eyes downward at the ashes on the hearth. Not relaxing his own gaze at the fire, but rather strengthening it with a fierce, firm grip upon his elbow-chair, the elder sits for a few moments rigid, and then, with thick drops standing on his forehead, and a sharp catch of his breath, becomes as he was before. On his so subsiding in his chair, his nephew gently and assiduously tends him. . . . (ch. 2)

This seizure and others like it lead directly to Jasper's incriminating collapse on learning (too late) that Edwin and Rosa had actually dissolved their engagement, so that the murder was "unnecessary." This last collapse is figured through the same, scattered images of bodily concentration: "a staring white face, and two quivering white lips, in the easy chair," "two muddy hands gripping its sides," "a lead-coloured face in the easy-chair, and on its surface dreadful starting drops or bubbles, as of steel," "a ghastly figure" with "a writhing action," and finally, "nothing but a heap of torn and miry clothes upon the floor" (ch. 15).

This Wicked Witch of the West-like deliquescence of Jasper, the passionately resisted, orgasmically structured incursion of trance and passivity into the site he has chosen for mastery and assertion, is not the end for him—only the beginning of the end. Here, too, as in the London plot, the Cloisterham agent of discovery is apparently to be an ignored female presence: Dick Datchery, who is thought by many critics to be Helena Landless in disguise. In Cloisterham, the "heterosexual" site, a woman becomes invisible to Jasper not by remaining a woman, but by becoming a man. Here, where an unswerving self-discipline and mobilization of will are meant to constitute Jasper's sexuality, it is the insidious pressure on Jasper of his own hunger to abdicate the imposition of will that makes his escape impossible.

Besides the Princess Puffer's evidence and the evidence of Jasper's self-betrayal through collapse, the third avenue to Jasper's discovery—although how distinct from those it was meant to prove, in the final writing, is unclear—is the evidence of a ring. Unknown to Jasper, Edwin was carrying a gold ring when he died; and if, as seems likely, Jasper disposed of the body in lime, the ring alone would escape corrosion and dissolution. When Edwin decides not to mention to anyone that he has the ring in his pocket, the narrative brings up a vein of imagery familiar from earlier novels:

> Among the mighty store of wonderful chains that are for ever forging, day and night, in the vast ironworks of time and circumstance, there was one chain forged in the moment of that small conclusion, riveted to the foundations of heaven and earth, and gifted with invincible force to hold and drag. (ch. 13)

On the subject of rings, Burton, in the cryptically macaronic language of his "Terminal Essay" (e.g., "the 'sanctus paederasta' being violemment soupçonné when under the mantle:—non semper sine plagâ ab eo surrexit"[13]), lists in his lexicon of the Greek "nomenclature of pathologic love"

> Catapygos, Katapygosyne = puerarius and catadactylium from Dactylion, the ring, used in the sense of Nerissa's, but applied to the corollarium puerile.[14]

This is reminiscent of the murder of Rogue Riderhood, in *Our Mutual Friend,* "girdled still with Bradley's iron ring," and the attack which that one in turn echoes by Bradley on Eugene: the ring represents the inseparably violent fates of two men bound together by a self-contradictory, repressive eros. It recalls, as well, the iron bonds that link the men in *Great Expectations.* In *Our Mutual Friend,* Bradley taunts Riderhood, "I'll hold you living, and I'll hold you dead!" Magwitch, similarly, having escaped the prison ship and even rid himself of the heavily significant leg iron, lets himself be recaptured only to torment the hated Compeyson. "I took him," he gloats. "He knows it. That's enough for me."

> "Let *him* go free? . . . Let *him* make a tool of me afresh and again? Once more? No, no, no. If I had died at the bottom there;" and he made an emphatic swing at the ditch with his manacled hands; "I'd have held to him with that grip, that you'd have been safe to find him in my hold."[15]

When Compeyson ultimately precipitates himself into a murderous clinch with Magwitch, letting himself be murdered in order to prevent Magwitch's escape from England, it is only a reprise of the same song—as, indeed, is the skulking Orlick's murderous imprisonment of Pip in the lime-kiln. Each of these men is bound, through a woman whom he is incapable of loving, to a far more intense relation with a man toward whom he can express nothing but the most intimate violence.

I have suggested, and the prose from Richard Burton confirms, that the image of male rape implicit in Dickens' use of the paranoid Gothic became more articulately available in its foreign siting, in imperialist literature. The *terminus ad quem* of this motif is unfortunately an account of a real rape, in T. E. Lawrence's *Seven Pillars of Wisdom*. Inevitably, it is a far more wracking account than Burton's voyeuristic, cosmopolitan retailing of "a favourite Persian punishment," or "a curious irritation and soreness in la parte-poste." At the same time, Lawrence when most personal (as here) is also most literary. The rhyme between Dickens' "rivalrous" male clinches, and Lawrence's account many decades later of a real rape and its desperate psychological aftermath, underlines the extent to which men's sensibility, like women's, had already been structured around rape. Here is one of Dickens' accounts: John Harmon, "the man from Somewhere," after his return from "somewhere" overseas, retrospectively attempts to piece together the attack on him by Riderhood and his former shipmate, one George Radfoot, who also dresses in his clothes and impersonates him (as Headstone does to Riderhood).

> "When [Radfoot] came back, I had his clothes on, and there was a black man with him, wearing a linen jacket, like a steward, who put the [opium-spiked] smoking coffee on the table in a tray and never looked at me. . . .
>
> "Now, I pass to sick and deranged impressions; they are so strong, that I rely upon them; but there are spaces between them that I know nothing about, and they are not pervaded by any idea of time.
>
> "I drank some coffee, when to my sense of sight he began to swell im-

mensely, and something urged me to rush at him. We had a struggle near the door. He got from me, through my not knowing where to strike, in the whirling round of the room, and the flashing of flames of fire between us. I dropped down. Lying helpless on the ground, I was turned over by a foot. I was dragged by the neck into a corner. I heard men speak together. I was turned over by other feet. I saw a figure like myself lying dressed in my clothes on a bed. What might have been, for anything I knew, a silence of days, weeks, months, years, was broken by a violent wrestling of men all over the room. The figure like myself was assailed, and my valise was in its hand. I was trodden upon and fallen over. I heard a noise of blows, and thought it was a wood-cutter cutting down a tree. I could not have said that my name was John Harmon—I could not have thought it—I didn't know it—but when I heard the blows, I thought of the wood-cutter and his axe, and had some dead idea that I was lying in a forest.

"This is still correct? Still correct, with the exception that I cannot possibly express it to myself without using the word I. But it was not I. There was no such thing as I, within my knowledge.

"It was only after a downward slide through something like a tube, and then a great noise and a sparkling and crackling as of fires, that the consciousness came upon me, 'This is John Harmon drowning! John Harmon, struggle for your life. John Harmon, call on Heaven and save yourself!' I think I cried it out aloud in a great agony, and then a heavy horrid unintelligible something vanished, and it was I who was struggling there alone in the water."[16]

Lawrence, too, experiences the loss of the sense of time, and the far more important loss of a sense of personal identity. He has been taken prisoner as a possible spy, and refused the sexual advances of the Turkish commander, who "half-whispered to the corporal to take me out and teach me everything."

To keep my mind in control I numbered the blows [of a whip], but after twenty lost count, and could feel only the shapeless weight of pain, not tearing claws, for which I had prepared, but a gradual cracking apart of my whole being by some too-great force whose waves rolled up my spine till they were pent within my brain, to clash terribly together. Somewhere in the place a cheap clock ticked loudly, and it distressed me that their beating was not in its time. I writhed and twisted, but was held so tightly that my struggles were useless. After the corporal ceased, the men took up, very deliberately, giving me so many, and then an interval, during which they would squabble for the next turn, ease themselves, and play unspeakably with me. This was repeated often, for what may have been no more than ten minutes. . . .

At last when I was completely broken they seemed satisfied. Somehow I found myself off the bench, lying on my back on the dirty floor, where I snuggled down, dazed, panting for breath, but vaguely comfortable. I had strung myself to learn all pain until I died, and no longer actor, but spectator, thought not to care how my body jerked and squealed. Yet I knew or imagined what passed about me.

I remembered the corporal kicking with his nailed boot to get me up; and this was true, for next day my right side was dark and lacerated. . . . I remembered smiling idly at him, for a delicious warmth, probably sexual, was swelling through me: and then he flung up his arm and hacked with the full length of his whip into my groin. This doubled me half-over, screaming, or, rather, trying impotently to scream, only shuddering through my open mouth. One giggled with amusement. A voice cried, "Shame, you've killed him." Another slash followed. A roaring, and my eyes went black: while within me the core of life seemed to heave slowly up through the rending nerves, expelled from its body by the last indescribable pang.[17]

In both the fictional and the autobiographical descriptions, one of the most chilling and authentic-sounding impressions is that, from the point of view of the bloodied, half-conscious offal on the floor, the other men in the room seem to be behaving to one another in a casual, ordinary barracks-room male fashion, wrestling together, laughing together, taking turn and turn about. Or are they assaulting one another murderously, as well? The distinction seems impossible to make. Certainly for Lawrence, the racial and cultural foreignness of the Turks (in relation to "his" Arabs, as well as to himself) seems an emblem for the wrenching disjunctions in his ability, as a man, to master the map of male homosocial desire. To begin with, he had moved from intensely charged but apparently unfulfilling bonds with Englishmen, to bonds with Arab men that had, for political reasons, far more space for fantasy and mystification and hence for the illusionistic charisma of will.[18] Many passages in *The Seven Pillars* are devoted to charting the alien but to him compelling geography of male homosociality in the Arab culture. Lawrence wrote (hubristically) of the bond with a particular Arab boy as the motive of his entire commitment to the fate of the Arabs as a race:

> I loved you, so I drew these tides of men into my
>   hands and wrote my will across the sky in stars
> To earn you Freedom, the seven pillared worthy house,
>   that your eyes might be shining for me
>   When we came.[19]

At the same time, he was conscious of nothing so much as the brittleness of the pseudo-mutuality that allowed him as an Englishman to manipulate the pride and affection of the Sherifs. In the "Twenty-Seven Articles" he wrote for a Foreign Office bulletin on "Handling Hedjaz Arabs," he advised,

> Win and keep the confidence of your [Arab] leader. Strengthen his prestige at your expense before others when you can. Never refuse or quash schemes he may put forward. . . . Always approve them, and after praise modify them insensibly, causing the suggestions to come from him, until they are in accord with your own opinion. When you attain this point, hold him to it, keep a tight grip of his ideas, and push him forward as firmly as possible, but secretly so that but no one but himself (and he not too clearly) is aware of your pressure.[20]

The expense of this proceeding in an unnaturally rigid and constant mobilization of the Englishman's will was clear to Lawrence.

> The beginning and ending of the secret handling of Arabs is unremitting study of them. Keep always on your guard; never say an inconsidered thing, or do an unnecessary thing: watch yourself and your companions all the time: hear all that passes, search out what is going on beneath the surface, read their characters, discover their tastes and their weaknesses, and keep everything you find out to yourself. Bury yourself in Arab circles, have no interests and no ideas except the work in hand, so that your brain shall be saturated with one thing only, and you realize your part deeply enough to avoid the little slips that would undo the work of weeks. Your success will be just proportioned to the amount of mental effort you devote to it.[21]

Even while articulating the stress and fragility of such a mental discipline, Lawrence loved it: it was his chosen eros. The rape at Deraa shattered this precarious, Jasper-like, exploitive equilibrium. "The citadel of my integrity," he wrote, "had been irrevocably lost."[22] The trauma of rape can never be simple. For Lawrence, the unprepared-for and hence unmasterable confrontation with yet another, arbitrarily different, brutally contradictory way of carving up the terrain of male bonding, sexuality, and domination, made the self-contradictory grounds of his previous costly and exciting poise too rawly obvious. "I lost my nerve at Deraa," he wrote.

Blond Lawrence among the Arabs, like dark Jasper among the complacent denizens of Cloisterham, had been acting out a story like Horner's in *The Country Wife:* in the arena of race and national culture rather than of gender, they had attempted to construct a position of apparent "androgyny" or halfway-ness that, while pretending to share equally in the qualities of two symmetrically opposite groups, really manipulated the *a*symmetry of their status for personal advancement. A kind of apotheosis of such manipulation on the plane of English imperialism is the eponymous little hero of Kipling's *Kim*.

> Though he was burned black as any native; though he spoke the vernacular by preference, and his mother-tongue in a clipped uncertain sing-song; though he consorted on terms of perfect equality with the small boys of the bazar; Kim was white.[23]

Combining the best of Indian urchin street-smarts and an English-style education, Kim's half-and-half-ness makes him the perfect spy in "the Great Game"—the game of espionage in the service of protecting English rule over India. And not surprisingly, the test in which Kim establishes his essential superiority as material for the Great Game is one in which he resists being hypnotized by an Indian man.

> Lurgan Sahib laid one hand gently on the nape of his neck, stroked it twice or thrice, and whispered. . . .
> To save his life, Kim could not have turned his head. The light touch held him as in a vice. . . . Another wave of prickling fire raced down his neck, as Lurgan Sahib moved his hand.
> . . . . So far Kim had been thinking in Hindi, but a tremor came on him, and with an effort like that of a swimmer before sharks, who hurls himself half out of the water, his mind leaped up from a darkness that was swallowing it and took refuge in—the multiplication-table in English![24]

And after his English multiplication-table and his English force of will have allowed him to repel the hypnosis,

> "Was that more magic?" Kim asked [Lurgan Sahib] suspiciously. The tingle had gone from his veins; he felt unusually wide awake.
> "No, that was not magic. It was only to see if there was—a flaw in a jewel. Sometimes very fine jewels will fly all to pieces if a man holds them in his hand, and knows the proper way."[25]

If Kim is able to act out Horner's imperialistic pseudo-"androgyny" in racial and national terms, what is the meaning of his story in gender terms? For Kim, who is practically still a child, the exploration of the map of male homosociality, like his many other explorations, is still an exciting pleasure. He is too young for anyone to expect him to route his passionate attachments to older men through a desire for women. In addition, the overseas setting and still more the quasimilitary, quasi-Jesuitic, quasi-sports-like espionage ethos of the novel seem largely to bracket the entire question of women. In gender terms, Kim's India is what Lawrence's warrior Arabia had delusively promised to be: a kind of postgraduate or remedial Public School, a male place in which it is relatively safe for men to explore the crucial terrain of homosociality. There are limits, but in these imagined subject territories, as to some degree in real ones, the schism of homophobia is not the most visible feature of geography.

At this advanced stage in the hypostatization of English homophobia, however, the relative relaxation of its proscriptive grasp on "abroad" has to be counterbalanced by a hectically heightened insistence on the unbridgeable gap between "abroad" and "home." Like Jasper, imperialist ideology in relation to "the Sotadic Zone" was somewhat self-permissive within a circumscribed geographical space, but only on the (impossible) condition that that space be hermetically isolated from the space of active, consequential self-constitution.

The trajectory of *The Mystery of Edwin Drood,* so far as we can reconstruct it, is double and self-contradictory in relation to this self-contradictory double bind. On the one hand, the novel in many ways connives in a view of Englishness, of culture and race, or simply of "psychology," that insulates Jasper's experience from that of the novel's wholesome and blond characters. Late in the existing part of the novel, for instance, it is explained why Rosa finds the question of Jasper's guilt such a confusing one to think about:

> for what could she know of the criminal intellect, which its own professed students perpetually misread, because they persist in trying to reconcile it with the average intellect of average men instead of identifying it as a horrible wonder apart. (ch. 20)

On the other hand, *Drood* shares the Gothic novel structure of beginning with a schema of discrete sets of paranoid doubles formed under the projective pressure of male homophobia, and then narrating the decomposition of that costly but apparently stable schema as the political and psychological contradictions that underlie male homophobia become increasingly clamorous. This trajectory in the novel seems to be moving toward a deeply founded critique of the impossibly but compulsorily self-ignorant terms of masculinity, of male homosocial desire, in English culture. At the moment when Jasper, the murderer of Edwin Drood, becomes convinced that the boy really is dead, he writes this in his diary:

> I now swear, and record the oath on this page, That I nevermore will discuss this mystery with any human creature until I hold the clue to it in my hand. That I never will relax in my secresy or in my search. That I will fasten the crime of the murder of my dear dead boy, upon the murderer. And That I devote myself to his destruction. (ch. 16)

The echo of Oedipus here invites the reader to expect the most scouring, universal application of the corrosives that are obviously destined to eat away the rigid and factitious compartmentalizations of Jasper's male desire. The partitions that sustain Jasper's emotional life are riddled with seepage; they are undermined from the start. The corrosive lime in the graveyard, like fever,

> burn[s] away
> Individual beauty from
> Thoughtful children[26]

leaving no individuated token of Edwin's personality—merely the anonymous, inherited, "riveted," male violence-perpetuating gold ring; as Orlick has tried to do to Pip at the lime-kiln, or George Radfoot to John Harmon at Limehouse Hole.[27]

One impulse in *Edwin Drood,* then, is toward a de-individualizing, relatively universal Gothic critique of the organization of male desire—a critique that would sweep away the factitious distinctions between exotic and domestic sites and bonds and pleasures. If it collapses the rigid, vulnerable structures of Jasper's relations to the man and the woman he "loves," can it stop short at Crisparkle's deeply congruent ones?

It can. In fact, as we have seen throughout our discussion of the Gothic, the organization and the manipulability of male bonds after the secularization of homophobia depend exactly on a visible *arbitrariness* in assigning "good" or "bad" names to the array of homosocial bonds. In a narrow, psychologizing view, *Edwin Drood* could well be called a novel about the homosexual panic of a deviant man. The jagged edge of a racial fault-line across the novel's plot and setting facilitates that coarse halving of

the view. A dilated view of the novel might suggest that it pairs the baffled homosexual panic of a dark man with the protected homosexual panic
of a blond man. And a view that encompassed a hypothetical male reader
would see something different again: that the clench, the depersonalized
iron ring of violent and unseeing response to the double bind of male
homosociality is being passed forward yet again.

CODA

Toward the Twentieth Century:
English Readers of Whitman

> Our journey had advanced—
> Our feet were almost come
> To that odd Fork in Being's Road—
> —Dickinson [1]

Our last several readings have situated us at the moment in English history just before the map of male homosocial desire becomes entirely legible to twentieth-century eyes. By the first decade of the present century, the gaping and unbridgeable homophobic rift in the male homosocial spectrum already looked like a permanent feature of the geography. A work like *In Memoriam,* already problematical in its relation to this difficult terrain by the time it appeared in 1850, would have had to be written very differently indeed by 1910.

It had for a long time been true—it had already been clear in the paranoid Gothic—that the schism in the male-homosocial spectrum created by homophobia was a schism based on minimal difference. It was all the more virulently fortified for that. Worse, as we discussed in chapter 5: the more insidious and undermining for that were its effects on the men whom it laid open to every form of manipulation. The deep structure of this double bind for men, the fact of profound schism based on minimal and undecidable differentiation, has persisted and intensified in the twentieth century. Homosexual panic is not only endemic to at any rate middle-class, Anglo-American men (presumably excluding some homosexuals), but a mainspring of their treatment of politics and power—not least, of course, in relation to women. [2]

At the same time that the principle of minimal differentiation has been powerfully operative, it has nevertheless been truer in the twentieth century than before that the men who were more or less firmly placed on the proscribed end of the homosocial spectrum have also been united powerfully by proscription and have worked powerfully to claim and create a difference—a difference beyond proscription. Thus, it is at this historical point that a discussion of male homosocial desire as a whole really gives way to a discussion of male homosexuality and homophobia as we know them.

This latter discussion is already richly in progress;[3] it is not the project of this book. However, I would like to limn in briefly here what seem to be the main ideological drive mechanisms between the mid-Victorian homosocial energies surveyed in the last four chapters, and the engines of repression and liberation as they now present themselves to us. I have chosen Walt Whitman as a figure to stand for the transition to our crystallized homosexual/homophobic world—not Whitman as he writes in America, but Whitman as he is read in England.

A louche and pungent bouquet of the sheepish and the shrewd, Whitman's individuality is most expressive in half-concealment. In fact, the play of calculation with haplessness in Whitman's self-presentation is so intricate, so energizing that that itself, more than the material concealed or revealed, creates an erotic surface, "Ebb stung by the flow, and flow stung by the ebb."[4] In this reading, not Whitman himself but the ideological uses made of his reticence will be the subject: Whitman not as a poet, but as a magnetic figure in the history of English sexual politics.

In the late comedy of Whitman's relations with Horace Traubel, the Boswell of his last years in Camden, the debility of age offers both a luxuriance of expressive openness and unaccountability—"How sweet the bed—the dear bed! When a fellow is physically in the dumps the bed gives him a sort of freedom"—and a pretext for any amount of cat-and-mouse about sexual secrets: "You'll hear that in due time—not tonight. That cat has too long a tail to start to unravel at the end of an evening." Every issue of revelation becomes a flirtation between the young man and the old. For instance, after Whitman shows Traubel a letter from Ellen Terry, "He regarded me with a whimsical eye: 'You have a hungry look: I think you want the letter. Well—take it along. You seem to cultivate that hungry look: it is a species of pantalooned coquetry.'"[5]

Indeed, a benign and generalized "pantalooned coquetry" was a dominant note in the Camden circle of those years. Whitman's most explicit

recorded statement about genital homosexuality arises from this context—arises from it but seems to disrupt or betray it, at the same time.
John Addington Symonds, an English admirer, wrote him, not once but
many times, to ask "exactly what he means by 'Calamus,' & whether, in
his propagation of the gospel of comradeship, he has duly taken into account the physical aspects of manly love."[6] On receiving these letters, "My
first instinct . . . is violently reactionary—is strong and brutal for no,
no, no," Whitman, in Camden, tells Traubel.[7] Brutal for no, no, no is in
fact the famous response he finally makes, after toying with Symonds' interest through a correspondence of nineteen years:

> that the calamus part has even allow'd the possibility of such construction as
> mention'd is terrible—I am fain to hope the pages themselves are not to be
> even mention'd for such gratuitous and quite at the time entirely undream'd
> & unreck'd possibility of morbid inferences—wh' are disavow'd by me & seem
> damnable.[8]

To this Symonds replied fairly meekly—"It is a great relief to me to know
so clearly and precisely what you feel about the question I raised"—but
he was not really satisfied by it, writing optimistically to Traubel, "I do
not think he quite understood what I was driving at." Traubel at any rate
must have been amused, after all that Whitman had confided in him about
the decades-long inquisition, by the suggestion that Whitman did not quite
understand what was being driven at. Symonds himself seems finally to
have swallowed Whitman's response with a quiet gulp of salt. Writing of
it to Edward Carpenter, he quotes Whitman's letter and postscript
("Though unmarried I have had six children"), remarking mildly, "It struck
me when I first read this p.s. that W.W. wanted to obviate 'damnable
inferences' about himself by asserting his paternity."[9] It has struck recent
biographers in the same way. The intensity with which Whitman relished
the long inquisition ("Who could fail to love a man who could write such
a letter?")[10] may show more of his complicated erotic velleities than the
"violently reactionary" final response.

At the time of Symonds' inquisition, the historical configuration of male
homosocial desire was in rapid flux—a flux that circulated around alternative readings of Whitman. Whitman's influence on the crystallization,
in the latter nineteenth century, of what was to prove a durable and broadly
based Anglo-American definition of male homosexuality, was profound
and decisive, but almost certainly not—in its final effect—at all what he
would have desired. This is true even if we set aside his late brutal "no"

as a characteristic and disingenuous defensiveness ("There is something in my nature *furtive* like an old hen!"),[11] and provisionally assume that the "Calamus" poems and the central notion of "adhesiveness" purposefully define male homosocial bonds in a way that does include the distinctively sexual. That is, even assuming that what Symonds was "driving at" was in fact, as genital behavior, also something Whitman had been driving at in his poetry, still the cultural slippage of the Atlantic crossing meant that the sexual-ideological packages sent by the Kosmic American were very different from the ones unpacked by the cosmopolitan Englishman. The most important differences lay in the assumed class contexts in which the sexual ideology was viewed, and in the standing of women—both of "femininity" and of actual women—in the two visions.

These very differences made for Whitman's adaptability as an English (far more than as an American) prophet of sexual politics for the nineteenth century. Perhaps most important must have been the productively bad conceptual fit between English and American ideas of class. The English system—still organized at the upper bound around an increasingly nonreferential "zero degree" of aristocratic lineage, privilege, and culture—was potently elaborated to cultural and symbolic perception, not least in the sexual realm, although less and less usefully descriptive of the real lines of concrete power and interest. Whitman spoke to English readers from a society without a feudal history, one whose most palpable social divisions were both more various and more dichotomous: rural/urban, northern/southern, eastern/western, cultured/primitive, native/immigrant, white/Black. Even the division male/female seems to have taken an added crudity from the anxious, sharply dichotomized landscape of social categories. Imprecise but reverberant translations from the American to the English permitted Whitman, the figure, to embody contradictory and seductive attributes that would not have been combined in an Englishman. A "working-class" figure himself, he nevertheless could seem by this translation both to practice and to sacralize something like the English homosexual system whereby bourgeois men had sexual contacts only with virile working-class youths. (John Addington Symonds was fascinated with the story of Peter Doyle.) Certainly Whitman's class ascription, in English terms, was elusive as no Englishman's could have been. Also, Whitman shared (and helped shape) an important American ambivalence toward programmatic politics: a conviction on the one hand that equality itself was deeply at the heart of every social question, and on the other hand that no individual issue or possible structural change could really begin to address the centrality of this radical idea. The ideologically over-charged quietism that resulted, in Whitman, reflected very different im-ages back to Edward Carpenter, Symonds, Wilde, and D. H. Lawrence, in their more mediated political landscape.

At another level, the ravishing and peculiar eros in *Leaves of Grass* re-sisted translation as insistently as it demanded it. The slippage back and forth between the masturbatory and the homosexual,[12] for instance, or the suppleness and rapidity with which the reader personally is enfolded in a drama of domination with the speaker,[13] made a transposition into physical terms, much less into programmatic ones, necessarily a distor-tion and, oddly, a desexualization of the original. Early Whitman's un-relenting emphasis in the poetry and in the biography on *incarnating* a phallic erethism—his erectness, his eternally rosy skin, his injections of life and health into scenes of death and wounds—had, again, at least a double effect. Put schematically, rather than having a phallus, he enacted one. Seeming at first to invite a naively celebratory, male-exalting afflatus of phallic worship, the deeper glamor of this pose lay in the drama (called *Leaves of Absence?*) of shame, concealment, and exhibition; of engorge-ment (related to shame) and vacancy; of boastful inadequacy; of being like a woman, since to have to enact rather than possess a phallus is (in this system) a feminine condition; of being always only everything or nothing, and the hilarious bravado of asserting a mere human personality or desire in the face of that. D. H. Lawrence, who was light-years from Whitman in character and feeling, probably learned this drama from him, but hated it; others (Carpenter, Symonds, probably Wilde) who re-sponded to its sheer splendor, had to flatten it out more—with plenty of help from Whitman himself—in order to describe what they were re-sponding to. It is easy to see how a translation into horizontal, social terms of this drama of labile absolutes invited almost any construction, as long as it was centered on the question of the male. It is more difficult to say how far the drama is properly a male homosexual one, or how resonantly it engages the question of women as women. Still, the vibrant obstacle itself, the difficult personal excitement of show and tell that I have already described, potentially repressive as it is, is part of Whitman's claim on the political imaginations of women and gay men as we are now constituted.

Whitman's electric effect on his English readers seems to have been protopolitical to a striking degree: *Leaves of Grass* operated most charac-teristically as a conduit from one man to another of feelings that had, in many cases, been private or inchoate. This is what Whitman intended for "Calamus" to effect in his own country, "the special meaning of this 'Calamus' cluster": "it is by a fervent accepted development of comradeship, the beautiful and sane affection of man for man . . . that the United States of the future (I cannot too often repeat) are to be the most effectually welded together, intercalated, annealed into a living union."[14] In England, to trace the path of individual copies of the book, beginning with the remaindered copies of the 1855 *Leaves* scattered abroad by an itinerant pedlar, would be to feel like the eye of a needle that was penetrating from layer to layer of the literate social fabric, bonding together a new whole of shared interests, around the connecting thread of manly love. Symonds wrote:

> our Master Walt has the power of bringing folk together by a common kinship of kind feeling.—I suppose this is the meaning of "Calamus," the essence of the doctrine of comradeship. He has not only preached the gospel of mutual goodwill, but has been a magnetic force ("telepathically" potent, as the Psychical Research people might say) to create the emotion.—[15]

Edward Carpenter asserted of Whitman's poems that "thousands date from their first reading . . . a new inspiration and an extraordinary access of vitality carrying their activities and energies into new channels."[16] Photographs of Whitman, gifts of Whitman's books, specimens of his handwriting,[17] news of Whitman, admiring references to "Whitman" which seem to have functioned as badges of homosexual recognition, were the currency of a new community that saw itself as created in Whitman's image.

The male homosexual culture and practice of nineteenth-century England, the landscape onto which Whitman burst, seems to have been sharply stratified by class. As we discussed in chapter 9, a "Sporus"-like homosexual role seems to have been available to aristocratic Englishmen and their personal dependents for at least two centuries and probably much longer. ("Kings seem peculiarly inclined to homosexuality," remarks Havelock Ellis.)[18] It was in some ways an effeminate role; the stereotypical effect of the male-male sexual liaison was to reduce perceived masculinity, rather than to redouble it. But this feminization occurred within a nonmeritocratic political context in which the power of the individual aristocrat was not, in any event, dependent on personal style so much as on material and hereditary rights, and in which (partly for that reason) the mutual exclusiveness of "masculine" and "feminine" traits in general was less stressed, less absolute, and less politically significant than it was to be for the nineteenth-century bourgeoisie. For instance, among the 27 case studies of homosexual men in Symonds and Ellis' *Sexual Inversion*, the eight who are discernibly "high bred," of independent means, or without profession have a far higher incidence of self-described femininity or effeminacy than the professionally or even the artistically employed men. One, for instance, "thinks he ought to have been a woman," while another "is decidedly feminine in his dress, manner of walking, love or ornaments and fine things. His body is excessively smooth and white, the hips and buttocks rounded. . . . His temperament is feminine, especially in vanity, irritability and petty preoccupations."[19]

With the expanding number, visibility, and scope of the educated middle class, a new range of male homosocial bonds emerged, connected to new configurations of male homosexuality. A nominally individualistic and meritocratic, often precarious, and authentically anxious path of economic and social life had to be forged by each man of this class; newly exclusive and enforced gender roles gave an apparent ideological distinctness to the amorphous new class; and as a result, as we discussed in chapter 9, young men who explored a range of forms and intensities of male homosocial bonds tried to do so without admitting culturally defined "femininity" into them as a structuring term. Even when men of this class formed overtly sexual liaisons with other men, they seem to have perceived the exclusion of women from their intimate lives as virilizing them, more than they perceived their choice of a male object as feminizing them.[20] Unlike aristocratic homosexual men whose strongest cultural bond was with Catholic Europe (especially with the countries where the permissive Code Napoleon was in force), the educated middle-class man looked to classical Sparta and Athens for models of virilizing male bonds, models in which the male homosocial institutions (education, political mentorship, brotherhood in arms) and the homosexual seemed to be fully continuous, and fully exclude the world of women.

We have discussed ideology as a mechanism for concealing or rationalizing contradictions within a status quo; but the unusually acute and rapid contradictions embodied in the nineteenth-century English middle class resulted in a body of sexual ideology that was both unusually rigid and proscriptive, and at the same time plethoric and full of narratives that overtly contradicted each other. Although the aristocratic homosexual mode was highly visible within narrow circles of Victorian society, and was to become widely disseminated by the end of the century, the initial force of Whitman's influence is easiest to trace in the internal dialectic within middle-class homosexual ideology. Symonds and Edward Carpenter, two of Whitman's English admirers, demarcate the different directions of Whitman's influence on that ideology. Each of these middle-class, Oxbridge-educated, homosexual men wrote books on homosexuality and on Whitman himself. Each saw himself as embodying and promoting Whitman's view of manly love in the service of new democratic ideals. Their uses of Whitman were, however, in effect very different.

Whitman thought J. A. Symonds not only "wonderfully cute" and remarkably persistent but "someways the most indicative . . . and significant man of our time."[21] Carpenter, however, saw "a certain lack of solidity and self-reliance in Symonds's nature" and concluded that his homosexual advocacy was damaged by "vacillation and timidity."[22] The limitations of Symonds' advocacy were part of his indicativeness of his time and class, however. Symonds' cultural and political position was toward the aristocratic end of the bourgeois homosexual spectrum I have sketched; in fact, his own (anonymous) case history in *Sexual Inversion* is one of the eight I grouped, from the evidence of the case descriptions alone, with the aristocratic ones (he calls himself "of independent means"). He is far from the most effeminately figured of these eight, judging by description ("only non-masculine in his indifference to sport, . . . never feminine in dress or habit").[23] The leisure and cosmopolitanism that were enforced by Symonds' ill health—his consumption made England a fatal environment for him—and subsidized by family money and connections, coexisted with a driving professionalism about his writing. He wrote not as an amateur or only as a connoisseur, but as a prolific, highly cultured journalist, and as if his family's livelihood depended on his earnings. (Fortunately, it did not.)[24]

A distinctive sexual-political narrative emerged from Symonds' ambiguous position at the upper threshold of the middle class. He liked to describe the potential political effects of "Calamus" love in terms drawn from chivalry, but appealing at the same time to the virilizing authority of the Greeks. To Whitman, he describes it as "the Dorian Chivalry of Comradeship."[25] In his book on Whitman, he sketches the course of the implicit narrative:

> medieval chivalry, the great emotional product of feudalism, though it fell
> short of its own aspiration, bequeathed incalculable good to modern society

by refining and clarifying the crudest male appetites. In like manner, this democratic chivalry, announced by Whitman, may be destined to absorb, control, and elevate those darker, more mysterious, apparently abnormal appetites, which we know to be widely diffused and ineradicable in the groundwork of human nature.

. . . The question [is] whether the love of man for man shall be elevated through a hitherto unapprehended chivalry to nobler powers, even as the barbarous love of man for woman once was.[26]

Responding to what Havelock Ellis, in *The New Spirit*, described as a confusion in Whitman's view of the position of women (" 'Manly love,' even in its extreme form, is certainly Greek, as is the degradation of women with which it is always correlated; yet the much slighter degradation of women in modern times Whitman sincerely laments"),[27] Symonds asked Ellis,

are we justified in taking for granted that if modern society could elevate manly love into a new chivalry, this would prejudice what the world has gained by the chivalrous ideal of woman?[28]

Symonds' appeal to chivalry as an ideal was not unaccompanied by a consciousness of "the dishonour, dishonesty, and disloyalty toward women which have always, more or less, prevailed in so-called good society."[29] Still, the value of feudalistic chivalry as a sexual-political ideal is treated as self-evident, needing only broader and more fervent application to turn it into genuine democracy.

Heroism steps forth from the tent of Achilles; chivalry descends from the arm-gaunt charger of the knight; loyalty is seen to be no mere devotion to a dynasty. . . . None of these high virtues are lost to us. On the contrary, we find them everywhere. They are brought within reach, instead of being relegated to some remote region in the past, or deemed the special property of privileged classes. . . . And so it is with the chivalrous respect for womanhood and weakness, with loyal self-dedication to a principle or cause, with comradeship uniting men in brotherhood.[30]

Practically, this version of Whitmanian democracy translated into a certain complaisance toward existing social arrangements. At least, the solution to social problems seemed to him not only readily available, but pleasurable.

I fully enter into Walt's feelings. Among my own dearest friends are a pos-
tillion, a stevedore, a gondolier, a farm servant, a porter in a hotel. I find the
greatest possible relief & rest in conversing with them. They do me so much
good by their simplicity & manly affection. Their real life is such a contrast
to that strange thought-world in which my studious hours are past—Italian
Renaissance, Greek Poets, Art, philosophy, poetry—all the lumber of my
culture. In fact the greatest thing I owe to Walt is his having thoroughly
opened my eyes to comradeship & convinced me of the absolute equality of
men. My friends of this kind think me an exception to the rest of the world.
But, having won their confidence, I see how enormously they appreciate the
fraternal love of a man socially & by education superior to them. I verily
believe that the social problems would find their solution if only the majority
of rich & cultivated people felt as I do, & acted so.[31]

The gondolier Symonds mentions was Angelo Fusato, with whom he had
a loving and long-term friendship. But when we read that Symonds trav-
eled to friends' houses accompanied by Angelo as a personal servant—
"He is an old peasant, has been with me for ten years, & is a very good
fellow. Just now I am really dependent on him while travelling"—we can
imagine that Symonds' imagined ideal democracy, firmly based as it was
on noblesse oblige and individual pastoralism and condescension, was not
structurally threatening to the class system as he experienced it. (His
biographer remarks about this visit, "Mrs. Ross's reaction, when con-
fronted by a dazzlingly handsome 'old peasant' of thirty-three, is not recorded!")[32] In fact, the difference between Symonds' political ideal and
the bourgeois English actuality of sexual exploitation, for cash, of proletarian men and women is narrow and arbitrary. It seems to lie mostly in
the sanguine Whitmanian coloration of Symonds' rhetoric and erotic investment.

  The view of women implicit in Symonds' "two chivalries" narrative is
also more conservative than he imagines. For an active intellectual in the
1880s and 1890s to base a liberal sexual-political argument on the assumption that women's worst problem was to hold on to the gains they had
made under late feudalism, suggests an almost aggressive lack of interest
in that part of the contemporary dialogue on gender issues. Similarly, he
seems simply not to have seen that research for the projected book on
sexual inversion might profitably include women as well as men,[33] even
though at least one well-known, long-established Lesbian pair was among
his acquaintance. He appeals to Whitman's "Primeval my love for the
woman I love" ("Fast Anchored Eternal O Love!") in defending Whitman's "respect for women."[34] But that poem is not a particularly femin-

ist one for Whitman; instead, it is one of those in which he most explicitly subordinates the love of women to

> the purest born,
> The ethereal, the last athletic reality, my consolation,
> . . . your love, O man,
> O sharer of my roving life.[35]

Symonds' ideal "Dorian Chivalry" is firmly based on the Victorian bourgeois assertion that women and men "naturally" occupy separate spheres
of labor and activity. "It will be complementary, by no means prejudicial
to the elder & more commonly acceptable [concept of chivalry]. It will
engage a different type of individual in different spheres of energy—aims
answering to those of monastic labour in common or of military self-de-
votion to duty taking there the place of domestic cares & procreative util-
ity."[36] The vision of peasant life that surrounded his actual erotic bonds
with men was also idealized as "the right sort of Socialism," and in terms
that made clear how tendentious against women his idyll of freedom was:

> I find a great deal of the emotion, in a wholly manly & admirable form,
> abroad among the people here. It does not interfere with marriage, when
> that is sought as a domestic institution, as it always is among men who want
> children for helpers in their work & women to keep their households.[37]

Symonds' lack of interest in women as sexual partners seems to have
allowed him to accept unquestioningly some of the most conservative aspects of his society's stylized and constricting view of them. If anything,
his homosexual enthusiasm may have helped him articulate assertions that
further devalued women. For instance, he devotes an appendix to *Essays
Speculative and Suggestive* to demonstrating that women are less beautiful,
objectively considered, than men.[38] In his letters, too, he dilates in a
Lawrentian vein on the "most beneficent results, as regards health and
nervous energy," of "the absorption of semen," especially one report that
attributes to that "the thriving of girls" immediately after marriage.[39] On
the whole, however, his misogyny was not greater and may well have been
less than that of an identically situated heterosexual man. But the high,
erotically-charged valuation of masculinity that he recognized in Whitman ratified, for him, the separation of men's from women's spheres that
was the repressive orthodoxy of his own class in his highly stratified society.

Even among the studies he himself collected for *Sexual Inversion,* there
were examples of men who did explicitly connect their homosexuality with
various aspects of the economic and sexual oppression of women. One
man, for instance, "feels that in prostituting males rather than females he
is doing a meritorious action." Another thinks it "certainly less wrong
than seducing and ruining women." A third asserts "that the economic
conditions of women make it altogether unfair to use them as merely
channels for satisfying sexual passion, that physical continence is impossible, and that it is, therefore, better to spread abroad that spirit of open
comradeship which is natural to many men and boys, and which results
when the body is impassioned in mutual sex satisfaction." Any of these
statements could be facile, ex post facto rationalizations, rather than records of serious thought on the subject. So perhaps could the opinion of
Case VI: "with regard to the morality of this complex subject, my feeling
is that it is the same as should prevail in love between man and woman—
namely, that no bodily satisfaction should be sought at the cost of another person's distress or degradation."[40] Case VI, however, we know
not to have been a glib rationalizer, but a committed and programmatic
socialist, feminist, and Whitmanite, Edward Carpenter.

Carpenter's birth and training were much like Symonds', with the difference that his early ill health passed over at the same time that he finally
arrived at an untormented accommodation with his sexual preference for
men. During the same years, he was turning his back on the Anglican
church (in which he had been ordained), the class of his birth, and Cambridge, moving north to lecture in industrial towns and finally to set up
as a small-scale farmer and sandalmaker, in partnership with three successive lovers (along with the wives of the first two). His difference from
Symonds in physical health and sexual self-acceptance went with a difference in general temperament: Symonds wrote to his daughter, "I have
been a very unhappy man," while Carpenter was good, sane and cheerful
to a degree that is always nerving but may verge on the fatuous. Symonds at any rate seems to have thought Carpenter's book of poetry,
Towards Democracy, incomprehensibly upbeat, although "certainly the most
important contribution which has as yet been made to the diffusion of
Whitman's philosophy of life, & what I think we may now call the new
religion."[41]

An example of Carpenter's sweet mental tone is the treatment in his 1916
autobiography of his enduring, quasimarital relationship with George
Merrill, a young man "bred in the slums quite below civilization," but "a

singularly affectionate, humorous, and swiftly intuitive nature."[42] The happiness of their relationship is candidly described; so is the opposition of their friends; but that opposition is chalked up to everything but homophobia.

> If the Fates pointed favorably I need hardly say that my friends (with a few exceptions) pointed the other way! I knew of course that George had an instinctive genius for housework, and that in all probability he would keep house better than most women would. But most of my friends thought otherwise. They drew sad pictures of the walls of my cottage hanging with cobwebs, and of the master unfed and neglected while his assistant amused himself elsewhere. They neither knew nor understood the facts of the case. Moreover they had sad misgivings about the moral situation. A youth who had spent much of his early time in the purlieus of public-houses and in society not too reputable would do me no credit, and would only by my adoption be confirmed in his own errant ways. Such was their verdict.[43]

Nevertheless, or perhaps because of this very buoyancy and even impercipience (a problem too in his poetry), Carpenter was a magnetic, ingenious and effective writer and organizer for socialist, anti-imperialist, and feminist causes. The openly unequal allocation of domestic roles between him and Merrill seems paradoxically to have been part of a realistic, unwishful, relatively nonexploitive relationship, in which Merrill represented *a* bond, but not the only bond and not a substitute for other, politically purposeful bonds, with working-class people. There is a similar apparent paradox in Carpenter's feelings about women. Where Symonds had had "no exact horror" of women's bodies, and indeed was potent within marriage, Carpenter felt "positive repulsion" for women "physically," and found "the thought of marrying or cohabiting with any such . . . odious." Again, "Anything effeminate in a man . . . repels me very decisively."[44] At the same time it was Carpenter, and not Symonds, who investigated women with the same interest as men, for his book on "homogenic love"; who wrote heartfelt poetry about women's wages and women's sexual choices, as well as about male beauty; and who saw the oppression of his sexual kind and his adoptive class as being inextricable from "the disparity of the sexes."[45]

Carpenter's active feminism subsisted even in the absence of a consistent rationale or narrative to support it. Some of his writing seems to appeal to notions of femininity not very unlike Symonds', and consistent with the prescriptive Victorian consensus that women's "passive" sexuality was or ought to be an epitome of their social relations.[46] His way of imagining male homosexuality sometimes appealed to the same stereotypes: in "O Child of Uranus," for instance, he describes

> Thy Woman-soul within a Man's form dwelling . . .
> With man's strength to perform, and pride to suffer without sign,
> And feminine sensitiveness to the last fibre of being. . . .

The potentially oppressive asymmetry of this vision becomes clearer when he describes how the (male) Uranian is "loved by either sex"; in a description that could be of Christian religion but could also be of some painful incidents in Whitman's life (Carpenter, for instance, was a friend of Anne Gilchrist), or his own, he writes,

> . . . women break their alabaster caskets, kiss and anoint thy feet, and
> bless the womb that bare thee,
> While in thy bosom with thee, lip to lip,
> Thy younger comrade lies.[47]

In spite of his celebratory tone here, however, he was alive to the sometimes punishing partiality of the Whitmanic "universal" eros, especially in its relation to women: "There is no doubt in my mind that Walt Whitman was before all a lover of the Male. His thoughts turned towards Men first and foremost, and it is no good disguising that fact."[48] Carpenter's own ability to focus erotically on the Male, sentimentalize intermittently about the Female, and yet work relatively unswervingly for the rights of actual women came not from any one of his erotic or intellectual commitments, but from the analytic skill and caution with which he navigated among them. Because he was a pioneer both of socialism and at the same time of the study of sexuality, he never confined his vision of *class* struggle to the *(male)* wage workplace, nor his vision of ideal *sexuality* to the *(bourgeois)* female-immobilizing one.

We have personified here, in the congruent but contrasting lives of these two bourgeois readers of Whitman, two truths of the English sex/gender system. The first is the general one that sexual meaning is inextricable from social meaning—in the English case, from class. The meanings of "masculinity" and "femininity" themselves are produced within a context of class difference, are ascribed for political reasons to classes by themselves and by other classes, and have different functions, manifestations, value, and consequences according to class. The second is derived from the first but more specific: that sexual preference, ascribed masculinity or femininity of personal style, and actual support for women's welfare, are issues that are almost always (and rightly) seen as profoundly linked, but that cannot be generalized or predicted through a positive or negative correlation with each other. The "natural" effeminacy of male homosexuals, their "natural" hypervirility, their "natural" hatred of women, their "natural" identification with women—this always-applicable reservoir of contradictory intuitions, to which our society is heir, must not be mistaken for a tool of analysis. Only a view of homosexuality that is not only fully historical, but plural, described in relation to class interests, and placed appropriately in the context of the various specific institutions and forms by which gender and class power are transmitted, will be of analytic value; but this view is only beginning to emerge.

What finally was the form taken by Whitman's sexual politics in the hands of the English book-writing class? D. H. Lawrence's essay on Whitman, probably influenced in its early versions by Carpenter,[49] goes beyond Carpenter in its critique of Whitman's subsumptive attitude toward femininity and his eugenic attitude toward women. This feminist critique, for Lawrence, is in the service of a higher gynephobia, however. For instance, he dislikes Whitman's empathy with prostitutes. To his mind, a woman becomes a prostitute either because "she is fascinated by the Priapic mysteries," in which case she ought to obtain satisfaction, or because

> her nature has turned evil under her mental lust for prostitution. She has lost her soul. She knows it herself. She likes to make men lose their souls—in which case she ought to be killed.[50]

Whitman's and Carpenter's more careful and political knowledge, that a woman might be a prostitute because she needed to eat, or was in bondage to someone else, seemed to Lawrence wishy-washy compared to his own visceral, fearful, economically blind account of a world in which every issue for every inhabitant revolved around bourgeois sexual prohibition and the worship or subversion of the phallus. Similarly, a higher homophobia overtakes his initial, ravished response to Whitman's "sheer, perfect *human* spontaneity, undecorated, unclothed."[51] Whitman's welcome to the proximity of death, of images of death, in "the new Democracy . . . based on the love of comrades"[52] comes itself to seem too effeminate, too passive and soft, as Lawrence's attitude toward his own homosexual desires becomes more proscriptive and abstract. He came to see "perverts" as trying to "utterly falsify the phallic consciousness, which is the basic consciousness, and the thing we mean, in the best sense, by common sense."[53] A less yielding, more muscularly imperious approach toward death and the love of men is necessary, as part of the very overcoming of women.

> There, in these *womenless* regions of *fight* and *pure* thought and *abstracted instrumentality,* let men have a new attitude to one another. Let them have a new reverence for their heroes, a new regard for their comrades: deep, deep as life and death . . . and the extreme bond of deathless friendship supports them over the edge of the known into the unknown. [Emphasis mine][54]

Thus, one ramification of Whitman's influence is toward an authoritarian realm steeled to conquest by sexual repression and compulsion. (I might remark here that while male homosexuality does not correlate in a transhistorical way with political attitudes toward women, homophobia directed at men by men almost always travels with a retinue of gynephobia and antifeminism.) Obviously, this is the reading of Whitman that he as a personality would least have recognized or welcomed: all force and abstraction, no eros. Nevertheless, it is this hating homophobic recasting of the male homosocial spectrum—a recasting that recognizes and names as central the nameless love, only in order to cast it out—that has been most descriptive of the fateful twentieth-century societies, notoriously but by no means exclusively the Fascist.

A fourth English admirer of Whitman, Oscar Wilde, offers an ikon that we recognize more easily in our own society, although it is really to a large extent the complement, the residue, of the Lawrentian version. Symonds and Carpenter's patient intellectual work for "understanding," and for seemingly inevitable progress, were overtaken by the true melodrama of Wilde's life: *Sexual Inversion* and *Homogenic Love* were both completed by the time of Wilde's conviction, but both had their publication interrupted and delayed in the ensuing panic. Meanwhile, their time had essentially passed. The middle-class-oriented but ideologically "democratic," virilizing, classicizing, idealistic, self-styled political version of male homosexuality, which these two men in their tendentiously different ways embodied and sought to publicize and legitimate, seems with the protracted public enactment of the trials to have lost its consensus and its moment. For the first time in England, homosexual style—and homophobic style—instead of being stratified and specified and kept secret along lines of class, became, as we saw in chapter 5, a household word—the word "Oscar Wilde."[55]

Even though the repressiveness of Wilde's fate was so graphic and in-flictive that "desublimation" would be an absurd name for it, his influ-ence as a figure did channel public imagery—both homophobic and homophilic—in a direction that divorced the sexual, and even the imag-inative, from the political. In chapters 3 and 4, we discussed Wycherley's and Sterne's reifications of wit and "sexualism" as referentially volatile signifiers of aristocratic privilege, which offered a certain dangerous le-verage on real political power to middle-class men who could command and manipulate them. In the witty and erotized Wildean homosexual role, the same qualities maintained the same relation of sublimatable reference to "the aristocratic." The referential status of "the aristocratic" itself, however, had changed radically—had itself, as we have seen, been subli-mated, feminized, and materially hollowed out.

At least partly in response to "Wilde," public, overt male homosexual style in England and America in this century has had few ties to the Ed-ward Carpenter tradition, pregnant as that seemed at the turn of the cen-tury. The durable stereotype that came to prevail has been close to Sy-monds only as Symonds resembled Wilde: a connoisseur, an interpreter of aristocratic culture to the middle class, a socialist insofar as socialism would simply expand the venue of leisure, privilege, and high culture. In this case, the feminization of the English homosexual, in conformity with the former aristocratic style, went with a loss of interest in the political fate of real women. It went with a loss of interest in, or hope for, polit-ical struggle in general. Potential alliances between gay men and other, comparably oppressed groups were not cultivated. The struggle for rights for male homosexuals themselves went into a long abeyance, except at the level of the individual, often closeted, career, and of a lively but quie-tistic collective culture. Until the emergence of the gay rights movements of the 60s and 70s, one saw only more and more clearly the mutual dis-tinctness of the aristocratic-style, ascriptively feminine, "tragic," and af-fluent or apolitical male homosexual stereotype on the one hand, and on the other the actively, projectively homophobic mass culture founded on male bonds very similar to the ones it criminalized and glamorized in him. This was the triumph of Lawrence and "Wilde," loveless compulsion and politics-less eros: the chiasmus of partial or schizoid readings of male homosocial desire that overtook attempts at a more inclusive interpreta-tion.

Notes

Introduction

1. The notion of "homophobia" is itself fraught with difficulties. To begin with, the word is etymologically nonsensical. A more serious problem is that the linking of fear and hatred in the "-phobia" suffix, and in the word's usage, does tend to prejudge the question of the cause of homosexual oppression: it is attributed to fear, as opposed to (for example) a desire for power, privilege, or material goods. An alternative term that is more suggestive of collective, structurally inscribed, perhaps materially based oppression is "heterosexism." This study will, however, continue to use "homophobia," for three reasons. First, it will be an important concern here to question, rather than to reinforce, the presumptively symmetrical opposition between homo- and heterosexuality, which seems to be implicit in the term "heterosexism." Second, the etiology of individual people's attitudes toward male homosexuality will not be a focus of discussion. And third, the ideological and thematic treatments of male homosexuality to be discussed from the late eighteenth century onward do combine fear and hatred in a way that is appropriately called phobic. For a good summary of social science research on the concept of homophobia, see Morin and Garfinkle, "Male Homophobia."

2. For a good survey of the background to this assertion, see Weeks, *Sex,* pp. 1–18.

3. Adrienne Rich describes these bonds as forming a "lesbian continuum," in her essay, "Compulsory Heterosexuality and Lesbian Existence," in Stimpson and Person, *Women,* pp. 62–91, especially pp. 79–82.

4. "The Female World of Love and Ritual," in Cott and Pleck, *Heritage,* pp. 311–42; usage appears on, e.g., pp. 316, 317.

5. "The Unhappy Marriage of Marxism and Feminism: Towards a More Progressive Union," in Sargent, *Women and Revolution,* pp. 1–41; quotation is from p. 14.

6. See, for example, Rubin, "Traffic," pp. 182–83.

7. Rubin, "Traffic," p. 180.

8. Crompton, "Gay Genocide"; but see chapter 5 for a discussion of the limitations of "genocide" as an understanding of the fate of homosexual men.

9. On this, see Miller, *New Psychology,* ch.1.

10. Dover, *Greek Homosexuality,* p. 91.

11. Arendt, *Human Condition,* p. 83, quoted in Rich, *On Lies,* p. 206.

12. On the Bohemian Grove, an all-male summer camp for American ruling-class men, see Domhoff, *Bohemian Grove;* and a more vivid, although homophobic, account, van der Zee, *Men's Party.*

13. The NOW resolution, for instance, explicitly defines sadomasochism, pornography, and "pederasty" (meaning pedophilia) as issues of "exploitation and violence," *as opposed to* "affectional/sexual preference/orientation." Quoted in *Heresies 12,* vol. 3, no. 4 (1981), p. 92.

14. For explorations of these viewpoints, see *Heresies, ibid.;* Snitow et al., *Powers;* and Samois, *Coming.*

15. MacKinnon, "Feminism," pp. 530–31.

16. Mitchell, *Gone,* p. 780. Further citations will be incorporated within the text and designated by chapter number.

17. For a discussion of these limitations, see Vicinus, "Sexuality." The variety of useful work that is possible within these boundaries is exemplified by the essays in Newton et al., *Sex and Class.*

18. On this, see McKeon, " 'Marxism.' "

19. Juliet Mitchell discusses this aspect of *The German Ideology* in *Woman's Estate,* pp. 152–58.

20. Mitchell, *Woman's Estate,* p. 154.

21. The best and clearest discussion of this aspect of Freud is Laplanche, *Life and Death,* especially pp. 25–47.

22. On this, see ch. 8.

23. For an especially useful discussion of the absence of women from the work of Girard, see Moi, "Missing Mother."

24. On this see (in addition to Snitow et al., *Powers*) Breines and Gordon, "Family Violence."

25. The following books are, to a greater or lesser extent, among the exceptions: Fernbach, *Spiral Path;* Mieli, *Homosexuality;* Rowbotham and Weeks, *Socialism;* Dworkin, *Pornography.*

26. The most influential recent statement of this position is Heilbrun, *Androgyny.*

27. See Irigaray, "Goods"; and Frye, *Politics,* pp. 128–51. Jane Marcus's work on Virginia Woolf makes use of Maria-Antonietta Macciocchi's homophobic formulation, "the Nazi community is made by homosexual brothers who exclude the woman and valorize the mother." Marcus says, "The Cambridge Apostles' notions of fraternity surely appeared to Woolf analogous to certain fascist notions of fraternity." Macciocchi's formulation is quoted in Jane Caplan, "Introduction to Female Sexuality in Fascist Ideology," *Feminist Review* 1 (1979), p. 62. Marcus's essay is "Liberty, Sorority, Misogyny," in Heilbrun and Higonnet, *Representation,* pp. 60–97; quotation is from p. 67.

28. On this see Hocquenghem, *Homosexual Desire,* pp. 42–67.

Chapter 1. Gender Asymmetry and Erotic Triangles

1. On this, see Bell et al., *Sexual Preferences*.
2. Review of *Homosexualities*, p. 1077.
3. On this see Gallop, *Daughter's Seduction*, pp. 15–32.
4. Kahn, *Man's Estate*, pp. 9–10.
5. *The Elementary Structures of Kinship* (Boston: Beacon, 1969), p. 115; quoted in Rubin, "Traffic," p. 174.
6. Rubin, *ibid*.
7. Irigaray, "Goods," pp. 107–10.

Chapter 2. Swan in Love: The Example of Shakespeare's Sonnets

1. Barthes, *Lover's Discourse*, p. 14.
2. On this see, for instance, Weeks, *Coming Out*, pp. 52, 57, 68; and see the Coda of this book.
3. Marx, *Grundrisse*, p. 106.
4. Shakespeare, *Sonnets*, p. 39, Sonnet 42. Further citations will be incorporated in the text, where possible by Sonnet number.
5. Krieger, *Window*, p. 80.
6. Barthes, *Lover's Discourse*, p. 14.
7. Wilde, *Portrait*, p. 68.
8. Fiedler, *Stranger*, pp. 25–26.
9. On shamanization, see Lewis, *Lion*, pp. 149–58 and passim; quotations are from Knight, *Mutual Flame*, pp. 36–37.

Chapter 3. *The Country Wife:* Anatomies of Male Homosocial Desire

1. For instance, Alan Bray's *Homosexuality* offers a salutary, sceptical survey of the received wisdoms concerning male homosexuality in this period; see, e.g., pp. 7–9.
2. Vieth, *"Country Wife."*
3. Lévi-Strauss concludes, "This explains why the relations between the sexes have preserved that affective richness, ardour, and mystery which doubtless originally permeated the entire universe of human communications" (*Elementary Structures*, p. 496). This is quoted by Rubin in "Traffic," p. 201. Rubin remarks, "This is an extraordinary statement. Why is he not, at this point, denouncing what kinship systems do to women, instead of presenting one of the greatest rip-offs of all time as the root of romance?"
4. Wycherley, *Country Wife*, I.i. Further citations will be incorporated in the text, and designated where possible by act and scene.
5. On this see Vieth, *"Country Wife."*
6. Quoted in McCarthy, *William Wycherley*, pp. 91–92.
7. Freud, *Jokes*, pp. 98–100.
8. Wycherley, *Plain Dealer*, p. 6.

Chapter 4. *A Sentimental Journey:* Sexualism and the Citizen of the World

1. Zaretsky, *Capitalism.*

2. See ch. 5 on changes in eighteenth-century homosociality.

3. Sterne, *Sentimental Journey,* p. 27. Further citations will be incorporated in the text.

4. On this see Cavell, *Must We Mean,* pp. 281–82.

5. To describe the modern, psychoanalytic family as "apparently egalitarian" or "classless" is a condensed formulation of its very complicated relation to the forms of hierarchy in the world around it. Hierarchically organized as this family is by both age and gender, it is "classless" in the obvious sense that its members share a social class rather than competing for one. (This is not true of the pre-industrial, extended, cohabitant family of, for instance, the Poysers in *Adam Bede;* and of course modern non-family groups are ideologically supposed to be distinct from the family precisely because they are organized around individual competition for social advancement.) Again, while social and political paternalism take their very name from the family, the paternalism of the family is, by contrast, "apparently egalitarian" because sons *are* to grow into the status of fathers, daughters of mothers—as workers are not to grow into the status of owners; nor, to complicate the matter, daughters of fathers. The view of the nuclear family as a haven in the heartless world of capitalist competition seems to be as ineradicable as it is riddled with contradiction. Good discussions can be found in Barrett, *Women's Oppression,* Olsen, "Family," and Zaretsky, *Capitalism.*

Chapter 5. Toward the Gothic: Terrorism and Homosexual Panic

1. Bray, *Homosexuality,* p. 92.

2. *Ibid.,* p. 102.

3. *Ibid.,* pp. 102–3.

4. Weeks, *Coming Out,* pp. 3–4.

5. On this see Sarotte, *Like a Brother,* and Hoch, *White Hero.* The unusually exacerbated and intensively, punitively regulated relation of male homosexuality to the military—the most male-homosocial of institutions, *and* the one where the manipulability of men is most at a premium—makes sense in this light. Weeks offers a short discussion, without interpretation, of the history of this regulation in *Coming Out,* pp. 12–13.

6. For examples of this see Whitehead, "Sexual Antagonism"; and Ehrenreich, *Hearts,* pp. 14–28.

7. On this see Weeks, *Coming Out,* pp. 185–237.

8. Richard Gilman devotes an entire book *(Decadence)* to the shiftiness of this term—without apparently having noticed how many of its uses can be simply explained by its being a euphemism for "homosexual."

9. See, for instance, Moers, *Literary Women,* and Gilbert and Gubar, *Madwoman.*

10. On Beckford, see Alexander, *Wealthiest Son;* on Lewis, see Peck, *Life,* pp. 65–66; on Walpole, see Lewis, *Horace Walpole,* p. 36.

11. Stone, *Family*, pp. 541–42; discussed in Bray, *Homosexuality*, p. 138, n.26.

12. On this see, for instance, George Steiner, "Cleric," esp. pp. 179–83. However, I have found it surprisingly difficult to find good, nonhomophobic material on the extent and possible effects of this male homosexual influence.

13. Crompton, "Gay Genocide," p. 67.

14. Sedgwick, *Coherence*, esp. pp. 14–20.

15. Maturin, *Melmoth*; these and other "unspeakable" incidents are to be found in chs. 3, 8, 9, 11, 39; the last-quoted is from ch. 28.

16. *Ibid.*, ch. 32.

17. Nichols, *Father*, pp. 92–99.

Chapter 6. Murder Incorporated: *Confessions of a Justified Sinner*

1. Dickens, *Drood*, p. 206.

2. On this see Sedgwick, *Coherence*, pp. 34–40. An especially good account of the form of Hogg's *Confessions* occurs in Kiely, *Romantic Novel*, pp. 208–32.

3. Hogg, *Confessions*, p. 3. Further citations will be incorporated in the text.

4. On the high valuation of stupidity in nineteenth-century gentlemen, see Girouard, *Return*, pp. 166–68 and 269–70.

5. For a suggestive discussion of the psychological meaning of "primmed" lips in relation to paranoid psychosis, see Kris, *Psychoanalytic Explorations*, pp. 128–50.

6. See, for example, Girard's discussion of *The Eternal Husband*, in his *Deceit*, p. 45–47.

7. Todd, *Women's Friendship*, pp. 404–5. Interestingly, Bradley Headstone in *Our Mutual Friend* has similar nosebleeds (IV.1).

8. Marcus, *Other Victorians*, pp. 257–62. Marcus himself concludes that the sadomasochistic pornography he is discussing has a male-homosocial basis.

9. Hardy, *Mayor*, ch. 33.

10. See, for instance, Praz, *Romantic Agony*, and Punter, *Literature of Terror*.

11. These critical debates have characteristically occurred between "Freudian" critics who locate apparently homosexual material, and "conservative" critics who deny that it "proves" anything. In America, however, psychoanalytic thinking about homosexuality has itself virtually never resisted homophobic recuperation; these critical debates have therefore reinforced, rather than challenged, the homophobic norms of literary scholarship. On this see Abelove, "Freud."

12. Examples can be found in, for instance, Martin, *Homosexual Tradition*; Boyers and Steiner, *Homosexuality*; and Kellogg, *Literary Visions*.

13. Jacobus, "Is there a Woman," pp. 130–35.

14. Gold, "It's Only Love," p. 148.

15. *Ibid.*, pp. 153–54.

16. Besides Barrett, *Women's Oppression*, especially interesting discussions of the enforcement of the family can be found in Olsen, "Family," and Miller, "Discipline."

Chapter 7. Tennyson's *Princess:* One Bride for Seven Brothers

1. Tennyson, *Princess,* p. 749 (Prologue, ll. 193–94). Further citations will be incorporated in the text, and designated by section and line numbers.

2. Dickens, *Great Expectations,* pp. 437–38 (ch. 53). Further citations will be incorporated in the text and designated by chapter number.

3. Orlick: chs. 15, 17, 35, 43, 53; Compeyson: chs. 3, 5, 40, 44, 47, 54; Drummle: chs. 25, 26, 38, 43.

4. Orlick: ch. 15; Compeyson: chs. 22, 42; Drummle: ch. 59. Drummle's violence against Estella is not originally complicitous with Pip, but does in fact form the ground of her final submission to Pip, and thus augments the collective total of male power: she says, "suffering has been stronger than all other teaching, and has taught me to understand what your heart used to be. I have been bent and broken, but—I hope—into a better shape" (ch. 59).

5. James, *Letters to A. C. Benson,* p. 40.

Chapter 8. *Adam Bede* and *Henry Esmond:* Homosocial Desire and the Historicity of the Female

1. On this see, for instance, Michelle Zimbalist Rosaldo, "Women, Culture, and Society: A Theoretical Overview," pp. 17–42 in Rosaldo and Lamphere, *Women.*

2. Kelly-Gadol, "Social Relation," p. 819.

3. My formulations here are most directly indebted to the incisive survey of this ground in Barrett, *Women's Oppression,* e.g., pp. 160–86.

4. For example, Nancy Chodorow summarizes this argument: "In precapitalist and early capitalist times, the household was the major productive unit of society. Husband and wife, with their own and/or other children, were a cooperative producing unit. A wife carried out her childcare responsibilities along with her productive work, and these responsibilities included training girls—daughters, servants, apprentices—for their work. Children were early integrated into the adult world of work. . . . Until very recently, women everywhere participated in most forms of production. Production for the home was in, or connected to, the home." ("Mothering, Male Dominance, and Capitalism," p. 88.)

5. On this two-axis understanding of the family, see Barrett, *Women's Oppression,* pp. 200–3.

6. Lakoff, *Language,* esp. pp. 53–57. My understanding of the bearings of "women's language" is additionally derived from O'Barr and Atkins, "Women's Language," esp. p. 96.

7. Eliot, *Adam Bede,* vol. I, ch. 4, p. 52. Further citations will be incorporated in the text and designated by volume and chapter number. (Vol. I of this two-volume edition ends with ch. 24.)

8. Unichappell Music BMI, © 1980, 1981 EMI Records, Ltd.

9. For more on this see Jeffrey Weeks, "Capitalism and the Organisation of Sex," pp. 11–20 in Gay Left Collective, *Homosexuality,* esp. pp. 14–15.

10. John Sutherland's brief but suggestive description of Henry Esmond himself as both "eighteenth-century man" and "nineteenth-century man," in his In-

troduction to the Penguin Edition (Harmondsworth, Sussex, 1970), pp. 20–21, along with Harry Shaw's discussion cited below, offer a useful, male-centered counterpart to the feminist historical argument.

11. Thackeray, *Henry Esmond*, Bk. I, ch. 9, p. 89. Further citations will be incorporated in the text and designated by book and chapter numbers.

12. A good discussion of the general problems of *Henry Esmond*'s historicity, which however fails to question the historical status of femininity and the family in the novel, is in Shaw, *Forms*, pp. 56–70.

13. Thackeray, *Virginians*, ch. 22.

14. For a related formulation of the relationship between the two novels, see Rawlins, *Thackeray's Novels*, p. 190.

15. Milton, *Paradise Lost*, iv, l. 110.

16. Tennyson, *Princess*, ii, 79–80.

17. See Introduction ii–iii, and, for instance, "Deferred Action; Deferred," in Laplanche and Pontalis, *Language*, pp. 111–14.

Chapter 9. Homophobia, Misogyny, and Capital: The Example of *Our Mutual Friend*

1. Sedgwick, "Trace at 46," p. 14.

2. Alan Bray presents an especially striking example of this phenomenon in *Homosexuality*, pp. 76–77.

3. Schwarzbach, *Dickens*, pp. 198–99.

4. Davis, *Flint*, pp. 266, 271.

5. This is not a necessary inference from the pun, becaue of the gender ambiguity of the word "fanny": it apparently referred to female genitals throughout the nineteenth century in England, but cf., for example, Pope's portrayal of the homosexual Lord Hervey as "Lord Fanny" in the eighteenth century ("pure white curd of asses' milk"); and Fanny Assingham.

6. On the whole I consider the term "male rape," where its meaning is clear in context, preferable to "homosexual rape," since men who rape men are often not homosexual either by self-attribution or by habitual sexual practice; the violent and often the specifically *homophobic* content of this crime are more relevant to our concerns here than its apparently *homosexual* orientation.

7. Dickens, *Our Mutual Friend*, Bk. IV, ch. 10, p. 812. Further citations will be incorporated in the text and designated by book and chapter number.

8. Brown, *Life*, p. 300. The association between possession and the control of the anus must have something to do with an odd feature of the male "rapes" discussed in this chapter and the next: except in the one case of literal rape, it is the participant who would ordinarily be termed passive—the one associated with the "iron ring" of the sphincter—who is presented as the *aggressor;* the phallus itself barely figures in these "rapes."

9. Boswell, *Christianity*, p. 43.

10. Ackerley, *My Father*.

11. Eliot, *Felix Holt*, Bk. III, ch. 10.

12. *Ibid.*, III, 3.

13. *Ibid.*, I, 2.
14. Disraeli, *Coningsby*, ch. 9.
15. Nelson, *Nobs*, p. 147.
16. Miller, *Toward a New Psychology*, ch. 1.

Chapter 10. Up the Postern Stair: *Edwin Drood* and the Homophobia of Empire

1. Dickens, *Great Expectations*, ch. 17.
2. Dickens, *Our Mutual Friend*, Bk. II, ch. 15.
3. Dickens, *Edwin Drood*, ch. 19. Further citations will be incorporated in the text, identified by chapter number.
4. Each interpreter of *Edwin Drood* has to pick her or his way through the thickets of speculation about the intended plot of the unfinished novel. I should say at the outset that I take the very common position that Jasper meant to kill Edwin; the quite common position that he succeeded; the widely held positions that Neville will die, that Rosa will marry Tartar, and that Helena will marry Crisparkle; and the precedented but not unassailable position that Datchery is Helena in disguise.
5. This latter was not distinguished later in the century from the Jewish-identified ethos of nascent psychoanalysis; the figure of Svengali in *Trilby* marks an important link.
6. Burton, *Thousand Nights*, vol. 10, pp. 206–7.
7. *Ibid.*
8. Kaplan, *Dickens*, pp. 165–215.
9. Again, *Trilby* offers an important parallel.
10. On this see Wilner, "Music."
11. Burton, *Thousand Nights*, vol. 10, p. 232.
12. *Ibid.*, p. 235.
13. *Ibid.*, p. 214.
14. *Ibid.*, p. 216.
15. Dickens, *Great Expectations*, ch. 5.
16. Dickens, *Our Mutual Friend*, Bk. II, ch. 13.
17. Lawrence, *Seven Pillars*, pp. 444–45.
18. On this, see Mack, *Prince*, e.g., pp. 216–25; and Said, *Orientalism*, pp. 240–43.
19. Lawrence, *Seven Pillars*, p. 5.
20. Quoted in Mack, *Prince*, p. 464.
21. Quoted in *ibid.*, p. 467.
22. Lawrence, *Seven Pillars*, p. 447.
23. Kipling, *Kim*, p. 1.
24. *Ibid.*, p. 218.
25. *Ibid.*, p. 219.
26. W. H. Auden, "Lullaby," *Collected Shorter Poems 1927–1957* (New York: Random House, 1964), p. 107.

27. Dickens, *Our Mutual Friend,* Bk. II, ch. 13. Of course, I emphasize the recurrent thematics of "lime" here as pointing to the repressive anal aspect of these bonds. A twentieth-century novel that is a striking literalization of the *Drood* I present here is V. S. Naipaul's virulent *Guerrillas:* the thematics of buggery/rape (of a white by a Black) and of the limepit are more explicit, but the structure, in which homophobia, misogyny, and racism are each used to demonstrate the validity of the others, is oddly close to one side of Dickens.

Coda. Toward the Twentieth Century: English Readers of Whitman

1. Emily Dickinson, *The Complete Poems,* ed. Thomas Johnson (Boston: Little, Brown, 1960), p. 303.

2. See Ehrenreich, *Hearts,* ch. 2; Hoch, *White Hero;* Fernbach, *Sprial Path.*

3. See, e.g., Weeks and Rowbotham, *Socialism;* Weeks, *Coming Out;* D'Emilio, *Sexual Politics.*

4. Whitman, *Leaves* 1855, p. 119.

5. Traubel, *With Walt Whitman,* I, 415; II, 360; I, 5.

6. Schueller and Peters, eds. *Letters,* III, 485.

7. Traubel, *With Walt Whitman,* I, 76.

8. Miller, *Whitman,* V, 72–73. In his valuable collection, *Gay American History,* Jonathan Katz braids together relevant documents of Whitman, Symonds, and Edward Carpenter, to offer the best overview of this correspondence.

9. Symonds, *Letters,* III, 492; III, 553; III, 819. And see Symonds, *Study,* p. 76, and Symonds and Ellis, *Sexual Inversion,* pp. 19–21.

10. Traubel, *With Walt Whitman,* I, 204.

11. Carpenter, *Days,* pp. 42–43.

12. On this see, among others, Calvin Bedient, "Whitman: Overruled," in Boyers and Steiner, *Homosexuality,* pp. 326–36.

13. On this see, among others, Savitch, "Whitman's Mystery."

14. Symonds, *Whitman,* p. 72.

15. Symonds, *Letters,* III, 543.

16. Carpenter, *Some Friends,* p. 16.

17. See Grosskurth, *Symonds,* p. 120.

18. Symonds and Ellis, *Sexual Inversion,* p. 17.

19. *Ibid.,* p. 64, 76.

20. This may have been true of nonurbanized, noncosmopolitan segments of the English aristocracy, as well; the bond, in Surtees' *Mr. Sponge's Sporting Tour,* between Lord Scamperdale and Jack Spraggon, "his 'particular' " (ch. 20), could easily bear such a construction.

21. Symonds and Ellis, *Sexual Inversion,* p. xiii.

22. Carpenter, *Friends,* pp. 11–12.

23. Symonds and Ellis, *Sexual Inversion,* p. 58; Symonds is Case XVIII, p. 62.

24. In addition, he disliked and mistrusted the air of excess and effeminacy that

seemed to him to characterize Wilde's aristocratic homosexual friends, such as
Roden Noel, and Wilde's own "morbid and perfumed" literary manner (*Letters*
III, 478).

25. *Ibid.*, III, 494.

26. Symonds, *Study*, pp. 84–85.

27. Ellis, *New Spirit*, p. 104.

28. Symonds, *Letters*, III, 459. Also see III, 448, 483.

29. Symonds, "Democratic Art," *Essays*, p. 245.

30. *Ibid.*, pp. 244–45.

31. Symonds, *Letters*, III, 825.

32. Grosskurth, *Symonds*, p. 271.

33. *Ibid.*, p. 290.

34. Symonds, *Letters*, III, 459.

35. "Fast Anchor'd Eternal O Love!" This is the reading of the 3d edition.

36. Symonds, *Letters*, III, 799.

37. *Ibid.*, III, 808.

38. Symonds, *Essays*, pp. 418–19; and see *Letters*, III, 455.

39. Symonds, *Letters*, III, 798; III, 811.

40. Symonds and Ellis, *Sexual Inversion*, pp. 57, 67, 49, 47.

41. Symonds, *Letters*, III, 712; III, 675.

42. Carpenter, *My Days and Dreams*, pp. 159–60.

43. *Ibid.*, p. 161.

44. Symonds and Ellis, *Sexual Inversion*, pp. 61, 46–47.

45. Carpenter, *My Days and Dreams*, p. 95. Some important reservations concerning Carpenter's feminism are, however, described by Sheila Rowbotham in "Edward Carpenter: Prophet of the New Life," in Rowbotham and Weeks, *Socialism*, pp. 25–138.

46. See, for instance, "As a Woman of a Man," *Towards Democracy*, p. 157.

47. *Ibid.*, p. 387.

48. Carpenter, *Friends of Walt Whitman*, p. 14.

49. For a good discussion of this relationship, see Delavenay, *D. H. Lawrence and Edward Carpenter*, passim but esp. pp. 221–34.

50. Lawrence, *Studies*, pp. 167–68, 175.

51. Lawrence, *The Symbolic Meaning* p. 264; quoted in Delavenay, *D. H. Lawrence and Edward Carpenter*, to which my discussion is indebted.

52. Lawrence, *Studies*, p. 169. See Carpenter, *Friends*, for Carpenter's sympathetic view of Anne Gilchrist's story; and see Rowbotham, *Socialism*, esp. pp. 96–99, for a similar relationship of Carpenter's.

53. Lawrence, *Letters*, II, 1049.

54. D. H. Lawrence, "Education of the People," in *Phoenix*, pp. 664–65, quoted in Delavenay, *D. H. Lawrence and Edward Carpenter*.

55. On "Wilde," see ch. 5.

BIBLIOGRAPHY

Abelove, Henry. "Freud, Male Homosexuality, and the Americans." In *Sexuality in Nineteenth-Century Europe.* Ed. Isabel Hull and Sander Gilman. Forthcoming.

Ackerley, J. R. *My Father and Myself.* London: Bodley Head, 1968.

Alexander, Boyd. *England's Wealthiest Son: A Study of William Beckford.* London: Centaur, 1962.

Altman, Dennis. *The Homosexualization of America, the Americanization of the Homosexual.* New York: St. Martin's, 1982.

Arendt, Hannah. *The Human Condition.* Chicago: University of Chicago Press, 1958.

Aspiz, Harold. *Walt Whitman and the Body Beautiful.* Urbana: University of Illinois Press, 1980.

Barrett, Michèle. *Women's Oppression Today: Problems in Marxist Feminist Analysis.* London: Verso, 1980.

Barry, Kathleen. *Female Sexual Slavery.* New York: Prentice-Hall, 1979.

Barthes, Roland. *A Lover's Discourse: Fragments.* Tr. Richard Howard. New York: Hill and Wang, 1978.

Beckford, William. *The Episodes of Vathek.* Rutherford, N.J.: Associated University Press, 1975.

—— *Vathek.* Ed. Roger Lonsdale. London: Oxford University Press, 1970.

Bell, Alan P., Martin S. Weinberg, and Sue Kiefer Hammersmith. *Sexual Preference: Its Development in Men and Women.* Bloomington: Indiana University Press, 1981.

Birkin, Andrew. *J. M. Barrie and the Lost Boys: The Love Story that Gave Birth to Peter Pan.* New York: Clarkson N. Potter, 1979.

Boswell, John. *Christianity, Social Tolerance, and Homosexuality: Gay People in Western Europe from the Beginning of the Christian Era to the Fourteenth Century.* Chicago: University of Chicago Press, 1980.

Boyers, Robert, and George Steiner, eds. "Homosexuality: Sacrilege, Vision, Politics." Special issue of *Salmagundi* 58–59 (Fall 1982–Winter 1983).

Bray, Alan. *Homosexuality in Renaissance England*. London: Gay Men's Press, 1982.

Breines, Wini, and Linda Gordon. "The New Scholarship on Family Violence." *Signs* 8, no. 3 (Spring 1983), pp. 490–531.

Brown, Norman O. *Life Against Death: The Psychoanalytical Meaning of History*. Middletown, Conn.: Wesleyan University Press, 1959; rept. 1970.

Burton, Richard F. "Terminal Essay." In *A Plain and Literal Translation of The Arabian Nights' Entertainments, Now Entituled The Book of the Thousand Nights and a Night, With Introduction Explanatory Notes on the Manners and Customs of Moslem Men and a Terminal Essay upon the History of The Nights*. Medina Edition, Vol 10. N. p.: Burton Club, 1886, pp. 63–302.

Carpenter, Edward. *My Days and Dreams: Being Autobiographical Notes*. London: George Allen & Unwin, 1916.

—— *Towards Democracy*. N.p.: Albert & Charles Boni, 1932.

—— *Some Friends of Walt Whitman: A Study in Sex Psychology*. London: British Society for the Study of Sex Psychology, n.d.

Cavell, Stanley. *Must We Mean What We Say: A Book of Essays*. New York: Scribner's, 1969.

Cavitch, David. "Whitman's Mystery." *Studies in Romanticism* 17, no. 2 (Spring 1978), pp. 105–28.

Chesebro, James W., ed. *Gayspeak: Gay Male and Lesbian Communication*. New York: Pilgrim Press, 1981.

Chitty, Susan. *The Beast and the Monk: A Life of Charles Kingsley*. New York: Mason-Charter, 1975.

Chodorow, Nancy. "Mothering, Male Dominance, and Capitalism." In *Capitalist Patriarchy and the Case for Socialist Feminism*. Ed. Zillah Eisenstein. New York: Monthly Review, 1979, pp. 83–106.

—— *The Reproduction of Mothering: Psychoanalysis and the Sociology of Gender*. Berkeley: University of California Press, 1978.

Cott, Nancy F. *The Bonds of Womanhood: "Women's Sphere" in New England, 1780–1835*. New Haven: Yale University Press, 1977.

Cott, Nancy F. and Elizabeth H. Pleck, eds. *A Heritage of Her Own: Toward a New Social History of American Women*. New York: Simon and Schuster, 1979.

Crew, Louie, ed.. *The Gay Academic*. Palm Springs, California: ETC Publications, 1978.

Crompton, Louis. "Gay Genocide: From Leviticus to Hitler." In *The Gay Academic*. Ed. Louie Crew. Palm Springs, Calif.: ETC Publications, 1978, pp. 67–91.

Davis, Earle. *The Flint and the Flame: The Artistry of Charles Dickens*. Columbia, Mo.: University of Missouri Press, 1963.

Delavenay, Emile. *D. H. Lawrence and Edward Carpenter: A Study in Edwardian Transition*. London: Heinemann, 1971.

Deleuze, Gilles, and Felix Guattari. *Anti-Oedipus: Capitalism and Schizophrenia*. Tr. Robert Hurley, Mark Seem, and Helen R. Lane. New York: Viking, 1977.

D'Emilio, John. *Sexual Politics, Sexual Communities: The Making of a Homosexual Minority in the United States, 1940–1970*. Chicago: University of Chicago Press, 1983.

Dickens, Charles. *David Copperfield*. Ed. Trevor Blount. Harmondsworth, Sussex: Penguin, 1966.

—— *Great Expectations*. Ed. Angus Calder. Harmondsworth: Penguin, 1965.

—— *The Mystery of Edwin Drood*. Ed. Margaret Cardwell. Oxford: Oxford University Press, 1972.

—— *Nicholas Nickleby*. Ed. Michael Slater. Harmondsworth: Penguin, 1978.

—— *Our Mutual Friend*. Ed. Stephen Gill. Harmondsworth: Penguin, 1971.

—— *The Posthumous Papers of the Pickwick Club*. Ed. Robert L. Patten. Harmondsworth: Penguin, 1972.

Dinnerstein, Dorothy. *The Mermaid and the Minotaur: Sexual Arrangements and Human Malaise*. New York: Harper & Row—Colophon, 1976.

Disraeli, Benjamin, Earl of Beaconsfield. *Coningsby, or The New Generation*. Hughenden Edition. London: Longmans, Green, 1881.

Domhoff, G. William. *The Bohemian Grove and Other Retreats: A Study in Ruling-Class Cohesiveness*. New York: Harper & Row, 1974.

Dover, K. J. *Greek Homosexuality*. New York: Random House—Vintage, 1980.

Driberg, Tom. *Ruling Passions*. New York: Stein and Day, 1978.

du Maurier, George. *Trilby: A Novel*. New York, 1899.

Dworkin, Andrea. *Pornography: Men Possessing Women*. New York: G. P. Putnam's Sons—Perigee Books, 1981.

Ehrenreich, Barbara. *The Hearts of Men: American Dreams and the Flight from Commitment*. New York: Anchor—Doubleday, 1983.

Eisenstein, Zillah, ed. *Capitalist Patriarchy and the Case for Socialist Feminism*. New York: Monthly Review, 1979.

—— The Radical Future of Liberal Feminism. New York: Longman, 1981.

Eliot, George. *Adam Bede*. Illustrated Cabinet Edition. 2 vols. Boston: Dana Estes, n.d.

—— *Felix Holt, The Radical*. Illustrated Cabinet Edition. 2 vols. Boston: Dana Estes, n.d.

Ellis, Havelock, *The New Spirit*. New York: The Modern Library, n.d.

Engel, Monroe. *The Maturity of Dickens*. Cambridge, Mass.: Harvard University Press, 1959.

Engels, Friedrich. *The Origin of the Family, Private Property, and the State, in the Light of the Researches of Lewis H. Morgan*. Introduction and Notes by Eleanor Burke Leacock. New York: International Publishers, 1972.

Fernbach, David. *The Spiral Path: A Gay Contribution to Human Survival*. Alyson Press, 1981.

Fiedler, Leslie. *Love and Death in the American Novel*. Revised ed. New York: Stein and Day, 1966.

—— *The Stranger in Shakespeare*. New York: Stein and Day, 1972.

Foucault, Michel. *The History of Sexuality: Volume I. An Introduction*. Tr. Robert Hurley. New York: Pantheon, 1978.

Freud, Sigmund. *The Standard Edition of the Complete Works of Sigmund Freud*. Tr. James Strachey. London: The Hogarth Press and The Institute For Psychoanalysis, 1953–74.

Frye, Marilyn. *The Politics of Reality: Essays in Feminist Theory*. Trumansburg, N.Y.: The Crossing Press, 1983.

Gallop, Jane. *The Daughter's Seduction: Feminism and Psychoanalysis*. Ithaca: Cornell University Press, 1982.

Gay Left Collective, ed. *Homosexuality: Power and Politics*. London: Allison & Busby, 1980.

Gilbert, Sandra, and Susan Gubar, *The Madwoman in the Attic: The Woman Writer and the Nineteenth-Century Literary Imagination*. New Haven: Yale University Press, 1979.

Gilman, Richard. *Decadence: The Strange Life of an Epithet*. New York: Farrar, Straus and Giroux, 1979.

Girard, René. *Deceit, Desire, and the Novel: Self and Other in Literary Structure*. Tr. Yvonne Freccero. Baltimore: Johns Hopkins University Press, 1972.

Girouard, Mark. *The Return to Camelot: Chivalry and the English Gentleman*. New Haven: Yale University Press, 1981.

Godwin, William. *Caleb Williams*. Ed. David McCracken. London: Oxford University Press, 1970.

Gold, Alex, Jr. "It's Only Love: The Politics of Passion in Godwin's *Caleb Williams*." *Texas Studies in Literature and Language* 19, no. 2 (Summer 1977), pp. 135–60.

Goodman, Paul. *Making Do*. New York: Macmillan, 1963; rept. New American/Signet, 1964.

Griffin, Susan. *Pornography and Silence: Culture's Revenge Against Nature*. New York: Harper & Row, 1981.

Grosskurth, Phyllis. *Havelock Ellis: A Biography*. New York: Knopf, 1980.

—— *John Addington Symonds: A Biography*. London: Longmans, 1964.

Halsband, Robert. *Lord Hervey: Eighteenth-century Courtier*. Oxford: Oxford University Press, 1974.

Hardy, Thomas. *The Life and Death of the Mayor of Casterbridge. The Works of Thomas Hardy*. Wessex Edition. 21 vols. London: Macmillan, 1912–1914. Vol. V.

Harry, Joseph, and Man Singh Das, eds. *Homosexuality in International Perspective*. New Delhi: Vikas Publishing House, 1980.

Heilbrun, Carolyn G. *Toward a Recognition of Androgyny*. New York: Harper & Row–Colophon, 1973.

Heilbrun, Carolyn G., and Margaret Higonnet, eds. *The Representation of Women in Fiction: Selected Papers from the English Institute, 1981*. New series, no. 7. Baltimore: Johns Hopkins University Press, 1983.

Herdt, G. H. *Guardians of the Flutes: Idioms of Masculinity: A Study of Ritualized Homosexual Behavior*. New York: McGraw Hill, 1981.

Hoch, Paul. *White Hero Black Beast: Racism, Sexism, and the Mask of Masculinity*. London: Pluto, 1979.

Hocquenghem, Guy. *Homosexual Desire*. Tr. Daniella Dangoor. London: Allison & Busby, 1978.

Hogg, James. *The Private Memoirs and Confessions of a Justified Sinner*. New York: Norton, 1970.

House, Humphry. *The Dickens World*. London: Oxford University Press, 1941.

Irigaray, Luce. "When the Goods Get Together." In *New French Feminisms*, ed. Elaine Marks and Isabelle de Courtivron. New York: Schocken, 1981, pp. 107–11.

Isherwood, Christopher. *Christopher and His Kind: 1929–1939*. New York: Avon-Discus, 1976.

Jacobus, Mary. "Is There a Woman in This Text?" *New Literary History* 14 (1982–83), pp. 117–41.

James, Henry. *Letters to A. C. Benson and August Monod*, ed. E. F. Benson. London: Elkins Mathews & Marrott, 1930.

Johnson, Edgar. *Charles Dickens: His Tragedy and Triumph*. 2 vols. New York: Simon and Schuster, 1952.

Kahn, Coppélia. *Man's Estate: Masculine Identity in Shakespeare*. Berkeley: University of California Press, 1981.

Kaplan, Fred. *Dickens and Mesmerism: The Hidden Springs of Fiction*. Princeton: Princeton University Press, 1975.

Kaplan, Justin. *Walt Whitman: A Life*. New York: Simon & Schuster, 1980.

Katz, Jonathan. *A Gay/Lesbian Almanac*. New York: Crowell, 1982.

Katz, Jonathan. *Gay American History*. New York: Thomas Y. Crowell, 1976; rept. Avon, 1978.

Kellogg, Stuart, ed. *Literary Visions of Homosexuality*. Special issue of *Journal of Homosexuality* 8, nos. 3–4 (Spring-Summer 1983).

Kelly-Gadol, Joan. "The Social Relation of the Sexes: Methodological Implications of Women's History." *Signs* 1, no. 4 (1976), pp. 809–823.

Kiely, Robert. *The Romantic Novel in England*. Cambridge, Mass.: Harvard University Press, 1972.

Killham, John. *Tennyson and "The Princess": Reflections of an Age*. London: University of London, The Athlone Press, 1958.

Kipling, Rudyard. *Kim*. London: Macmillan, 1908; rept. 1960.

Klein, Richard. Review of *Homosexualities in French Literature*. *MLN* 95, no. 4 (May 1980), pp. 1070–80.

Knight, G. Wilson. *The Mutual Flame: On Shakespeare's Sonnets and the Phoenix and the Turtle*. London: Methuen, 1955.

Krieger, Murray. *A Window to Criticism: Shakespeare's Sonnets and Modern Poetics*. Princeton: Princeton University Press, 1964.

Kris, Ernst. *Psychoanalytic Explorations in Art*. London: Allen & Unwin, 1953.

Kristeva, Julia. *Powers of Horror: An Essay on Abjection*. Tr. S. Roudiez. New York: Columbia University Press, 1982.

Lakoff, Robin. *Language and Women's Place*. New York: Harper & Row, 1975.

Langguth, A. J. *Saki: A Life of Hector Hugh Munro*. New York: Simon and Schuster, 1981.

Laplanche, Jean. *Life and Death in Psychoanalysis*. Tr. Jeffrey Mehlman. Baltimore: Johns Hopkins University Press, 1976.

Laplanche, Jean, and J.-B. Pontalis. *The Language of Psychoanalysis*. Tr. Donald Nicholson-Smith. New York: Norton, 1973.

Lawrence, D. H. *The Collected Letters of D. H. Lawrence*. Ed. Harry T. Moore. 2 vols. London: Heinemann, 1962.

—— *Phoenix: The Posthumous Papers of D. H. Lawrence*. London: Heinemann, 1936.

—— *Studies in Classic American Literature*. New York: Viking, 1923.

—— *The Symbolic Meaning*. Arundel: Centaur Press, 1962.

Lawrence, T. E. *Seven Pillars of Wisdom: A Triumph*. Garden City, N.Y.: Doubleday, Doran, 1935.

Lennon, Florence Becker. *Victoria Through the Looking-Glass: The Life of Lewis Carroll*. New York: Simon & Schuster, 1945.

Lévi-Strauss, Claude. *The Elementary Structures of Kinship*. Boston: Beacon Press, 1969.

Lewis, Wilmarth Sheldon. *Horace Walpole*. Bollingen Series 25–9. New York: Pantheon, 1960.

Lewis, Wyndham. *The Lion and the Fox: The Role of the Hero in the Plays of Shakespeare*. London: Methuen, 1951.

Macciocchi, Maria-Antonietta. "Female Sexuality in Fascist Ideology." *Feminist Review* 1 (1979), pp. 59–82.

Mack, John E. *A Prince ot Our Disorder: A Life of T. E. Lawrence*. Boston: Little, Brown, 1976.

MacKinnon, Catharine A.. "Feminism, Marxism, Method, and the State: An Agenda for Theory." *Signs* 7, no. 3 (Spring 1982), pp. 515–44.

Marcus, Steven. *The Other Victorians: A Study of Sexuality and Pornography in Mid-Nineteenth-Century England*. New York: Basic Books, 1966.

Martin, Robert K. *The Homosexual Tradition in American Poetry*. Austin: University of Texas Press, 1979.

Marx, Karl. *Grundrisse: Foundations of the Critique of Political Economy*. Tr. Martin Nicolaus. New York: Random House–Vintage, 1973.

Maturin, Charles Robert. *Melmoth the Wanderer*. Ed. Douglas Grant. Oxford: Oxford University Press, 1968.

McCarthy, B. Eugene. *William Wycherley: A Biography*. Athens, Ohio: Ohio University Press, 1979.

McConnell-Ginet, Sally, Ruth Borker, and Nelly Furman, eds. *Women and Language in Literature and Society*. New York: Praeger, 1980.

McKeon, Michael. "The 'Marxism' of Claude Lévi-Strauss." *Dialectical Anthropology* 6 (1981), pp. 123–50.

Mieli, Mario. *Homosexuality and Liberation: Elements of a Gay Critique*. London: Gay Men's Press, 1977.

Miller, D. A. "Discipline in Different Voices: Bureaucracy, Police, Family, and *Bleak House*." *Representations* 1, no. 1 (1983), pp. 59–89.

Miller, Jean Baker. *Toward a New Psychology of Women*. Boston: Beacon Press, 1976.

Miller, J. Hillis. *Charles Dickens: The World of his Novels*. Cambridge, Mass.: Harvard University Press, 1958.

Mitchell, Juliet. *Women's Estate*. New York: Random House–Vintage, 1973.

Mitchell, Margaret. *Gone With The Wind*. New York: Avon, 1973.

Miyoshi, Masao. *The Divided Self: A Perspective on the Literature of the Victorians*. New York: New York University Press, 1969.

Moers, Ellen. *Literary Women*. New York: Doubleday, 1976.

Moi, Toril. "The Missing Mother: The Oedipal Rivalries of René Girard." *Diacritics* 12, no. 2 (Summer 1982), pp. 21–31.

Morgan, Ted. *Maugham: A Biography*. New York: Simon & Schuster, 1980.

Morin, Stephen M., and Ellen M. Garfinkle. "Male Homophobia." In

Gayspeak: Gay Male and Lesbian Communication. Ed. James W. Chesebro. New York: Pilgrim Press, 1981, pp. 117–29.

Naipaul, V. S. *Guerrillas.* New York: Random House, 1975.

Nichols, Beverley. *Father Figure.* New York: Simon & Schuster, 1972.

Nelson, Michael. *Nobs and Snobs.* London: Gordon & Cremonesi, 1976.

O'Barr, William M., and Bowman K. Atkins. " 'Women's Language' or 'Powerless Language'?" In *Women and Language in Literature and Society,* ed. Sally McConnell-Ginet, Ruth Borker, and Nelly Furmin. New York: Praeger, 1980, pp. 93–110.

Olsen, Frances E. "The Family and the Market: A Study of Ideology and Legal Reform." *Harvard Law Review* 97, no. 7 (May 1983), pp. 1497–1578.

Osborne, Charles. *W. H. Auden: The Life of a Poet.* New York: Harcourt Brace Jovanovich, 1979.

Peck, Louis F. *A Life of Matthew G. Lewis.* Cambridge, Mass.: Harvard University Press, 1962.

Pleck, Joseph H. *The Myth of Masculinity.* Cambridge, Mass.: MIT Press, 1981; rept. 1983.

Plummer, Kenneth, ed. *The Making of the Modern Homosexual.* London: Hutchinson, 1981.

Praz, Mario. *The Romantic Agony.* Tr. Angus Davidson. London: Oxford University Press, 1970.

Punter, David. *The Literature of Terror: A History of Gothic Fiction from 1765 to the Present Day.* London: Longman, 1980.

Radcliffe, Ann. *The Italian, or the Confessional of the Black Penitents.* Ed. Frederick Garber. From 1797 ed. Oxford: Oxford University Press, 1971.

Ray, Gordon. *The Buried Life: A Study of the Relation Between Thackeray's Fiction and His Personal History.* London: Oxford University Press, 1952; rept. Folcroft, 1970.

Rawlins, Jack P. *Thackeray's Novels: A Fiction That Is True.* Berkeley: University of California Press, 1974.

Reiter, Rayna, ed. *Toward an Anthropology of Women.* New York: Monthly Review Press, 1975.

Rich, Adrienne. *On Lies, Secrets, and Silence: Selected Prose 1966–1978.* New York: Norton, 1979.

Rosaldo, Michelle Z., and Louise Lamphere, eds. *Women, Culture, and Society.* Stanford: Stanford University Press, 1974.

Rowbotham, Sheila, and Jeffrey Weeks. *Socialism and the New Life: The Personal and Sexual Politics of Edward Carpenter and Havelock Ellis.* London: Pluto Press, 1977.

Rubin, Gayle. "The Traffic in Women: Notes Toward a Political Economy of Sex." In *Toward an Anthropology of Women*. Ed. Rayna Reiter. New York: Monthly Review Press, 1975, pp. 157–210.

Ryan, Mary P., and Judith R. Walkowitz, eds.. *Sex and Class in Women's History*. London: Routledge & Kegan Paul, 1983.

Said, Edward W. *Orientalism*. New York: Random House–Vintage, 1978; rept. 1979.

Samois, ed. *Coming to Power: Writing and Graphics on Lesbian S/M*. Boston: Alyson, 1982.

Sargent, Lydia, ed. *Women and Revolution: A Discussion of the Unhappy Marriage of Marxism and Feminism*. Boston: South End Press, 1981.

Sarotte, Georges-Michel. *Like a Brother, Like a Lover: Male Homosexuality in the American Novel and Theater from Herman Melville to James Baldwin*. Tr. Richard Miller. New York: Doubleday-Anchor, 1978.

Schwarzbach, F. S. *Dickens and the City*. London: Athlone, 1979.

Sedgwick, Eve Kosofsky. "The Character in the Veil: Imagery of the Surface in the Gothic Novel." *PMLA* 96, no. 2 (March 1981), pp. 255–70.

—— *The Coherence of Gothic Conventions*. New York: Arno, 1980.

—— "Trace at 46." *Diacritics* 10, no. 1 (March 1980), pp. 3–20.

Shakespeare, William. *Shakespeare's Sonnets*. Ed. and with analytic commentary by Stephen Booth. New Haven: Yale University Press, 1977.

Shaw, Harry E. *The Forms of Historical Fiction: Sir Walter Scott and His Successors*. Ithaca: Cornell University Press, 1983.

Shelley, Mary. *Frankenstein, or the Modern Prometheus*. Ed. James Kinsley and M. K. Joseph. Oxford: Oxford University Press, 1980.

Snitow, Ann, Christine Stansell, and Sharon Thompson, eds. *Powers of Desire: The Politics of Sexuality*. New York: Monthly Review Press–New Feminist Library, 1983.

Steiner, George. "The Cleric of Treason." *New Yorker* 56 (December 8, 1980), pp. 158–95.

Sterne, Laurence. *A Sentimental Journey Through France and Italy*. Ed. Graham Petrie. Hammondsworth: Penguin, 1967.

Stimpson, Catharine R., and Ethel Spector Person, eds. *Women: Sex and Sexuality*. Chicago: University of Chicago Press, 1980.

Stoehr, Taylor. *Dickens: The Dreamer's Stance*. Ithaca: Cornell University Press, 1965.

Stone, Lawrence. *The Family, Sex, and Marriage in England, 1500–1800*. New York: Harper & Row, 1977.

Surtees, R. S. *Handley Cross, or, Mr. Jorrocks's Hunt*. London: Bradbury, Agnew, n.d.

—— *Mr. Sponge's Sporting Tour*. London: Bradbury, Agnew, n.d.

Symonds, John Addington. *Essays Speculative and Suggestive*. London: Smith, Elder, 1907.

—— *The Letters of John Addington Symonds*. Ed. Herbert M. Schueller and Robert L. Peters. 3 vols. Detroit: Wayne State University Press, 1969.

—— *A Study of Walt Whitman*. London: Nimmo, 1893.

Symonds, John Addington, and Havelock Ellis. *Sexual Inversion*. London: Wilson and Macmillan, 1897. Rept. New York: Arno, 1975.

Tennyson, Alfred, Lord. *The Princess: A Medley*. In *The Poems of Tennyson,* ed. Christopher Ricks. London: Longmans, 1969, pp. 743–844.

Thackeray, William Makepeace. *The History of Henry Esmond, Esq. Written By Himself.* Biographical Edition. New York: Harper, 1903.

—— *The Virginians*. Biographical Edition. New York: Harper, 1899.

Tiger, Lionel. *Men In Groups*. New York: Random House, 1969.

Todd, Janet. *Women's Friendship in Literature*. New York: Columbia University Press, 1980.

Traubel, Horace. *With Walt Whitman in Camden*. Boston: Small, Maynard, 1906.

Trollope, Anthony. *Works*. New York: Dodd, Mead, 1921–29.

van der Zee, John. *The Greatest Men's Party on Earth: Inside the Bohemian Grove*. New York: Harcourt Brace Jovanovich, 1974.

Vicinus, Martha. "Sexuality and Power: A Review of Current Work in the History of Sexuality." *Feminist Studies* 8, no. 1 (Spring 1982), pp. 133–56.

Vieth, David M. *"The Country Wife:* An Anatomy of Masculinity." *Papers on Language and Literature* 2 (1966), pp. 335–50.

Warner, Sylvia Townsend. *T. H. White: A Biography*. London: Jonathan Cape with Chatto & Windus, 1967.

Weeks, Jeffrey. *Coming Out: Homosexual Politics in Britain from the Nineteenth Century to the Present*. London: Quartet Books, 1977.

—— *Sex, Politics, and Society: The Regulation of Sexuality Since 1800*. London: Longman, 1981.

Whitehead, Ann. "Sexual Antagonism in Hertfordshire." In *Dependence and Exploitation in Love and Marriage,* ed. Diana Leonard Barker and Sheila Allen. London: Longman, 1976, pp. 169–203.

Whitman, Walt. *Leaves of Grass*. Ed. Malcolm Cowley. Reprint of 1855 edition. New York: Penguin, 1959.

—— *Leaves of Grass: A Textual Variorum of the Printed Poems*. Ed. Sculley Bradley, Harold W. Blodgett, Arthur Golden, William White. 3 vols. New York: New York University Press, 1980.

—— *Whitman: The Correspondence*. Ed. Edward Haviland Miller. 6 vols. New York: New York University Press, 1969.

Wilde, Oscar. *The Picture of Dorian Gray*. London, 1891.

—— *The Portrait of Mr. W. H.* Ed. Vyvyan Holland. London: Methuen, 1958.

Wilner, Joshua David. "Music Without Rhythm: Incorporation and Intoxication in the Prose of Baudelaire and De Quincey." Ph.D. diss., Yale University, 1980.

Wycherley, William. *The Country Wife*. Ed. Thomas H. Fujimura. Regents Restoration Drama Series. Lincoln, Neb.: University of Nebraska Press, 1965.

—— *The Plain Dealer*. Ed. Leo Hughes. Regents Restoration Drama Series. Lincoln, Neb.: University of Nebraska Press, 1967.

Zaretsky, Eli. *Capitalism, The Family, and Personal Life*. New York: Harper-Colophon, 1976.

INDEX